Lecture Notes in Computer Science   8310

Commenced Publication in 1973
Founding and Former Series Editors:
Gerhard Goos, Juris Hartmanis, and Jan van Leeuwen

T0213858

Magnus Jonsson   Alexey Vinel
Boris Bellalta   Ninoslav Marina
Desislava Dimitrova   Dieter Fiems (Eds.)

Multiple Access Communications

6th International Workshop, MACOM 2013
Vilnius, Lithuania, December 16-17, 2013
Proceedings

 Springer

Volume Editors

Magnus Jonsson
Halmstad University, Sweden
E-mail: magnus.jonsson@ide.hh.se

Alexey Vinel
Tampere University of Technology, Finland
E-mail: alexey.vinel@tut.fi

Boris Bellalta
Universitat Pompeu Fabra, Barcelona, Spain
E-mail: boris.bellalta@upf.edu

Ninoslav Marina
University of Information Science and Technology "St. Paul the Apostle"
Ohrid, Republic of Macedonia
E-mail: ninoslav.marina@uist.edu.mk

Desislava Dimitrova
University of Bern, Switzerland
E-mail: dimitrova@iam.unibe.ch

Dieter Fiems
Ghent University, Belgium
E-mail: dieter.fiems@ugent.be

ISSN 0302-9743   e-ISSN 1611-3349
ISBN 978-3-319-03870-4   e-ISBN 978-3-319-03871-1
DOI 10.1007/978-3-319-03871-1
Springer Cham Heidelberg New York Dordrecht London

Library of Congress Control Number: 2013954718

CR Subject Classification (1998): C.2, H.4, D.2, K.6.5, C.2.4, H.3

LNCS Sublibrary: SL 5 – Computer Communication Networks and
Telecommunications

Typesetting: Camera-ready by author, data conversion by Scientific Publishing Services, Chennai, India
Printed on acid-free paper
Springer is part of Springer Science+Business Media (www.springer.com)

Preface

It is our great pleasure to present the proceedings of the 6th International Workshop on Multiple Access Communications (MACOM) that was held in Vilnius during December 16–17, 2013.

Our gratitude goes to the Technical Program Committee and external reviewers for their efforts in selecting 16 high-quality contributions to be presented and discussed in the workshop.

The contributions gathered in these proceedings describe the latest advancements in the field of multiple access communications, with an emphasis on OFDM techniques, channel coding, spectrum management, medium access control protocols, and different aspects of wireless access networks.

Finally, we would like to take this opportunity to express our gratitude to all the participants, together with the local organizers, who helped to make MACOM 2013 a very successful event.

December 2013

Magnus Jonsson
Alexey Vinel
Boris Bellalta
Ninoslav Marina
Desislava Dimitrova
Dieter Fiems

Organization

MACOM 2013 was organized by VGTU, Vilnius, Lithuania.

Executive Committee

General Co-chairs

Ninoslav Marina	UIST, Macedonia
Boris Bellalta	UPF, Spain
Alexey Vinel	TUT, Finland

TPC Co-chairs

Magnus Jonsson	HH, Sweden
Toni Stojanovski	UIST, Macedonia
Dieter Fiems	Ghent University, Belgium
Desislava Dimitrova	University of Bern, Switzerland

Local Chair

Arturas Medeisis	VGTU, Lithuania

Publicity and Web Chair

Jaume Barcelo	UPF, Spain

Publication Chair

Nikita Lyamin	HH, Sweden

Technical Program Committee

Konstantin Avrachenkov	Inria Sophia Antipolis, France
Abdelmalik Bachir	Imperial College London, United Kingdom
Boris Bellalta	Universitat Pompeu Fabra, Spain
Torsten Braun	University of Bern, Switzerland
Raffaele Bruno	IIT-CNR, Italy
Peter Buchholz	TU Dortmund, Germany
Claudia Campolo	University Mediterranea of Reggio Calabria, Italy
Cristina Cano	Hamilton Institute, Ireland
Eduardo Cerqueira	Federal University of Para, Brazil

Tugrul Dayar	Bilkent University, Turkey
Desislava Dimitrova	University of Bern, Switzerland
Alexander Dudin	Belarusian State University, Belarus
Dieter Fiems	Ghent University Belgium
Andres Garcia-Saavedra	Universidad Carlos III de Madrid, Spain
Elena Hadzieva	UIST, Macedonia
Andras Horvath	University of Turin, Italy
Ganguk Hwang	KAIST, Korea
Magnus Jonsson	Halmstad University, Sweden
Dragi Kimovski	UIST, Macedonia
Vinay Kolar	IBM Research, India
Reza Malekian	UIST, Macedonia
David Malone	NUI Maynooth, Ireland
Vincenzo Mancuso	Institute IMDEA Networks, Spain
Ninoslav Marina	Princeton University, USA
David Morales	Universitat Pompeu Fabra, Spain
Dmitry Osipov	IITP RAS, Russia
Edison Pignaton de Freitas	University of Brasilia, Brazil
Vicent Pla	Universitat Politecnica de Valencia, Spain
Zsolt Saffer	Budapest University of Technology and Economics, Hungary
Predrag Spasojevic	Rutgers University, USA
Toni Stojanovski	UIST, Macedonia
Rob van der Mei	Centrum voor Wiskunde en Informatica, The Netherlands
Maria-Angeles Vzquez-Castro	Universidad Autonoma de Barcelona, Spain
Alexey Vinel	Tampere University of Technology, Finland
Yan Zhang	Simula Research Laboratory and University of Oslo, Norway
Dmytro Zubov	UIST, Macedonia

Additional Reviewers

Konstantin Avrachenkov	Magnus Jonsson	Toni Stojanovski
Boris Bellalta	Dragi Kimovski	Dmitry Osipov
Raffaele Bruno	Vinay Kolar	Zsolt Saffer
Peter Buchholz	Dieter Fiems	Predrag Spasojevic
Cristina Cano	Andres Garcia-Saavedra	Susanna Spinsante
Tugrul Dayar	Reza Malekian	Maria-Angeles
Desislava Dimitrova	David Malone	Vzquez-Castro
Alexander Dudin	Rob van der Mei	Jose Vidal
Elena Hadzieva	Vincenzo Mancuso	Alexey Vinel
Andras Horvath	Vicent Pla	Yan Zhang
Ganguk Hwang	Luis Sanabria-Russo	Dmytro Zubov

Technical Sponsors

- Wireless Networking for Moving Objects (WINEMO). IC0906 COST action.
- CISNETS (TEC2012-32354) project funded by the Spanish Government.

Table of Contents

Wireless Networks

Information Theory

A Modified Scheme for PAPR Reduction in OFDM System Based on Clipping Method

Jing Yan, Jianping Wang, and Zhen He

Department of Communication Engineering, School of Computer and Communication
Engineering, University of Science and Technology Beijing, Beijing, 100083, China
yanjing_1230@126.com, zhenhe688@163.com, jpwang@ustb.edu.cn

Abstract. Reducing the peak-to-average power ratio (PAPR) of Orthogonal
frequency division multiplexing (OFDM) has become the most popular technology for high data rate transmission in recent years. However, most of the
proposed schemes either have a high computational complexity or poor bit error
rate (BER) performance. Among them, signal clipping is the simplest method to
improve the OFDM system's PAPR performance, but it results in serious degradation of the BER performance. In this paper, a modified Clipping scheme
based on quantization method is proposed by quantizing the transmitted signal
to a group of preset threshold. Simulation results show that the new scheme can
significantly improve the BER and the out-of-band radiation performance while
guaranteeing the PAPR performance of the QAM-OFDM system.

Keywords: OFDM, PAPR, Quantization, signal Clipping.

1   Introduction

Orthogonal Frequency Division Multiplexing (OFDM) is the most popular multi-
carrier modulation technique. The essential of this technique is to convert a high-rate
data stream into several low-rate streams which are modulated to the mutually orthogonal sub-carriers afterwards [1]. Thus, the symbol period can be extended effectively
and the frequency selective fading effect due to multi-path can be reduced. However,
a major issue with an OFDM system is the extraordinarily high value of peak-to-
average power ratio (PAPR). If the PAPR exceeds the nonlinearity limits of high-
power amplifier, channel in-band interference and out-of-band radiation may occur
[2].

Several schemes have been proposed for reducing the PAPR of multicarrier
system, which can be classified into three classes [3]: clipping algorithm, coding
algorithm and probability algorithm. Among them, signal clipping is the simplest
algorithm, but clipping will process nonlinear distortion on OFDM time-domain signal, which will lead to serious in-band distortion and out-of-band radiation. A lot of
research has been done to reduce the out-of-band radiation in clipping scheme, the
Clipping and Filtering (CF) [4]and Repeat clipping and filtering algorithm (RCF)
proposed by Jean Armstrong [5] are the most classic ones. By repeatedly clipping
and filtering operation, the peak re-growth caused by filtering can be reduced, while

M. Jonsson et al. (Eds.): MACOM 2013, LNCS 8310, pp. 1–7, 2013.
© Springer International Publishing Switzerland 2013

simultaneously improving the PAPR performance. Based on these two classic schemes, much more methods have been proposed. Luqing wang [6] proposed a simplified Clipping and Filtering technique, which scales the clipping noise generated in the first iteration to get a new CF technique significantly reducing the computational complexity. In [7], the Partial Transmit Sequences (PTS) technique is combined with the CF algorithm, which can reduce the in-band noise caused by nonlinear operation. In [8], the SFBC encoding is used in the relay which enables the source to transmit clipped SISO-OFDM signals without an increase in PAPR and computational complexity. An adaptive clipping control algorithm is proposed in [9], which uses a new suboptimal PRT set selection scheme based on the genetic algorithm (GA) to solve the NP-hard problem. All these methods provide effective solutions to reduce the PAPR of the OFDM signals at different costs.

In this paper, we presents a new clipping scheme to reduce the PAPR of the OFDM system called Quantization Clipping (QC), for the first time quantified theory is applied to the signal clipping technology. The QC method could significantly reduce the out-of-band radiation and improve the BER performance of the system while ensuring the PAPR performance.

2   Quantization Clipping Scheme

In an OFDM system with N sub-carriers, the input symbol in frequency domain can be written as $X=[X_0, X_1, ..., X_{N-1}]$, where X_k, $k=0,1,...,N-1$ represents the complex data of the k-th subcarrier and they are independent with each other. Then the complex OFDM symbol in time domain can be shown as:

$$x(t) = \frac{1}{\sqrt{N}} \sum_{n=0}^{N-1} X_n e^{j2\pi\left(\frac{n}{NT}\right)t} \quad , 0 \leq t < NT \tag{1}$$

Where $x(t)$ is the modulated time domain signal and $j = \sqrt{-1}$. T represents a period of input symbol; NT is the length of the valid data block.

The PAPR of OFDM signal sequence X is defined as the ratio of maximum to the average power of the signal, which can be expressed as

$$PAPR = \frac{\max\limits_{0 \leq t \leq N-1} |x(t)|^2}{E\left[|x(t)|^2\right]} \tag{2}$$

For the data block with the length of N, N points sample values obtained by the N-point IFFT (i.e. the Nyquist sampling rate values) are not able to accurately reflect the PAPR characteristics of the continuous time domain signal. To approximate PAPR in discrete time domain, an over-sampled version can be used. The over-sampled time-domain signal xn can be obtained by using a LN-point IFFT operation, with extending X to a vector with the length of LN by inserting $(L-1)N$ zeros in the middle, i.e. $Xn=[X_0,...,X_{N/2-1},0,...,0,X_{N/2},...,X_{N-1}]$, $n=0, 1, ..., NL-1$. Where L is the oversampling factor, and usually $L \geq 4$ is used to capture the peaks of the time-domain signal.

In a multi-carrier system, a large PAR occurs rarely, so use the maximum PAPR to measure the performance of the OFDM system performance does not mean much. It is more useful to consider PAPR as a random variable and use a statistical description given by the complementary cumulative density function (CCDF), defined as the probability that PAPR exceeds a given threshold.

The fundamental principle of conventional Clipping algorithm is to detect the peak of the time domain OFDM signal before it is supplied to the power amplifier. If any part of the signal exceeds the threshold, a nonlinear processing should be implied to limit the amplitude of the signal within the pre-set threshold; otherwise let the signal through without interference [4]. The schematic diagram of clipping scheme is shown in Fig. 1.

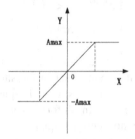

Fig. 1. The schematic diagram of traditional Clipping scheme

The clipped time domain signal can be written as:

$$\hat{x}(t) = \begin{cases} x(t) , & |x(t)| \leq A \\ Ae^{j\phi(t)}, & |x(t)| > A \end{cases} \tag{3}$$

Where A is the clipping threshold, and $\phi(t)$ represents the phase of $x(t)$.

The conventional Clipping scheme processes serious distortion on the input signal and results in bad BER performance. So we propose the introduction of the quantization algorithm into it. The principal of quantization algorithm is to divide the input signal into a series of quantization intervals according to its range, and then give the signal for each interval, a preset quantization value. The quantization can be expressed mathematically as follows [10, 11]:

$$f' = y_Q(f) = S * round(\frac{f}{S}) \tag{4}$$

Where f represents the number of quantization operation, S represents the quantization step, f' is the quantization operation results of f, 'round' means rounding operation, $y_Q(f)$ is a many-to-one irreversible quantization function[11].

Unlike the traditional clipping algorithm which has only one threshold value, the newly proposed quantized clipping algorithm contains several different preset threshold values so that the input signal would firstly be processed in such a way that the signal values between different intervals will be quantized to different threshold values. The new algorithm will set distortion to a smaller level, thus reduces the bit error rate and out-of-band radiation of the OFDM system effectively.

If there are n threshold, $n + 1$ quantization interval is generated, a QC scheme with 4 threshold values (i.e. 5 quantified intervals) can be expressed as:

$$\hat{x}(t) = \begin{cases} A_0 e^{j\phi_0(t)} & |x(t)| \le A_1 \\ A_1 e^{j\phi_1(t)} & A_1 < |x(t)| \le A_2 \\ A_2 e^{j\phi_2(t)} & A_2 < |x(t)| \le A_3 \\ A_3 e^{j\phi_3(t)} & A_3 < |x(t)| \le A_4 \\ A_4 e^{j\phi_4(t)} & |x(t)| > A_4 \end{cases} \tag{5}$$

Where $x'(t)$ denotes the quantified signal , $x(t)$ input signal, $\emptyset_0(t)$, $\emptyset_1(t)$, $\emptyset_2(t)$, $\emptyset_3(t)$, (t), $\emptyset_4$ phase of input signal. A set of threshold values A_0, A_1, A_2, A_3, A_4 should meet the inequality $A_0 < A_1 < A_2 < A_3 < A_4$ and equation $A_2-A_1 = A_3-A_2 = A_4-A_3 = \Delta$, where Δ is the quantization step size. In uniform quantization, the quantization step size Δ is a fixed value, but for non-uniform quantization, Δ is variable. The implementation process of quantization algorithm is given as under:

(1)Framing intervals: Determine the appropriate quantization step according to the range and variation characteristics of the input signal, and then divide the signal interval into a set of intervals.

The most important parameter for performance is Clipping Ratio (CR), which is defined as:

$$CR = 20\log \frac{A}{\sigma} \tag{6}$$

A denotes limiting threshold, σ is the the root mean square of signal power:

$$\sigma = \sqrt{\frac{(x_0)^2 + (x_1)^2 + \cdots + (x_{N-1})^2}{N}} \tag{7}$$

x_0, ..., x_{N-1} is the input signal, N the number of subcarriers.

As A denotes clipping threshold, a bigger CR corresponds a higher threshold, and the effect of reducing PAPR gets worse, and vice verse.

(2) The number of subintervals: For uniform quantization, by dividing the signal range by the chosen quantization step size Δ, we get the quotient m as the number of subintervals and a remainder r, as shown in bellow:

$$m = [length(x)/\Delta] \, , \, r = length(x) - m * \Delta \qquad (8)$$

Length(x) represents the length of the input signal *x(t)*. For non-uniform quantization, the number of subintervals is determined by the threshold number n.

(3) Determine the quantitative value: Set a quantized value to each interval by certain rules, Quantization value in this algorithm is selected by the formula (3).

(4) The quantized signal: the input signal is denoted by x, quantized signal $\hat{x}$ and step size Δ. When $x \geq 0$, the expression of input signal in the k-th quantization interval is shown as follow:

$$\hat{x} = A_{k-1} e^{j\phi(t)} \, , A_{k-1} < x(t) \leq A_k, \, k=0,1,...,m \qquad (9)$$

3   Simulation Result

In this part, we compare the PAPR reduction performance of the conventional Clipping scheme and the Quantization Clipping scheme. The numerical analysis has been performed for the OFDM system specified in the IEEE 802.16 standard for the mobile wireless metropolitan area network (WMAN), which uses 2048 sub-carriers and 16-QAM modulations.

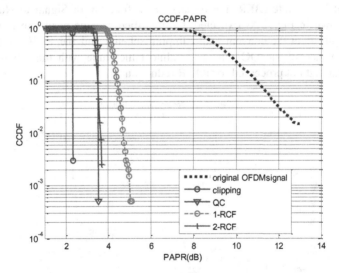

Fig. 2. The PAPR performance of the Conventional Clipping and QC scheme for N=2048

The complementary cumulative distribution functions (CCDFs) of PAPR are numerically obtained for the conventional Clipping scheme with *CR=1.0* and the modified Clipping scheme with *CR1=1.0, CR2=1.1, CR3=1.2, CR3=1.2, CR4=1.3* respectively. Fig.2 compares the PAPR reduction performance of the QC scheme, conventional clipping scheme and the conventional repeated clipping and filtering (RCF) scheme for 16-QAM with N=2048. The performance of the modified scheme is not as good as that of the conventional SLM scheme, but is similar with that of the RCF scheme with 2 iterations.

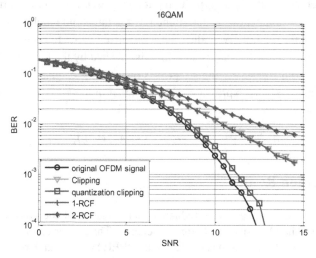

Fig. 3. The BER performance of the Conventional Clipping and QC scheme for N=2048

The Bit Error Rate (BER) performance as a function of Signal to Noise Ratio (SNR) is shown in Fig.3. As expected, the modified scheme results in much better noise immunity than the conventional Clipping scheme and the RCF schemes. The BER performance of the QC scheme is almost the same with that of an original OFDM signal that not processed for PAPR reduction.

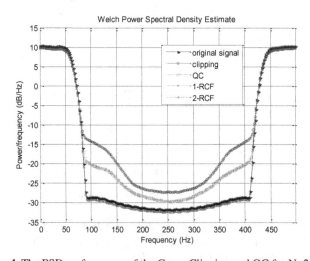

Fig. 4. The PSD performance of the Conv. Clipping and QC for N=2048

Fig.4 compares the PSD reduction performance of the modified and conventional Clipping schemes with N=2048. We can see that the conventional RCF scheme results in almost no out-of-band radiation and the conventional Clipping method leads to 6-dB lower out-of-band radiation than the one obtained for system without PAPR reduction. Our proposed technique results in 2-dB lower out-of-band radiation than the conventional Clipping scheme. The performance improves significantly compare to the conventional clipping scheme.

4   Conclusion

In this paper, we have proposed a novel scheme, called Quantization Clipping, in which the quantization algorithm is combined with the conventional clipping scheme to reduce the PAPR. By comparing the traditional clipping algorithm and the QC scheme, it has been found that the new scheme is not only simple, but also can greatly reduce the BER and out-of-band radiation of the system while improving the PAPR performance.

References

1. Vahlin, A., Holte, N.: Optimal Finite Duration Pulses for OFDM. IEEE Trans. Comm. 44(1), 10–14 (1996)
2. Merchan, S., Amada, A.G., Garcia, J.L.: OFDM performance in amplifier nonlinearity. IEEE Trans. Broadcast. 44(1), 106–114 (1998)
3. Jiang, T., Wu, Y.: An overwiew: Peak-to-average power ratio reduction techniques for OFDM signals. IEEE Trans. Broadcast. 54(2), 257–268 (2008)
4. Armstrong, J.: New OFDM Peak-to-average Power Reduction scheme. In: Proc. IEEE Vehicular Technology Conf., vol. 1, pp. 756–760 (2001)
5. Armstrong, J.: Peak-to-average power reduction for OFDM by repeated clipping and frequency domain filtering. IEEE Electron. Lett. 38(5), 246–247 (2002)
6. Wang, L.Q., Chintha, T.: A Simplified Clipping and Filtering Technique for PAR Reduction in OFDM Systems. IEEE Signal Process. Lett. 12(6), 453–456 (2005)
7. Wang, J., Guo, Y.: PTS-clipping method to reduce the PAPR in ROF-OFDM system. IEEE Trans. on Consumer Electronics 55(2), 356–359 (2009)
8. Kim, Y.-J., Kwon, U.-K.: An Effective PAPR Reduction of SFBC-OFDM for Multinode Cooperative Transmission. IEEE Signal Process. Lett. 16(11), 925–928 (2009)
9. Wang, Y., Chen, W.: Genetic Algorithm Based Nearly Optimal Peak Reduction Tone Set Selection for Adaptive Amplitude Clipping PAPR Reduction. IEEE Trans. Broadcast. 58(3), 462–471 (2012)
10. Chen, B., Wornell, G.W.: Digital Watermarking and Information Embedding Using Dither Modulation. In: IEEE Second Workshop on Multimedia Signal Processing, pp. 273–278 (1998)
11. Chen, B., Wornell, G.W.: Quantization Index Modulation: A Class of Provably Good Methods for Digital Watermarking and Information Embedding. IEEE International Theory 47(4), 1423–1443 (2001)

Impulse Noise Mitigation for OFDM by Time-Frequency Spreading

Jiri Blumenstein[1], Roman Marsalek[1],
Ales Prokes[1], and Christoph Mecklenbräuker[2]

[1] Department of Radio Electronics, Brno University of Technology, Czech Republic
[2] Institute of Telecommunications, Vienna University of Technology
xblume00@phd.feec.vutbr.cz
http://www.nt.tuwien.ac.at/ltesimulator

Abstract. This paper deals with the impulse interferences in modern vehicles and assesses the suitability of establishing in-vehicle wireless links replacing standard data cable bundles. According to our experiments, the standard UMTS Long Term Evolution (LTE) is highly affected by impulse noise. We compare it with a novel 2D signal spreading method exploiting the orthogonal Walsh-Hadamard sequences in order to spread the transmitted signal in time and frequency. This method requires minor modification of the 3GPP LTE standard while no additional bandwidth nor noticeable computational power is required. In the presence of impulse noise, the novel 2D spreading method outperforms the standard compliant LTE significantly.

As a system model, we used an open source LTE downlink simulator developed at Vienna University of Technology and the Middleton Class A impulse noise model.

Keywords: OFDM, 2D Signal spreading, Impulse noise, Channel estimation.

1 Introduction

One of today's most painful topics in car industry is weight and cost savings. However, we also see a trend of an ever increasing number of various electronic devices, whether we consider comfort or so-called infotainment systems on one hand or some sensors and control units on the other which are critical for safety or for example engine management. Both these examples of in-vehicle electronic devices increase the weight of modern cars significantly. For example, the total length of an average car cable bundle could easily reach 4 kilometers with the weight around 50 kilograms [1]. Not only are these cable bundles heavy and costly, but also its installation and durability represents a challenging engineering task.

Therefore, this paper deals with an idea of replacing some of these cable bundles with wireless connections. This is well suitable namely for noncritical infotainment systems which often require major data throughput. The issue to

M. Jonsson et al. (Eds.): MACOM 2013, LNCS 8310, pp. 8–20, 2013.
© Springer International Publishing Switzerland 2013

tackle is, however, the adverse radio environment of the car compartment. Article [2] presents an interesting finding regarding radio channel characteristics. Primarily, the large coherence times and almost constant dominant signal component seems as beneficial behavior for wireless communication systems.

This is in contrast with findings presented in [3]. Since combustion engine ignition is recognized as a source of perceptible impulse noise, in [4] authors performed a measurement of such impulse noise on in-vehicle power lines. They confirmed that the impulse noise is a phenomenon which is represented significantly in combustion engine vehicles, moreover they also provide characteristics of in-car impulse noise.

Although most papers, e.g. [3], deal with impulse noise on in-vehicle power lines, it is shown in [5] that such noise is radiated also into the radio environment. Widely exploited Middleton's model of impulse noise is presented in [6] with application in [7–9]. For example, in [9] the authors investigate the influence of impulse noise on the performance of a WLAN receiver.

This paper investigates the influence of the Middleton Class A impulse noise model [6] on the performance of LTE, which is picked as one of the most current wireless communication standards. Thanks to the wide range of Modulation and Coding Schemes (MCSs) and possible bandwidth settings, LTE is capable of operating in a variety of radio environments making it potentially suitable for in-vehicle applications. Moreover, we compare the throughput performance of standard compliant LTE with a novel method based on two-dimensional signal spreading employed in LTE. We presented the method in [10], however, in this paper the method is modified, as will be shown later.

Since LTE allows a certain degree of freedom in implementing the channel estimator, we therefore compare two possible candidates, namely the Least Square (LS) and Linear Minimum Mean Square Error (LMMSE). Thus, when we consider standard compliant LTE, we mean those LS and LMMSE based channel estimators [11].

Given standard LTE with pilot based Channel State Information (CSI) estimation, individual impulses of impulse noise could superimpose individual symbols (i.e. pilots) of the known training sequence causing the CSI estimate to be highly unreliable and misleading.

The two-dimensional spreading method utilizes the averaging principle while integrating data chips spread through a certain amount of time slots and subcarriers. In contrast with [10], the spreading is done over the known training sequence as well as over the data signal. This feature makes the CSI estimate rather robust mainly considering impulse noise.

Our simulation results are based on an open-source LTE downlink simulator developed at TU Vienna. After registering at [12], the simulator is freely available. We believe that this approach enhances the credibility and repeatability of our results. The simulator's detailed description is stated in [13, 14] and the corresponding uplink part also in [15].

The reminder of the paper is organized as follows: In the section System Model, we briefly introduce chosen features of the LTE and the the state-of-the

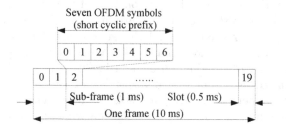

Fig. 1. The description of LTE resources in time domain. In case of 'normal' cyclic prefix we utilize 7 OFDM symbols in one subframe.

art as well as the novel impulse noise resistant 2D spreading channel estimation method. In the section Experiment and Results, the comparison of the LS, LMMSE and the 2D spreading method is stated. In the section Conclusion we sum up the paper. Symbols and notation used thorough the paper are summarized in Table 1.

2   System Model

Our system model is based on the LTE simulator which models the physical layer signal processing including modulation, channel coding, multiplexing etc. according to [11, 16–18].

To appropriately describe the differences between the state-of-the art and our novel method, the time-frequency structure of the LTE needs to be stated a priori.

In order to cope with the Inter Symbol Interference (ISI), the LTE utilizes the Orthogonal Frequency Division Multiplexing (OFDM) with Cyclic Prefix (CP) to encode the data on multiple orthogonal subcarriers, thus extending the symbol durations. The number of subcarriers is $N_s \in \{128, 256, 512, 1024, 1536, 2048\}$ which corresponds to the occupied system bandwidth $BW \in \{1.4, 3, 5, 10, 15, 20\}$ MHz with 15 kHz spacing.

In the time domain, the notation is as follows. One frame duration is 10 ms and consist of 10 subframes. One subframe then represents 2 slots, each with duration of 0.5 ms. The slots are the divided into 7 OFDM symbols (with so called normal CP). This is depicted in Figure 1.

Given the 3rd Generation Partnership Project (3GPP) standard LTE, the channel estimation is based on pilot symbols which are known at both the receiver and transmitter sides. After reception of the symbols, they are compared with the known values stored in the database, thus the CSI can be calculated. The 3GPP pilot grid pattern is visible in Figure 2.

Table 1. Notations and used symbols

$\mathbb{N}, \mathbb{R}, \mathbb{C}$	Natural, Real and Complex number system respectively.
$\mathbb{N}_{0 \leq 1}^{SF \times n}$	Binary $SF \times n$ matrix
$\mathbf{Z}^{\mathrm{H}}$	Hermitian transpose of $\mathbf{Z}$
$\mathbf{X}_{\mathbf{d}(i,*)}$	i-th row of the matrix $\mathbf{X_d}$
Ξ	Orthogonal Walsh-Hadamard matrix
$\otimes$	Kronecker product
$\odot$	Hadamard product

2.1 LS Channel Estimation

The received signal vector $\mathbf{y} \in \mathbb{C}^{1 \times n}$ can be written as:

$$\mathbf{y} = \mathbf{Zh} + \mathbf{v}, \tag{1}$$

so that $\mathbf{h} \in \mathbb{C}^{1 \times n}$ is a vector of channel coefficients, n is the number of transmitted symbols depending on the system bandwidth BW. The $\mathbf{v} \in \mathbb{C}^{1 \times n}$ is an interference vector described later in section 2.4. The $\mathbf{Z} \in \mathbb{C}^{n \times n}$ is a diagonal matrix written as:

$$\mathbf{Z} = \mathrm{diag}(\mathbf{z}), \tag{2}$$

where $\mathbf{z}$ is permuted data and pilot composite vector $\tilde{\mathbf{z}} = [\mathbf{z_p}^{\mathrm{T}}, \mathbf{z_d}^{\mathrm{T}}]^{\mathrm{T}}$. The permutation procedure is according to $\mathbf{z} = \mathbf{P}\tilde{\mathbf{z}}$ where the matrix $\mathbf{P}$ is a permutation matrix given by [17].

The LS estimation is then performed according to:

$$\hat{\mathbf{h}}_{\mathrm{p}}^{\mathrm{LS}} = \mathbf{Z}_{\mathrm{p}}^{\mathrm{H}}\mathbf{y}_{\mathrm{p}}. \tag{3}$$

The vector $\mathbf{y}_{\mathrm{p}} \in \mathbb{C}^{1 \times b}$ represents the received pilot signal of length b and $\mathbf{Z}_{\mathrm{p}}^{\mathrm{H}}$ is the Hermitian transpose of the transmitted signal matrix $\mathbf{Z}$ at specific pilot positions. The channel coefficients between the pilot symbols have to be obtained by interpolation.

2.2 LMMSE Channel Estimation

The Linear Minimum Mean Square Error (LMMSE) estimation requires knowledge of the second-order statistic of the noise and radio channel. It is seen in [19] that the LMMSE estimator represents filtered LS:

$$\hat{\mathbf{h}}_{\mathrm{LMMSE}} = \mathbf{A}_{\mathrm{LMMSE}}\hat{\mathbf{h}}_{\mathrm{p}}^{\mathrm{LS}}, \tag{4}$$

by minimizing MSE, we obtain the filtering matrix $\mathbf{A}_{\mathrm{LMMSE}}$:

$$\mathbf{A}_{\mathrm{LMMSE}} = \mathbf{R}_{\mathbf{h},\mathbf{h_p}} \left(\mathbf{R}_{\mathbf{h_p},\mathbf{h_p}} + \sigma^2 \mathbf{I} \right)^{-1}, \tag{5}$$

where $\mathbf{R}_{\mathbf{h},\mathbf{h_p}}$ is the channel crosscorrelation matrix and $\mathbf{R}_{\mathbf{h_p},\mathbf{h_p}}$ is the channel autocorrelation matrix. $\mathbf{I}$ is the identity matrix and σ^2 is the noise variance.

2.3 2D Spreading Based Channel Estimation

Transmitter. A report on implementation and performance of the 2D spreading method is to be found in [10]. However, hereinafter in this paper we utilize signal spreading not only over the data payload, but also over the pilot signal exploited for channel estimation. Let us have a transmitted signal vector $\mathbf{x}$:

$$\mathbf{x} = [\mathbf{x_d}^T, \mathbf{x_p}^T]^T, \tag{6}$$

which consists of data vector $\mathbf{x_d}^T \in \mathbb{C}^{1\times(n-b)}$ and $\mathbf{x_p}^T \in \mathbb{C}^{1\times b}$ representing the pilot signal vector. The n is the overall number of transmitted symbols contained in one subframe. This corresponds with the system bandwidth BW. The b is the number of pilot symbols in a subframe.

The received signal $\mathbf{y}$ is then written as:

$$\mathbf{y} = \mathbf{X_s}\mathbf{h} + \mathbf{v}, \tag{7}$$

where the $\mathbf{h}$ and $\mathbf{v}$ vectors symbolize the channel coefficients and Gaussian noise respectively. The matrix $\mathbf{X_s} \in \mathbb{C}^{n\times n}$ is a diagonal matrix representing the spreading operation of the pilots and data. The matrix $\mathbf{X_s}$ is composed as:

$$\mathbf{X_s} = \mathrm{diag}\left(\underbrace{w_{SF}\left(\mathbf{x_p} \otimes \Xi_{(SF,*)}\right)}_{\text{pilot sequence}} + \underbrace{\sum_{i=1}^{SF-1} w_i\left(\mathbf{X}_{\mathbf{d}(i,*)} \otimes \Xi_{(i,*)}\right)}_{\text{data}} \right), \tag{8}$$

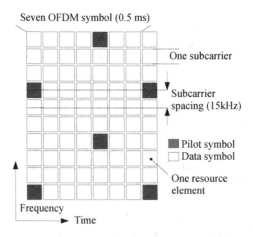

Fig. 2. The LTE time-frequency grid diagram. The dark gray resource elements represent pilot symbols known at the receiver side. Comparing the known specimen and received pilots we obtain the CSI. Between those points the CSI can be interpolated only.

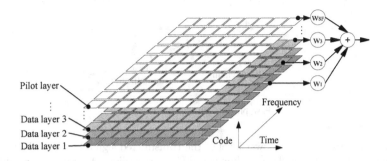

Fig. 3. Proposed novel 2D spreading based time-code-frequency grid. The first $SF-1$ code layers are devoted to data transmission, whereas the SF-th code layer carries the pilot signal. Due to this pilot layer arrangement, simplification of an LTE Frame Builder is necessary. The **w** is a vector of constant weight factors for adjusting the per-layer SNR. Here we assume a weight factor of 2 for the pilot layer and 1 for data layers.

where

$$\mathbf{X_d} = \begin{bmatrix} x_1 & \cdots & x_{n/SF} \\ x_{n/SF+1} & \ddots & \vdots \\ \vdots & \cdots & x_n \end{bmatrix}, \tag{9}$$

and

$$\Xi = \begin{bmatrix} \xi_{1,1} & \cdots & \xi_{1,SF} \\ \vdots & \ddots & \vdots \\ \xi_{SF,1} & \cdots & \xi_{SF,SF} \end{bmatrix}. \tag{10}$$

The SF is the spreading factor, the $\otimes$ is the Kronecker product, the matrix $\Xi \in \mathbb{N}_{0 \leq 1}^{SF \times SF}$ stands for the SF-th order Walsh-Hadamard matrix and the $\mathbf{X_{d(i,*)}}$ denotes the i-th row of the matrices $\mathbf{X_d}$. For simplicity, $\mathbf{x_p} = \mathbf{1}_{1,n/SF}$, i.e. vector of ones of length $\frac{n}{SF}$. The $\mathbf{x_p}$ is known at the transmitter as well as the receiver side so this is the pilot sequence, later referred to as a pilot layer.

We also introduce $\mathbf{w} \in \mathbb{R}_{>0}^{1 \times SF}$ representing constant weight factors for adjusting the per-layer Signal to Noise Ratio (SNR). The w_i is then an element of the vector $\mathbf{w}$. Here we assume a weight factor of 2 for the pilot layer and 1 for data layers. At the transmitter side, we ensure the same signal power level as in the case of a standard LTE downlink signal via RMS based power normalization, as seen in Figure 4.

The graphical illustration of Equation 8 is in Figure 3, where we can observe the pilot layer overlaying the data layers while their power is weighted by the vector $\mathbf{w}$.

Receiver. The processing of the received signal $\mathbf{y} = (y_1, y_2, \ldots, y_n)$ includes multiplication with the rows of the despreading matrix $\Theta \in \mathbb{N}_{0 \leq 1}^{SF \times n}$ and integration as known from the Code Division Multiple Access (CDMA) principle.

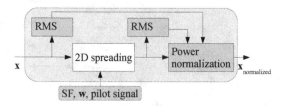

Fig. 4. To ensure the same power level of the transmitted signal for both the standard compliant LTE and novel 2D spreading based LTE, we utilize RMS power normalization

$$
\mathbf{Y} = \begin{pmatrix} \mathbf{y}_1 \\ \mathbf{y}_2 \\ \vdots \\ \mathbf{y}_{SF} \end{pmatrix}, \text{ where } \mathbf{y}_v = \frac{1}{\text{SF}} \left(\mathbf{y} \odot \mathbf{\Theta}_{(v,*)} \right), \tag{11}
$$

where the $\odot$ stands for the Hadamard product, the despreading matrix $\mathbf{\Theta}$ is the $\frac{n}{SF}$ replicated $\mathbf{\Xi}$ matrix. This is written as:

$$
\mathbf{\Theta} = \left[\mathbf{\Xi}_1, \mathbf{\Xi}_2, \dots, \mathbf{\Xi}_{\frac{n}{SF}} \right] : \mathbf{\Xi}_m = \mathbf{\Xi}, \forall m \in \left(1, 2, \dots, \frac{n}{SF} \right). \tag{12}
$$

The resulting matrix $\mathbf{Y_d} \in \mathbb{C}^{\frac{n}{SF} \times SF}$ is constructed by partial summation of elements y from the matrix $\mathbf{Y} \in \mathbb{C}^{n \times SF}$ defined in Equation 11:

$$
\mathbf{Y_d} = \begin{pmatrix} \mathbf{y_{d1}} \\ \mathbf{y_{d2}} \\ \vdots \\ \mathbf{y_{d \frac{n}{SF}}} \end{pmatrix},
$$

where $\mathbf{y_{di}} = \left(\sum_{k=1}^{SF} \{ y_{(k, SF(i-1)+1)} \}, \sum_{k=1}^{SF} \{ y_{(k, SF(i-1)+2)} \} \cdots \right.$

$$
\left. \dots, \sum_{k=1}^{SF} \{ y_{(k, iSF)} \} \right), \forall i = \left(1, 2, \dots, \frac{n}{SF} \right). \tag{13}
$$

Since the pilot vector is a vector of ones, the CSI is expressed as the SF-th code layer of the $\mathbf{Y_d}$ matrix. The pilot layer is transmitted in a spread form, therefore it needs to be spread again in order to obtain a complete CSI estimate over all assigned time-frequency recourses:

$$
\hat{\mathbf{h}}^{2D} = \mathbf{y_{d \frac{n}{SF}}} \otimes \mathbf{\Xi}_{(SF,*)}. \tag{14}
$$

As a result, no interpolation is needed and the computational demands are at the same level as in the case of the LS estimator. The LMMSE method is considerably more demanding.

2.4 Interference Model

Our system model exploits two noise models, namely the Additive White Gaussian Noise (AWGN) and the Middleton's Class A impulse noise model. The overall interference vector **v** from (1) is constructed according (15), where the variables **n** and **m** stand for the AWGN and the Middleton's Class A impulse noise models respectively.

$$\mathbf{v} = \mathbf{n} + \mathbf{m}. \tag{15}$$

Here one element of **n** is defined according to:

$$n = 10^{-\frac{SNR}{20}} \left(N(0,1) + jN(0,1)\right), \tag{16}$$

where $N(0,1)$ denotes zero-mean, normally distributed pseudo-random number with variance one. The j stands for basic imaginary unit.

The vector **m** represents the Middleton's Class A impulse noise, the most accepted model of asynchronous impulse noise [7]. The Class A is a narrowband noise model wherein the interference spectrum is narrower than the receiver bandwidth [8]. The Probability Density Function (PDF) of exploited Calss A impulse noise is given as:

$$f_x(x) = e^{-A} \sum_{k=0}^{K} \frac{A^k}{k!\sqrt{2\pi\sigma_m^2}} e^{\frac{x^2}{2\sigma_k^2}}, \tag{17}$$

where

$$\sigma_k^2 = \frac{\frac{k}{A} + \Gamma}{1 + \Gamma}, \tag{18}$$

is impulse noise variance, $A = v_i T_s$ is impulse index, v_i is mean impulse rate, T_s is mean impulse duration and K is the number of terms in the Class A PDF that should be considered while generating the noise samples (according to theory [6], $K = \infty$). The model assumes that the individual impulses are Poisson distributed in time, however increasing the impulse index A, the noise becomes arbitrarily close to Gaussian.

In the time domain, the LTE signal (black) and impulse noise (gray) are shown in Figure 5, whereas Figure 6 shows the Q-Q plot comparing quantiles of the impulse noise with normal data distribution. As we can see, utilized impulse noise represents data set with fat-tail distribution which takes extreme low and high values more frequently compared with normal distribution.

More detailed description of Middleton Class A impulse noise model can be found in [6,9].

According to Equation 15, the vector noise **v** is a composite of AWGN and impulse noise. Therefore we define the Signal to Interference and Noise Ratio (SINR) as follows:

$$SINR = \frac{P_{\text{sig}}}{P_{\text{imp.noise}} + P_{\text{AWGN}}}, \tag{19}$$

where P_{sig}, $P_{\text{imp.noise}}$ and P_{AWGN} represents the power of the transmitted signal, impulse noise and AWGN respectively.

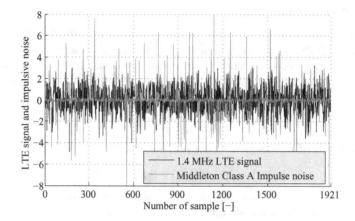

Fig. 5. Strong interfering impulse noise (gray) affecting the 1.4 MHz LTE downlink signal (black). The black signal represents one subframe, i.e. 1 ms. Note that no Gaussian noise is plotted, however, in our simulations Gaussian noise is present.

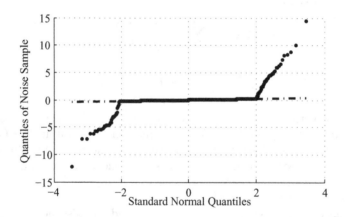

Fig. 6. Q-Q plot of impulse noise samples versus standard normal data samples. Compared to quantiles of the normal distribution, the PDF of the impulse noise takes extreme low and high values more frequently.

3   Experiment and Results

This section describes the utilized simulation setting as well as achieved results. As stated in [2], the fading characteristics of the in-vehicle radio channel features large coherence times and an almost constant dominant signal component. Due to the lack of suitable in-vehicle Power Delay Profile (PDP) models, we chose the PedA channel model [16] as the model which mostly corresponds with statements presented in [2].

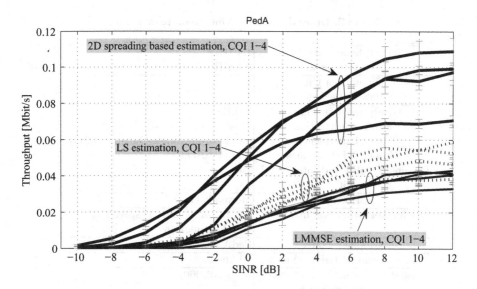

Fig. 7. The throughput comparison of two standard compliant LTE representatives, namely LS and LMMSE and novel 2D spreading based method. The impulse noise, as described in section 2.4, and the Gaussian noise are present. Data is provided with 95% confidence intervals.

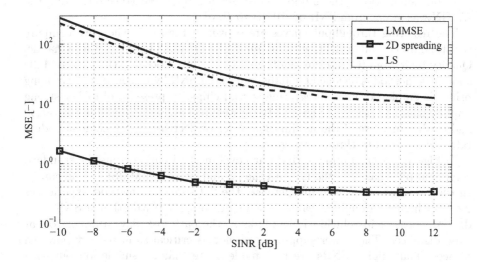

Fig. 8. MSE of the channel estimate. The error floor is caused by strong impulse noise interference. The 2D spreading averages the pilot values, thus provides more robust CSI.

Table 2. Utilized system setting, main parameters

System bandwidth BW	1.4 MHz
Carrier frequency	2.1 GHz
Number of UE	1
Number of eNodeBs	1
Subcarrier spacing	15 kHz
Subframe duration	1 ms
Transmission Scheme	Single-Input Single-Output (SISO)
Number of subframes	2 000 - 10 000
Channel Quality Indicator (CQI)	1-4
SF	48
CP length	'normal' [17]
Channel estimation method	LS, LMMSE and 2D spreading based estimation
Channel model	PedA [16]
User Terminal (UE) velocity	20 km/h
Number of symbols contained in one subframe	$n \in (816, 960)$

In Table 2 we present the major system parameters of our simulations. The Middleton's Class A noise model setting is derived from the study [3] and is as follows, $A = 0.1$, $\Gamma = 0.009$ and $K = 5$, producing impulse noise depicted in Figure 5 with Q-Q plot in Figure 6.

In our simulations, the impulse noise setting remained constant, while the AWGN was swept from SNR of -10 dB to 10 dB.

The resulting throughput curves are shown in Figure 7, where we compare the standard compliant LTE with modified 2D spreading based LTE for Channel Quality Indicators (CQIs) ranging from 1 to 4. This is because the proposed 2D spreading method is beneficial mainly under poor SNR by reason of the averaging principle employed while integrating spread chips. In presence of rather strong impulse noise, as visible in Figure 5, the system reaches its throughput saturation and further increase of the modulation order or decrease of the channel coding rate will not lead to throughput gain.

In Figure 7 we can observe that our novel method outperforms the standard compliant pilot based methods (both the LS and even the LMMSE) significantly. In the presence of impulse interference, the 2D spreading method experiences $2\times - 3\times$ higher throughput values reaching throughput saturation at SNR = 15 dB. We consider in-vehicle wireless links so the path loss plays a minor role at close distances. The power supply is also not as critical as in battery powered devices. Thus higher SNRs are reasonable. Note that for simulation purposes we utilized the narrowest system bandwidth $BW = 1.4$ MHz which is currently supported in the 3GPP LTE. Higher throughput could be obtained by increasing the bandwidth, or suppressing the impulse noise.

In Figure 8 present MSE of the channel estimate. The error floor is caused by strong impulse noise interference. The 2D spreading averages the pilot values, thus provides more robust CSI.

It is also worth noting that the performance of the LMMSE estimator is slightly worse compared with the LS approach. Our LMMSE estimator utilizes the estimated channel crosscorrelation matrix $\mathbf{R}_{h,h_p}$ and the channel autocorrelation matrix $\mathbf{R}_{h_p,h_p}$ (from Equation 5). The matrixes are estimated using 50 channel realizations. However, when the impulse noise is present, the estimated $\mathbf{R}_{h,h_p}$ and $\mathbf{R}_{h_p,h_p}$ are affected by extreme values of the impulse noise, thus worsens the MSE of the channel estimate.

4   Conclusion

This paper examines the influence of impulse noise on the Long Term Evolution (LTE) from the point of view of in-vehicle wireless communication links. Moreover, we propose a novel 2D spreading method which is more resistant against impulse interference.

Our proposed method reaches $2\times - 3\times$ higher throughput values than state-of-the art methods (LS and LMMSE) applied to the standard compliant LTE while requiring no additional bandwidth nor significant computational requirements. Computational demands of the 2D spreading based method are comparable with the LS method, thus much more favorable than in the case of LMMSE. Implementation of the 2D spreading requires minor changes on the physical layer part of the 3GPP standard.

To enhance the credibility of our results, we implemented our method into the state-of-the art simulation tool developed at TU Vienna [12].

Acknowledgment. This work was supported by the Czech Science Foundation project No. 13-38735S Research into wireless channels for intra-vehicle communication and positioning, and was performed in laboratories supported by the SIX project, No. CZ.1.05/2.1.00/03.0072, the operational program Research and Development for Innovation. The cooperation in the COST IC1004 action was supported by the MEYS of the Czech Republic project no. LD12006 (CEEC).

References

1. Leen, G., Heffernan, D.: Expanding automotive electronic systems. Computer 35(1), 88–93 (2002)
2. Moghimi, A., Tsai, H.-M., Saraydar, C., Tonguz, O.: Characterizing intra-car wireless channels. IEEE Transactions on Vehicular Technology 58(9), 5299–5305 (2009)
3. Degardin, V., Lienard, M., Degauque, P., Simon, E., Laly, P.: Impulsive noise characterization of in-vehicle power line. IEEE Transactions on Electromagnetic Compatibility 50(4), 861–868 (2008)
4. Degardin, V., Laly, P., Lienard, M., Degauque, P.: Impulsive noise on in-vehicle power lines: Characterization and impact on communication performance. In: 2006 IEEE International Symposium on Power Line Communications and Its Applications, pp. 222–226 (2006)

5. Ahmed, A.: Study of impulse noise in wireline and mimo wireless communication. Communications, Systems and Electronics School of Engineering and Science Jacobs University Bremen, Tech. Rep. (2011)
6. Middleton, D.: Canonical and quasi-canonical probability models of class a interference. IEEE Transactions on Electromagnetic Compatibility (2), 76–106 (1983)
7. Acciani, G., Amoruso, V., Fornarelli, G., Giaquinto, A.: Som-based approach for the analysis and classification of synchronous impulsive noise of an in-ship plc system. ISRN Artificial Intelligence 2012 (2012)
8. Evans, B.L.: In-platform radio frequency interference mitigation for wireless communications
9. Bhatti, S.A., Shan, Q., Glover, I.A., Atkinson, R., Portugues, I.E., Moore, P.J., Rutherford, R.: Impulsive noise modeling and prediction of its impact on the performance of WLAN receiver. In: The 17th European Signal Processing Conference, EUSIPCO 2009 (2009)
10. Blumenstein, J., Simko, M., Marsalek, R., Fedra, Z., Prokopec, J., Rupp, M.: Two dimensional signal spreading in umts lte: Exploiting time-frequency diversity to increase throughput. In: Wireless Personal Communications, pp. 1–11 (2012), http://dx.doi.org/10.1007/s11277-012-0864-3
11. 3GPP Technical Specification Group RAN, "E-UTRA; physical layer procedures," 3GPP, Tech. Rep. TS 36.213 (March 2009)
12. LTE simulator homepage, http://www.nt.tuwien.ac.at/ltesimulator/
13. Mehlführer, C., Wrulich, M., Ikuno, J.C., Bosanska, D., Rupp, M.: Simulating the Long Term Evolution physical layer. In: European Signal Processing Conference (EUSIPCO), Glasgow, Scotland (August 2009)
14. Mehlführer, C., Colom Ikuno, J., Simko, M., Schwarz, S., Wrulich, M., Rupp, M.: The vienna lte simulators - enabling reproducibility in wireless communications research. EURASIP Journal on Advances in Signal Processing 2011(1), 29 (2011), http://asp.eurasipjournals.com/content/2011/1/29
15. Blumenstein, J., Ikuno, J.C., Prokopec, J., Rupp, M.: Simulating the long term evolution uplink physical layer. In: 2011 Proceedings of ELMAR, pp. 141–144. IEEE (2011)
16. 3GPP Technical Specification Group RAN, "E-UTRA; LTE physical layer – general description," 3GPP, Tech. Rep. TS 36.201 Version 8.3.0 (March 2009)
17. 3GPP Technical Specification Group RAN, "E-UTRA; physical channels and modulation," 3GPP, Tech. Rep. TS 36.211 Version 8.7.0 (May 2009)
18. 3GPP Technical Specification Group RAN, "E-UTRA; multiplexing and channel coding," 3GPP, Tech. Rep. TS 36.212 (March 2009)
19. Omar, S., Ancora, A., Slock, D.T.M.: Performance analysis of general pilot-aided linear channel estimation in lte ofdma systems with application to simplified mmse schemes. In: IEEE 19th International Symposium on Personal, Indoor and Mobile Radio Communications, PIMRC 2008, pp. 1–6 (2008)

Analog Joint Source Channel Coding for Gaussian Multiple Access Channels

Mohamed Hassanin[1], Oscar Fresnedo[2], Javier Garcia-Frias[1], and Luis Castedo[2]

[1] Department of Electrical and Computer Engineering, University of Delaware
hassanin@udel.edu, jgarcia@ee.udel.edu
[2] Department of Electronics and Systems, University of A Coruna
ofresnedo@udc.edu, luis@udc.edu

Abstract. We investigate the problem of transmiting independent sources over the Gaussian Multiple Access Channel (MAC) using a CDMA-like access scheme that allows users to transmit at different rates. Rather than using standard digital communications systems, we focus on analog joint source-channel coding techniques to encode each user's source. We analyze the performance of the proposed scheme and demonstrate its optimality. Simulation results with practical analog joint source-channel codes optimized for point-to-point communications show that the resulting performance is very close to the theoretical limits.

Keywords: Analog Joint Source Channel Coding, Multiple Access Channels, CDMA.

1 Introduction

The use of digital communications systems based on the Shannon separation principle between source and channel coding [1] has led to ubiquitous communications in our society. In this framework, continuous signals are first acquired and source encoded in the digital domain, and then sent over a channel using digital transmission methods. It is well known that in point-to-point communications this approach is optimal provided that there are no constraints in terms of complexity and delays. However, to approach the optimal distortion-cost trade-off, sources have to be compressed using powerful quantization and encoding methods, and data has to be transmitted using digital channel codes. The utilization of capacity approaching digital source and channel codes requires significant delay and high computational complexity. Moreover, full redesign of the digital system is required whenever we want to change either the data rate or the distortion target.

Recently, systems based on analog joint source-channel coding have been discussed in the literature [2–4]. In this approach, the concatenation of the (vector) quantizer, the source encoder and the channel encoder typical of digital systems is substituted by an end-to-end analog encoder. This discrete-time, continuous-amplitude system directly processes the acquired samples using a non-linear

M. Jonsson et al. (Eds.): MACOM 2013, LNCS 8310, pp. 21–32, 2013.

transformation, whose output is transmitted directly through the channel after proper modulation. For the same performance, these schemes may present more robustness and require less encoding/decoding complexity than traditional digital systems.

Most of the work on analog coding (see [2, 3, 5, 6] and references therein) deals with transmission of memoryless sources over AWGN channels or static wireless channels, but recent extensions to optical environments, relay channels and MIMO systems have appeared in the literature [7–9]. In all these cases, the resulting performance is very close to the theoretical limits, while requiring less complexity than traditional digital schemes. In this paper, we extend the use of analog joint source-channel coding to Multiple Access Channels (MAC). Specifically, we encode each user's data by applying space-filling curves as those used in point-to-point analog joint source-channel coding schemes and then utilize a CDMA-like access scheme. Different from standard CDMA, the input to the access scheme is an analog value, but the basic idea of orthogonalizing the channel still holds.

Previous work on analog joint source-channel coding for the MAC has focused on the two user case and includes the work in [10], which extends the Nested Quantization digital technique proposed in [11]. The technique used in [10] is called Scalar Quantizer Linear Coding (SQLC) and, to our knowledge, it provides the best results so far for the two-user MAC using analog joint source-channel coding. Different from this work, our scheme utilizes standard analog mappings (designed for point-to-point communication) and achieves a performance very close to the theoretical limits.

The remainder of the paper is organized as follows. Section 2 presents the proposed CDMA-like access scheme. Analysis is performed and the optimality of the scheme is proved for several cases of interest. Section 3 introduces analog joint source-channel coding, discusses the theoretical limits and proposes practical systems for several cases of interest. Section 4 presents the simulation results and section 5 concludes the paper.

2   Proposed CDMA-Like Access Scheme

Let us assume a Multiple Access Channel (MAC) with N users. User i data, x^i, is transmitted to a common receiver so that

$$y = \sum_{i=1}^{N} x^i + z, \tag{1}$$

where z is i.i.d AWGN with zero mean and variance σ_z^2. Without loss of generality, we assume that the noise power is unity, $\sigma_z^2 = 1$. Let P_i be the i-th user received power per channel use. The different rates users may achieve, R_i, $i = 1, \ldots, N$ must satisfy the following inequalities $\forall J \subset \mathcal{P}(\{1, 2 \cdots N\})$, where $\mathcal{P}(\cdot)$ is the power set [12]

$$\sum_J R_i \leq \frac{1}{2} \log_2(1 + \sum_J P_i) \qquad \forall i \in J. \tag{2}$$

where

Equation (2) defines a polyhedron in N dimensions, and each inequality in (2) defines an edge of the polyhedron. The *maximum* sum rate is

$$\sum_{i=1}^{N} R_i \leq C_{MAC} = \frac{1}{2} \log_2(1 + \sum_{i=1}^{N} P_i). \tag{3}$$

For the N users to transmit over the MAC, we propose the utilization of a $K \times K$ orthogonal codebook, $\mathbf{C}_{K \times K}$, with $K \geq N$. To that end, we start off with an orthogonal matrix of size K, such as the Hadamard matrix, and assign m_i columns to user i so that $\sum_{i=1}^{N} m_i = K$. We then scale each user's columns by $\eta_i = \frac{1}{\sqrt{m_i}}$. The scaled columns assigned to user i are denoted by $\underline{\mu}_1^i\, \underline{\mu}_2^i\, \cdots \underline{\mu}_{m_i}^i$. As shown in Figure 1, we group the columns assigned to user i into one submatrix denoted by $\mathbf{C}_{K \times m_i} = [\underline{\mu}_1^i\, \underline{\mu}_2^i\, \cdots \underline{\mu}_{m_i}^i]$. This $\mathbf{C}_{K \times m_i}$ is the access codebook that user i uses to send the data as explained in Figure 2.

$$\mathbf{C}_{K \times K} = [\mathbf{C}_{K \times m_1} | \mathbf{C}_{K \times m_2} \cdots | \mathbf{C}_{K \times m_N}],$$

with

$$\mathbf{C}_{K \times m_i} = [\underline{\mu}_1^i\, \underline{\mu}_2^i\, \cdots \underline{\mu}_{m_i}^i]$$

$$= \begin{bmatrix} \underline{\mathbf{c_1}} \\ \underline{\mathbf{c_2}} \\ \vdots \\ \underline{\mathbf{c_K}} \end{bmatrix} = \begin{bmatrix} c_1^i(1) & c_1^i(2) & \cdots & c_1^i(m_i) \\ c_2^i(1) & c_2^i(2) & \cdots & c_2^i(m_i) \\ \vdots & \vdots & \cdots & \vdots \\ c_K^i(1) & c_K^i(2) & \cdots & c_K^i(m_i) \end{bmatrix}$$

Fig. 1. The codebook $\mathbf{C}_{K \times K}$ is obtained by scaling the Hadamard matrix columns corresponding to user i by the factor $\eta_i = \frac{1}{\sqrt{m_i}}$. The $K \times K$ access codebook is partitioned into N sub matrices, $\mathbf{C}_{\mathbf{K} \times \mathbf{m_i}}$ with $1 \leq i \leq N$, where $\mathbf{C}_{K \times m_i}$ is the access code for user i.

In the proposed scheme, each user makes use of K time intervals (with $K \geq N$) to send its information. The data user i transmits over this time frame is $\underline{\mathbf{x}}^i = [x_1^i\, x_2^i\, \cdots\, x_{m_i}^i]$ (Note that in general different users may have different channel data rates $\frac{m_i}{K}$). At time $1 \leq k \leq K$, user i utilizes code $\underline{\mathbf{c}}_k^i = [c_k^i(1)\, c_k^i(2)\, \cdots\, c_k^i(m_i)]$ (the kth row of $\mathbf{C}_{\mathbf{K}\mathbf{x}\mathbf{m_i}}$), and transmits $\underline{\mathbf{x}}^i \underline{\mathbf{c}}_k^{i\,T}$, so that the received signal $\underline{\mathbf{y}} = [y_1\, y_2\, \cdots y_K]$ is given by

$$y_k = \sum_{i=1}^{N} \underline{\mathbf{x}}^i \underline{\mathbf{c}}_k^{i\,T} + z_k = \sum_{i=1}^{N} \sum_{j=1}^{m_i} x_j^i c_k^i(j) + z_k, \qquad 1 \leq k \leq K. \tag{4}$$

As noted before, the data to be sent by user i, $\underline{\mathbf{x}}^i$, is *repeated* during the K signaling times. Therefore, the overall power received from each is KP_i. Figure 2 illustrates the proposed scheme for the case of a two user case ($N = 2$) with

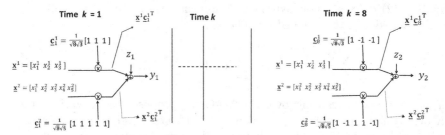

Fig. 2. Proposed scheme for two users ($N = 2$) with $K = 8$, $m_1 = 3$ and $m_2 = 5$. The upper branch corresponds to user 1 and the lower to user 2. Note the data of each user x_j^i is fixed for all the signaling times $1 \leq k \leq 8$.

$$
\mathbf{H_{8x8}} = \frac{1}{\sqrt{8}}
\begin{bmatrix}
1 & 1 & 1 & 1 & 1 & 1 & 1 & 1 \\
1 & -1 & 1 & -1 & 1 & -1 & 1 & -1 \\
1 & 1 & -1 & -1 & 1 & 1 & -1 & -1 \\
1 & -1 & -1 & 1 & 1 & -1 & -1 & 1 \\
1 & 1 & 1 & 1 & -1 & -1 & -1 & -1 \\
1 & -1 & 1 & -1 & -1 & 1 & -1 & 1 \\
1 & 1 & -1 & -1 & -1 & -1 & 1 & 1 \\
1 & -1 & -1 & 1 & -1 & 1 & 1 & -1
\end{bmatrix}
\tag{5}
$$

Fig. 3. 8×8 Hadamard matrix. Here $K = 8$, $m_1 = 3$ and $m_2 = 5$. To generate the matrix $\mathbf{C_{8 \times 8}}$, the first 3 columns are assigned to user 1 and then scaled by $\frac{1}{\sqrt{3}}$. The remaining 5 columns are assigned to user 2 and scaled by $\frac{1}{\sqrt{5}}$.

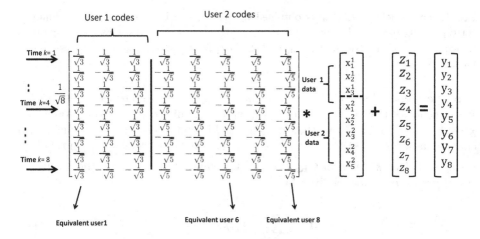

Fig. 4. Equivalent CDMA system corresponding to Figure 2. The first $m_1 = 3$ equivalent users correspond to the 3 different symbols of user 1 in our proposed scheme, while the next $m_2 = 5$ equivalent users correspond to the 5 different symbols of user 2.

$m_1 = 3$ and $m_2 = 5$ using the Hadamard matrix in Figure 3 to construct the access codes.

Notice that since the input source samples are i.i.d, the proposed scheme is equivalent to a CDMA system with K users and K spread sequences (the columns of the matrix $\mathbf{C}_{K \times K}$), with the first m_1 users of the equivalent scheme corresponding to the m_1 symbols of user 1, the next m_2 users of the equivalent scheme corresponding to the m_2 symbols of user 2, and so on. Figure 4 shows the equivalent CDMA system corresponding to Figure 2.

Note that the off diagonal entries of $\mathbf{C}_{K \times K} \mathbf{C}_{K \times K}{}^T$ are zero because each $\underline{\mu}_j^i$ is a scaled column of an orthogonal matrix. Hence $\mathbf{C}_{K \times K} \mathbf{C}_{K \times K}{}^T = \mathbf{D}$ is a $K \times K$ diagonal matrix with N distinct values (m_i entries of value $\frac{1}{m_i}$, where $1 \leq i \leq N$). Thus, the proposed scheme is equivalent to K orthogonal Single-Input Single-Output (SISO) channels and its sum rate capacity in terms of bits per channel use is

$$C_{scheme} = \frac{1}{K} \left[\sum_{i=1}^{N} \sum_{j=1}^{m_i} \left(\frac{1}{2} \log_2 \left(1 + \frac{KP_i}{m_i} \right) \right) \right], \tag{6}$$

where we have divided by K because the proposed system uses the MAC K times. Note that the power of each parallel SISO channel is the power of the spreading sequence $\underline{\mu}_j^{i\,T} \underline{\mu}_j^i = \frac{1}{m_i}$ multiplied times the overal power KP_i received from user i.

From (3), the maximum sum rate is

$$C_{MAC} = \frac{1}{2} \log_2(1 + \sum_{i=1}^{N} P_i) =$$
$$\frac{1}{2} \log_2 \left[1 + \sum_{i=1}^{N} \sum_{j=1}^{m_i} (\frac{P_i}{m_i}) \right]. \tag{7}$$

It can be easily shown that C_{scheme} and C_{MAC} are equal if and only if

$$\frac{P_i}{m_i} = \frac{P_j}{m_j} \qquad \forall j \neq i \ \ with \ \ 1 \leq i, j \leq N. \tag{8}$$

This result is not surprising since the equivalent CDMA scheme achieves the MAC capacity when all the K equivalent users have the same power.

Particularizing the above result for the 2-user case ($N = 2$) gives the optimal m_1 and m_2: $\frac{P_1}{m_1^*} = \frac{P_2}{m_2^*}$, such that $m_1^* + m_2^* = K$. Solving for the optimal m_i, $i = 1, 2$ yields

$$m_i^* = \frac{KP_i}{P_1 + P_2} \qquad i = 1, 2 \tag{9}$$

Since m_i is the number of columns assigned to user i, it should be an integer. Even though m_i^* may not be integers, if the code size K is chosen large enough (m_1, m_2) can be chosen as close to the optimal (m_1^*, m_2^*) as desired.

We can break up (6) to obtain the rate achieved by each user. For example, for the two user case, $N = 2$, we have

$$R_1 = \frac{1}{K}\left(\sum_{j=1}^{m_1}\frac{1}{2}\log_2(1 + \frac{KP_1}{m_1})\right) \tag{10}$$

$$R_2 = \frac{1}{K}\left(\sum_{j=m_1+1}^{K}\frac{1}{2}\log_2(1 + \frac{KP_2}{m_2})\right). \tag{11}$$

Figure 5 shows the maximal rates achieved by each user for the two user case when $P_1 = 8$ and $P_2 = 1$. The MAC capacity region is obtained from (2). In the Figure, we choose $K = 64$. As indicated in (8), there exists a point in the graph in which the proposed scheme achieves the MAC capacity.

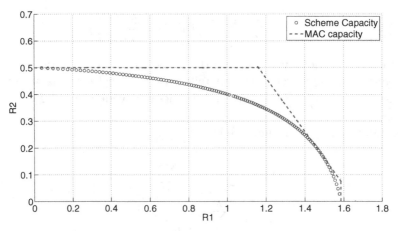

Fig. 5. MAC capacity and the proposed scheme capacity for $P_1 = 8$, $P_2 = 1$ and codebook size $K = 64$. Each point of the blue curve is obtained from (10) and (11) by sweeping m_1 from 0 to 64.

Note that Figure 5 is similar to the one obtained with an orthogonal FDMA (TDMA) system. However, the proposed scheme has the advantage of the relative easiness of the analysis and the potential to extend it to situations where the users are correlated. We also note that orthogonal systems would require the use of different rates in the analog joint source-channel encoder for each user, while here the rate is incorporated into the access scheme itself, which facilitates the design.

3   Analog Joint Source Channel Coding

To simplify the problem, we will consider the case of a MAC with two users transmitting independent Gaussian sources, S, of mean zero and variance σ_S^2.

Previous to the access scheme, we assume each user processes its source using an $M:1$ analog joint source channel encoder. When $M = 1$, the source samples, s_j^i, $j = 1, \ldots, m_i$ are input directly to the access scheme so that $x_j^i = \sqrt{\frac{P_i}{\sigma_S^2}} s_j^i$, $j = 1, \ldots, m_i$ while for $M = 2$ two consecutive source symbols (s_{2j}^i, s_{2j+1}^i) are encoded by a space-filling curve to generate the channel symbol x_j^i.

Under the Mean Squared Error (MSE) distortion criteria, the rate distortion function of any of the aforementioned sources is given by [12]

$$R(D_i) = \begin{cases} \frac{1}{2} \log_2(\frac{\sigma_S^2}{D_i}) & \text{for } D_i < \sigma_S^2, \\ 0 & \text{otherwise} \end{cases} \tag{12}$$

where D_i is average MSE distortion incurred by the source of user i.

Considering optimal power allocation for each of the users as given by (8), the theoretical limit for this problem is given by

$$M \left[\frac{m_1}{K} \log(\frac{\sigma_S^2}{D_1}) + \frac{m_2}{K} \log(\frac{\sigma_S^2}{D_2}) \right] < \frac{1}{2} \log(1 + P_1 + P_2). \tag{13}$$

By defining

$$\overline{SDR} = \frac{m_1}{K} \log_{10}(\frac{\sigma_S^2}{D_1}) + \frac{m_2}{K} \log_{10}(\frac{\sigma_S^2}{D_2}), \tag{14}$$

(13) can be re-written as

$$\overline{SDR} < \frac{5}{M} \log_{10}(1 + P_1 + P_2). \tag{15}$$

Notice the change in the base of the logarithm.

Again, it is important to remark that (15) does not hold for all combinations of P_1 and P_2, but it does when the power allocation for each user is optimized according to (8), and in general it holds for any combination of powers where the sum rate is maximized as indicated in (3). Notice that (15) represents the minimum "average" distortion incurred by the system when user i performs bandwidth compression by a factor of M and utilizes m_i access codes. We will use (15) to represent the Optimum Performance Theoretically Attainable (OPTA) in terms of $\overline{SDR}$ vs $SNR = 10 \log_{10}(P_1 + P_2)$, and compare this optimal performance with simulation results obtained from the proposed system when, for each SNR value, the power allocation for each user, $SNR_i = 10 log_{10} P_i$, is optimized following (8).

3.1 Uncoded Transmission ($M = 1$)

As explained before, the source samples, s_j^i, $j = 1, \ldots, m_i$, are input directly to the access scheme so that $x_j^i = \sqrt{\frac{P_i}{\sigma_S^2}} s_j^i$, $j = 1, \ldots, m_i$. Notice that with this scheme user i transmits m_i source symbols using K signaling intervals.

At the receiver site, we perform MMSE decoding on the received vector $\mathbf{y}$ to obtain the MMSE estimate of the transmitted vector $\mathbf{s}$ comprising user 1 and user 2 data. We observe that the received vector $\mathbf{y}$ can be expressed as $\mathbf{y} = \mathbf{H\Gamma s} + \mathbf{z}$, where $\mathbf{\Gamma}$ is a diagonal scaling matrix containing either $\sqrt{\frac{P_1}{\sigma_S^2}}$ or $\sqrt{\frac{P_2}{\sigma_S^2}}$. The MMSE estimate of the transmitted data is given by

$$\hat{\underline{\mathbf{s}}} = ((\mathbf{H\Gamma})^T \mathbf{H\Gamma} + 2\mathbf{I})^{-1}(\mathbf{H\Gamma})^T \mathbf{y}. \tag{16}$$

Since $\mathbf{H}^T\mathbf{H} = \mathbf{I}$, (16) reduces to

$$\hat{\underline{\mathbf{s}}} = (\mathbf{\Gamma}^T\mathbf{\Gamma} + 2\mathbf{I})^{-1}(\mathbf{H\Gamma})^T\mathbf{y}, \tag{17}$$

which, given the orthogonalization produced by the CDMA-like access scheme, is just the result of applying a matched filter.

3.2   2:1 Bandwidth Reduction ($M = 2$)

As indicated before, in this case each one of the users utilizes a space-filling curve to encode two consecutive source symbols (s_{2j}^i, s_{2j+1}^i) into symbol x_j^i. Therefore, user i transmits $2m_i$ source symbols over $m_1 + m_2$ signaling intervals. Systems based on the use of space filling curves were proposed independently by Shannon and Kotelnikov [14, 15]. Here, we consider the non-linear Archimedean spiral defined parametrically as

$$\begin{cases} u = \dfrac{\Delta_i}{\pi}\theta\sin\theta \\ v = \dfrac{\Delta_i}{\pi}\theta\cos\theta \end{cases} for \ \theta \geq 0, \qquad \begin{cases} u = -\dfrac{\Delta_i}{\pi}\theta\sin\theta \\ v = \dfrac{\Delta_i}{\pi}\theta\cos\theta \end{cases} for \ \theta < 0, \tag{18}$$

where Δ_i is the distance between two neighboring spiral arms in the curve corresponding to user i and θ is the angle from the origin to the point (u, v) on the curve. The Archimedean spiral is studied in detail in [5]. Notice that if Δ_i is fixed, then there is a one to one mapping between the angle, θ, and the pair on the curve (u, v). The mapping function $M_{\Delta_i}(s_{2j}^i, s_{2j+1}^i)$ takes any source pair (s_{2j}^i, s_{2j+1}^i) and projects it to the closest point on the spiral, that is

$$\hat{\theta}_j^i = M_{\Delta_i}(s_{2j}^i, s_{2j+1}^i) = $$
$$\arg\min_{\theta}\{(s_{2j}^i \pm \frac{\Delta_i}{\pi}\theta\sin\theta)^2 + (s_{2j+1}^i - \frac{\Delta_i}{\pi}\theta\cos\theta)^2\}. \tag{19}$$

After the mapping, $\hat{\theta}_j^i$ is processed by the function $T_{\alpha_i}(\hat{\theta}_j^i) = (\hat{\theta}_j^i)^{\alpha_i}$ to produce x_j^i. For each user, both parameters (Δ_i, α_i) are optimized according to the corresponding power allocation P_i [6], where, for each SNR, P_i, the optimal power allocation, is chosen according to (8).

The decoder is composed of two main components. First, the MMSE outer detector (similar to the MMSE detector that was used in section 4.B) that decouples the two users data. Secondly, the inner decoder after the MIMO detector which performs Maximum Likelihood (ML) decoding on the 2:1 spiral compression system. Given the received vector $\mathbf{y}$, the MMSE estimate of the transmitted

Encoder

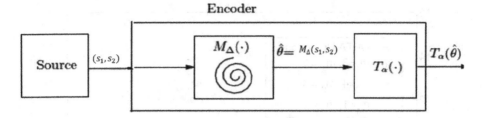

Fig. 6. System diagram of an encoder based on the 2:1 Archimedean spiral

vector $\mathbf{x}$ is obtained as in (16). Then the ML estimate of θ of user i is calculated by inverting the transformation $T_{\alpha_i}(\cdot)$

$$(\hat{\theta}^i_j)_{ML} = T_{\alpha_i}^{-1}(\hat{x}^i_j). \tag{20}$$

Finally, we perform the inverse mapping on $(\hat{\theta}^i_j)_{ML}$ according to (18) to obtain the ML estimates of the original transmitted source pair $(\hat{s}^i_{2j}, \hat{s}^i_{2j+1})$ of each user.

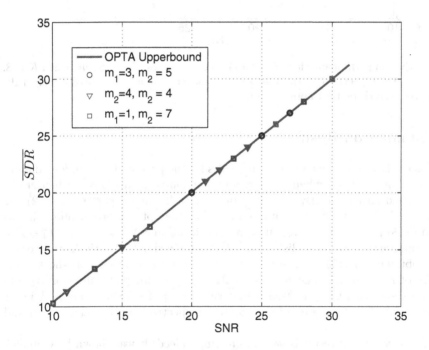

Fig. 7. System performance for $M = 1$ and different values of m_1 and m_2 when $K = 8$. Note that irrespectively of the values of m_1 and m_2 the scheme achieves the SDR upperbound exactly.

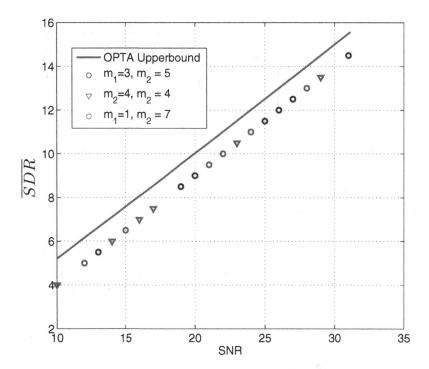

Fig. 8. System performance for $M = 2$ and different values of m_1 and m_2 when $K = 8$. Notice that irrespectively of the values of m_1 and m_2, the achieved SDR is only 1 dB away from the theoretical upperbound.

4   Simulation Results

In this section we present simulation results for the proposed system for different values of m_1 and m_2 when $K = 8$ and the source symbols of each user are transmitted either directly ($M = 1$) or using a 2:1 spiral curve ($M = 2$). As described before, in our simulations we utilize the optimal power allocation as given in (8) for an overall system power specification $SNR = 10 \log_{10}(P_1 + P_2)$, and compare the "average" distortion $\overline{SDR}$ as defined in (14) with the theoretical limit obtained in (15). Notice that this limit does not depend on the specific values of m_1 and m_2. The results for $M = 1$ and different values of m_1 and m_2 are shown in Figure 7. Notice that the proposed scheme is *optimal*, i.e. it achieves the distortion bound for all SNRs irrespectively of the values of m_1 and m_2.

The above shown result is very interesting indeed. It was shown by Gobblick [16] that for point-to-point communications, uncoded transmission of Gaussian sources through Gaussian channels is optimal when one source symbol is transmitted per channel use. Our system achieves this optimal performance since the use of the access codes converts the MAC channel into K orthogonal parallel SISO channels.

Simulation results for the $M = 2$ case and different values of m_1 and m_2, with $K = 8$, are shown in Figure 8. Notice that irrespectively of the values of m_1 and m_2, our system is only about 1 dB away from the OPTA for a wide range of SNRs.

5   Conclusion

We have proposed the use of a CDMA-like access scheme for the transmission of independent users through a MAC using analog joint source-channel coding. The proposed access scheme allows for the use of different rates for each user, and achieves the theoretical limit when the power is allocated optimally to each user. The sources are encoded by standard space-filling curves optimized for point-to-point AWGN channels. Simulation results show the optimality of the practical analog coding schemes when each user transmits the source symbols directly through the channel. The resulting performance when 2:1 spiral mappings are used to encode each source lies within 1 dB of the theoretical limit.

Acknowledgement. This work was supported in part by NSF Awards EECS-0725422 and CIF-0915800 and Xunta de Galicia, MINECO of Spain, and FEDER funds of the EU under grants 2012/287, TEC2010-19545-C04-01 and CSD2008-00010.

References

1. Shannon, C.: A Mathematical Theory of Communication. The Bell System Technical Journal (27), 379–423 (1948)
2. Ramstad, T.: Shannon Mappings for Robust Communication. Telektronikk 98(1), 114–128 (2002)
3. Chung, S.: On the Construction of Some Capacity-Approaching Coding Schemes. Ph.D. thesis, Massachusetts Institute of Technology (2000)
4. Gastpar, M., Rimoldi, B., Vetterli, M.: To Code, or not to Code: Lossy Source-Channel Communication Revisited. IEEE Transactions on Information Theory 49(5), 1147–1158 (2003)
5. Hekland, F., Floor, P., Ramstad, T.: Shannon-Kotelnikov Mappings in Joint Source-Channel Coding. IEEE Transactions on Communications 57(1), 94–105 (2009)
6. Hu, Y., Garcia-Frias, J., Lamarca, M.: Analog Joint Source-Channel Coding Using Non-Linear Curves and MMSE Decoding. IEEE Transactions on Communications 59(11), 3016–3026 (2011)
7. Brante, G., Souza, R., Garcia-Frias, J.: Spatial Diversity Using Analog Joint Source-Channel Coding in Wireless Channels. IEEE Transactions on Communications 61(1), 301–311 (2012)
8. Fresnedo, O., Vázquez-Araujo, F., Castedo, L., González López, M., García-Frias, J.: Analog Joint Source-Channel Coding in MIMOrcia Rayleigh Fading Channels. In: Proceedings of 20th European Signal Processing Conference (EUSIPCO 2012), Bucharest, Romania (August 2012)

9. Fresnedo, O., Vázquez-Araujo, F., Castedo, L., García-Frias, J.: Analog Joint Source-Channel Coding for OFDM Systems. In: Proceedings of 14th IEEE International Workshop on Signal Processing Advances in Wireless Communications (SPAWC 2013), Darmstadt, Germany (June 2013)

10. Floor, P., et al.: Zero-Delay Joint Source-Channel Coding for a Bivariate Gaussian on a Gaussian MAC. IEEE Transactions on Communications 60(10), 3091–3102 (2012)

11. Servetto, S.: Lattice Quantization with Side Information, Codes, Asymptotics, and Applications in Sensor Networks. IEEE Transactions on Information Theory 53(2), 714–731 (2007)

12. Cover, T., Thomas, J.: Elements of Information Theory. Wiley-Interscience, New York (1991)

13. Lapidoth, A., Tinguely, S.: Sending a Bivariate Gaussian Source over a Gaussian MAC. IEEE Transactions on Information Theory 56(6), 2714–2752 (2010)

14. Shannon, C.: Communication in The Presence of Noise. In: Proceedings of IRE, pp. 10–21 (January 1949)

15. Kotel'nikov, V.: The Theory of Optimum Noise Immunity. McGraw-Hill Book Company, Inc., New York (1959)

16. Goblick, T.: Theoretical Limitations on the Transmission of Data from Analog Sources. IEEE Transactions on Information Theory 11(10), 558–567 (1965)

Inner Convolutional Codes and Ordered Statistics Decoding in a Multiple Access System Enabling Wireless Coexistence[*]

Dmitry Osipov[1,2]

[1] Institute for Information Transmission Problems Russian Academy of Sciences,
19 Bolshoy Karetny Lane Moscow 127994, Russia
[2] National Research University Higher School of Economics,
20 Myasnitskaya Ulitsa Moscow 101000, Russia
d_osipov@iitp.ru

Abstract. The problem of wireless coexistence will become crucial in years to come. Future generation communication systems will have to endure interference induced by communication systems operating within the same frequency bands. Coded DHA FH OFDMA using ordered statistics is well suited for the task. This paper addresses the problem of transmission rate increase in a coded DHA FH OFDMA system. It will be demonstrated that using q-ary convolutional codes constructed from punctured Reed-Solomon codes as inner codes in a coded DHA FH OFDMA provides rates sufficiently higher than those ensured by block inner codes ensuring at the same time reasonable decoding complexity, relatively small codeword length and low probability of error.

Keywords: multiple access, wireless coexistence, ordered statistics, convolutional code.

1 Introduction

In recent decades spectral rate maximization in a wireless communications has become the major goal for the researchers in the field. However since the demand for wireless services grows drastically and the available bandwith is limited the problem of wireless coexistence will become crucial in years to come. Recently proposed solutions are for the most part aimed at avoiding the signal transmitted by the coexisting wireless system [1–3]. However the problem of wireless coexistence can be treated in another way: since in years to come available frequency band will be highly overloaded future generation systems should withstand severe interference. This can be done by a proper signal-code construction choice. In this paper a coded DHA FH OFDMA system will be considered [4,5]. It has been demonstrated that coded DHA FH OFDMA can perform even under severe jamming [5,6]. This paper addresses the problem of rate increase in a coded DHA FH OFDMA.

---

[*] This work has been supported by the RFBR (research project No. 12-07-31035 mol_a)

M. Jonsson et al. (Eds.): MACOM 2013, LNCS 8310, pp. 33–38, 2013.

This paper is organized as follows. In section 2 a short sketch of a coded DHA FH OFDMA system with noncoherent RANK receiver(decoder) is given. In section 3 an inner q-ary convolutional code and Viterbi algorithm in RANK metric employment in a coded DHA FH OFDMA will be proposed. In section 3 the effectiveness of the proposed approach to inner code choice will be verified by means of simulation. Finally in section 4 the obtained results and future work perspectives will be discussed.

2   Transmission and Reception

Let us consider a multiple access system in which U_A active users transmit information via a channel split into Q identical nonoverlapping subchannels by means of OFDM. Information that is to be transmitted is encoded into a codeword of a (n, k, d) q-ary code $(q < Q)$. Whenever a user is to transmit a $q-$ary symbol it places 1 in the position of the vector $\bar{a}_g$ corresponding to the symbol in question within the scope of the mapping in use (in what follows it will be assumed that all positions of the vector are enumerated from 1 to Q, moreover without loss of generality we shall assume that the 1st subchannel corresponds to 0, the 2nd subchannel corresponds to 1 and so on). Then a random permutation of the aforesaid vector is performed and the resulting vector $\pi_g(\bar{a}_g)$ is used to form an OFDM symbol (permutations are selected equiprobably from the set of all possible permutations and the choice is performed whenever a symbol is to be transmitted). Therefore in order to transmit a codeword a user is to transmit n OFDM symbols. A sequence of OFDM symbols, corresponding to a certain codeword that has been sent by a certain user, will be referred to as a frame. Note that frames transmitted by different users need not be block synchronized, i.e. if within the time interval a certain user transmits a frame that corresponds to a codeword, symbols transmitted by another user within the same time period do not necessarily all comprise one codeword. Moreover, it will be assumed that transmissions from different users are uncoordinated, i.e. none of the users has information about the others. In what follows we shall assume that all users transmit information in OFDM frames and the transmission is quasisynchronous. In terms of the model under consideration this assumption means that transmissions from different users are symbol synchronized.

Within the scope of reception of a certain codeword the receiver is to receive n OFDM symbols corresponding to the codeword in question. Note that the receiver is assumed to be synchronized with transmitters of all users. Therefore all the permutations done within the scope of transmission of the codeword in question are known to the user. The receiver measures energies at the outputs of all subchannels (let us designate the vector of the measurements as b_g where g is the number of the OFDM symbol) and applies inverse permutation to each vector b_g corresponding to the respective OFDM symbol thus reconstructing initial order of elements and obtaining vector $\tilde{b}_g = \pi_g^{-1}(b_g)$. Let us consider a matrix X that consists of vectors $\tilde{b}_g = \pi_g^{-1}(b_g)$ that correspond to the codeword transmitted by the user under consideration. Let us note that matrix X corresponds to the received codeword. The detector is to decide on the transmitted codeword by analyzing the matrix X.

The straightforward decoding algorithm clearly boils down to computing the sum of elements corresponding to each codeword (i.e. total energy corresponding to the respective codeword) and choosing the codeword that corresponds to the maximum sum. Hereinafter we shall refer to it as "maximum energy algorithm" or MEA. For AWGN channels with high SNR values MEA is equivalent to maximum likelihood (ML) decoding. However in real life scenarios SNR can be low either due to severe fading or due to the signal transmitted by a system employing DS CDMA. Therefore MEA is not suitable for both Gaussian channels with low SNR and fading channels. To overcome this problem several robust metrics based on ordered statistics were proposed. Hereinafter we shall consider a metric proposed in [6]. Within the scope of the calculation of the metric in question each element of the matrix is associated with the number of elements of the matrix that are smaller than the respective element (following the terminology of [6] this value will be refereed to as rank). Thus a metric associated with each codeword is simply the sum of ranks of the elements corresponding to this codeword i.e. the algorithm is almost equivalent to MEA but for the fact that it is RANK matrix not the matrix X that is used to compute the decision statistics.

3   Inner Code Choice

Let us consider the problem of inner code choice in a coded DHA FH OFDMA system in terms of both computational complexity and transmission rate. First of all one can notice that whatever metric is used the distance of the inner code is crucial. This is easily explainable since one can argue that if two codewords coincide in certain positions (i.e. certain elements of the matrix correspond to both codewords) these are the postions in which the codewords differ from each other which makes the decoder choose one codeword over another. Thus it is desirable to choose inner code with maximum possible code distance (code length being fixed). Therefore it seems that Reed-Solomon codes are perfect candidates for inner codes in a coded DHA FH OFDMA. However since the decoding algorithms that were mentioned in the previous section boil down to exhaustive search due to complexity considerations the number of information symbols is to be relatively small even if a small field is used (e.g. if we use $q = 8$ and $k = 4$ we need to compute $M = q^k = 4096$ decision statistics and choose the maximum one. Obviously the decision statistics can be computed in parallel. However this will require 4096 computing units and still 4096 values shall be sorted.) On the other hand the length of the resulting code (and thus the cardinality of the finite field in use) is to be great enough to guarantee that the probability of erroneous decision will be below the desired value. Therefore it is advisable to use relatively large fields which means that the number of information symbols is to be very small in order to provide reasonable computational complexity. Thus the resulting rate of the code will be very low. Punctured Reed-Solomon codes can be considered as a good tradeoff to a certain extent but the resulting rate will remain relatively low. Thus even MDS codes that can be considered (in a sense) optimal can hardly provide desirable transmission rates. On the other hand convolutional codes can provide relatively high rates, sufficient code length and can be decoded e.g. with a Viterbi algorithm which is known to have complexity exponential with overall constraint length but linear with the number of information symbols (as opposed to exhaustive search which is exponential with the number of information symbols.)

Let us consider a q-ary convolutional code with rate $1/c$, memory m and s_i information symbols (the length of the resulting codeword is therefore $l = s_i \cdot c$) constructed in following way: the information bit and the content of the shift register are encoded with systematic $(q - 1, m + 1)$ Reed-Solomon code (further on this code will be referred to as component code). Each tuple consists the information symbol and $c-1$ parity symbols (in other word each tuple is obtained by shortening and puncturing of the component code).To preserve code rate we will use direct truncation. Since RANK metric employed in [6] is an additive one Viterbi algorithm [7] can be used to decode the code under consideration.

4   Simulation

Let as consider a DHA FH OFDMA system with the inner convolutional code described above. Hereinafter we shall assume that the system under consideration operates within a AWGN channel ($Q = 4096$). However since we are aiming at investigating the case when the system in question experiences severe interference we shall assume that the SNR is -20dB (let us note, however, that this is the signal-to-noise ratio within all the bandwidth available to all users. Since the user under consideration uses information obtained via narrowband subchannels the effective SNR per subchannel will be sufficiently higher) and there are $U_A = 500$ users operating within the same band. Those users will be further on referred to as "interfering" and we shall assume that each interfering user transmits a signal within a certain subchannel and the power of this signal at the receiver side is 100 times greater than that of the signal transmitted by the user under consideration. Hereinafter we shall consider the case with $m = 1$. Thus the decoder will consist of q units (each corresponding to a certain memory state) and each unit is to perform $q \cdot (c - 1)$ additions s_i times and to compare q branch metrics (each comparison is in fact a sorting i.e. the complexity of each comparison will be $O(q \cdot log(q))$. Please note that to calculate the RANK matrix all the elements of the matrix X are to be sorted. In this respect the proposed algorithm does not differ from the one described in [6]. If q is large it is reasonable to choose small values of s_i and c to make the complexity of the decoding procedure and the RANK matrix calculation procedure low and to provide acceptable code rates. In what follows we shall consider the case $q = 256$ In Table 1. Symbol Error Rates (SERs) obtained for $s_i = \{6, 8\}$ and $c = \{6, 8\}$ are presented

As can be seen even for relatively high rates (1/6 and 1/8 respectively) SER ensured by the convolutional code in use is very low. Increase in c (by 4/3) results in more than 10 times decrease in SER.Therefore relatively short and high-rate

Table 1. SER provided by short convolutional inner code

c (tuple length in symbols)	6	8
s (number of information symbols)		
6	$5, 1 * 10^{-3}$	$3, 33 \cdot 10^{-4}$
8	$2, 9 * 10^{-3}$	$1, 249 \cdot 10^{-4}$

outer codes can provide low probability of decoding failure (i.e. either decoding denial or erroneous decoding.) For instance if punctured (48,34) RS code over $GF(256)$ is used as outer code and convolutional code with $c = 6$ and $s_i = 6$ as inner code it is easy to show that the probability of the fact that the decoding will result in either decoding denial (which is more likely) or erroneous decoding will be less then $1, 44 \cdot 10^{-10}$ (please note that the frame length will be 1728 OFDM symbols and resulting code rate will be more then 1/10).

Since each tuple of the code in use is a codeword of the punctured RS code it seems reasonable to compare the performance of the system employing a convolutional code with rate 1/c and punctured RS code with the same rate.

Table 2. Convolutional code vs. short punctured RS code of the same rate

	Convolutional code (c=6)		Punctured RS code (n=6)
Number of information symbols of the convolutional code, s	s=6	s=8	
Symbol Error Rate	$5, 1 \cdot 10^{-3}$	$2, 9 \cdot 10^{-3}$	$3, 26 \cdot 10^{-2}$
	Convolutional code (c=8)		
Number of information symbols of the convolutional code, s	s=6	s=8	
Symbol Error Rate	$3, 3 \cdot 10^{-4}$	$1, 25 \cdot 10^{-4}$	$1, 3 \cdot 10^{-3}$

As can be seen from Table 2 SER ensured by punctured RS code with rate 1/c is about 10 time greater than that ensured by the convolutional code of the same rate (for $s_i = 8$), which means shorter outer codes with higher rates can be applied if inner convolutional code is used. On the other hand the complexity of the decoding procedure is considerably greater for the convolutional code both due to the fact that the code itself is s_i times longer and since the number of matrix elements to be sorted is much greater. Thus the choice between moderate length convolutional codes and very short punctured RS codes as inner code for a coded DHA FH OFDMA system should be considered as a tradeoff between complexity decrease and SER decrease.

5 Conclusion and Future Work

Hereinabove a coded DHA FH OFDMA system with inner q-ary convolutional code has been considered. It has been demonstrated that using q-ary convolutional codes (constructed from Reed-Solomon codes) as inner codes in a coded DHA FH OFDMA provides rates sufficiently higher than those ensured by block inner codes with reasonable decoding complexity, relatively small codeword length (which means that overall length of the frame corresponding to the codeword of the resulting concatenated code and thus the delay will decrease as well) and low probability of error (per symbol). Thus a coded DHA FH OFDMA with inner convolutional codes employing Viterbi decoding in RANK metric can be considered as a very promising candidate for future generation communication systems.

However the problem is to be investigated in more detail.Hereinafter we have considered an AWGN channel only. However most systems operate in multipath fading channels. Simulations results obtained in [6] show that RANK decoder can be successfully employed in a fading environment. Since the proposed decoding algorithm is a modification of the decoding algorithm introduced in [6](obtained by replacing exhaustive search by a Viterbi algorithm) the proposed multiple access system can operate in fading channels too. However obtaining desirable probability of error (per symbol) in a fading channel will require longer and probably more powerful convolutional codes. It should be noted that the problem of inner code parameters (i.e. length, rate, overall constraint length, component block code parameters etc.) choice is closely related to the problem of outer code choice. Moreover the overall complexity of the decoding procedure can be further reduced e.g. by replacing Viterbi decoding by list decoding. These problems are subject to future investigation.

References

1. Golmie, N., Chevrollier, N., Rebala, O.: Bluetooth Adaptive Frequency Hopping and Scheduling. In: Proceedings of Military Communications, MILCOM 2003, Boston, MA, pp. 1138–1142 (October 2003)
2. Golmie, N.: Bluetooth Dynamic Scheduling and Interference Mitigation. Mobile Networks and Applications 9(1), 21–31 (2004)
3. Chiasserini, C.F., Rao, R.R.: Coexistence Mechanisms for Interference Mitigation between IEEE 802.11 WLANs and Bluetooth. In: Proceedings of IEEE INFOCOMM 2002, pp. 590–598 (2002)
4. Osipov, D., Frolov, A., Zyablov, V.: Multiple Access System for a Vector Disjunctive Channel. Problems of Information Transmission 48(3), 243–249 (2012)
5. Osipov, D., Frolov, A., Zyablov, V.V.: Multitone jamming-proof q-ary code-based signal-code construction. In: Collected Works of the 34th Conference of Young Scientists and Specialists Information Technologies and Systems, Gelendzhik, Russia, October 2-7, pp. 168–173 (2011) (in Russian)
6. Kondrashov, K., Afanassiev, V.: Ordered statistics decoding for semi-orthogonal linear block codes over random non-Gaussian channels. In: Proc. of the Thirteenth International Workshop on Algebraic and Combinatorial Coding Theory, Pomorie, Bulgaria, June 15-21, pp. 192–196 (2012)
7. Viterbi, A.J.: Error Bounds for Convolutional Codes and an Asymptotically Optimum Decoding Algorithm. IEEE Trans. Information Theory IT-13, 260–269 (1967)

Delay-Doppler Space Division-Based Multiple-Access Solves Multiple-Target Detection

Yutaka Jitsumatsu[1], Tohru Kohda[1], and Kazuyuki Aihara[2,*]

[1] Dept. Informatics, Kyushu University
744 Motooka, Nishi-ku, Fukuoka, 819-0395, Japan
{jitumatu,kohda}@inf.kyushu-u.ac.jp
[2] Institute of Industrial Science, The University of Tokyo
4-6-1 Komaba Meguro-ku, Tokyo 153-8505, Japan
aihara@sat.t.u-tokyo.ac.jp

Abstract. Non-coherent signal with unknown delay and Doppler is recovered by Gabor Division/Spread Spectrum System (GD/S³). A transmitted signal in GD/S³ is expressed by a Gabor expansion whose expansion coefficient is a product of time domain (TD) and frequency domain (FD) spread spectrum (SS) codes. A receiver in GD/S³ employs multiple TD integrators with TD SS codes and a prescribed delay and FD integrators with FD SS codes and a prescribed Doppler. These integrators estimate and update Doppler and delay cooperatively and individually. The receiver of GD/S³ is applicable to a multiple-target problem by borrowing an idea from code division multiple access (CDMA) philosophy. Namely, a delay-Doppler space is partitioned into four sub-spaces and their associated two-dimensional (2D) SS codes are assigned. Four delay-Doppler targets can be resolved and detected by four pairs of TD and FD correlators using the assigned SS codes.

Keywords: Spread Spectrum Multiple Access, Code Division Multiple Access, multi-path detection, delay-Doppler determination.

1 Introduction

Synchronization is the first task to be established in any communication system before data transmission [1–3]. Estimation of the time delay and Doppler's shift is an old problem in radar and sonar [4–9], but recently it has attracted much attention in mobile communications [10], Global Positioning System (GPS) [11], ultra wideband (UWB), and underwater acoustic (UWA) communications [12].

---

* This research is supported by the Aihara Innovative Mathematical Modelling Project, the Japan Society for the Promotion of Science (JSPS) through the "Funding Program for World-Leading Innovative R&D on Science and Technology (FIRST Program)," initiated by the Council for Science and Technology Policy (CSTP).

M. Jonsson et al. (Eds.): MACOM 2013, LNCS 8310, pp. 39–53, 2013.

Consider a narrow-band single-path channel model with a received signal, defined by

$$r(t) = \Re[\alpha \widetilde{s}(t - t_d)e^{j(2\pi(f_c+f_D)(t-t_d)+\varphi)} + \widetilde{\xi}(t)e^{j2\pi f_c t}], \tag{1}$$

where $\Re[\cdot]$ denotes the real part, $\widetilde{s}(t)$ and $\widetilde{\xi}(t)$ are complex lowpass equivalent of a transmitted signal and a narrow-band white Gaussian noise, α, t_d, f_c, f_D and φ are an attenuation factor, a propagation time delay, a carrier frequency, a Doppler's shift, and an initial phase. Suppose $\alpha = 1$. Main task in communication is to recover data symbols, that are embedded in $\widetilde{s}(t)$, from $r(t)$ without information for f_D, t_d and φ. The conventional phase locked loop (PLL) minimizes the phase distortion caused by φ under the condition $f_D \simeq 0$, and a single parameter estimation for t_d is performed. However, if f_D is larger than the locking range of the PLL, synchronization is no longer maintained.

Usually two dimensional estimation is performed on a Time Domain (TD) signal, which results in a brute-force detection. How can we give a simultaneous t_d and f_D determination without their prescribed information? This question is at the heart of signal processing for communication.

Recently, Compressed Sensing (CS) technique has been applied to radar [13–15]. In [14], a new algorithm realizing super-resolution radar is proposed. The method in [15] is based on a signal recovery of signals with finite rate of innovation. Advantage of CS-based radar is that multiple targets can be identified with improved resolution.

The main concern of delay-Doppler determination is how to design a transmitted signal $s(t) = \Re[\widetilde{s}(t)e^{j2\pi f_c t}]$. To do it, we use the classical Gabor's expansion [16], defined by

$$\widetilde{s}(t) = \sum_{q=1}^{P} \sum_{q'=1}^{P'} d_q \widetilde{v}(t - qT)e^{j2\pi q' F(t-\frac{qT}{2})}, \tag{2}$$

where d_q is a data symbol with address $\boldsymbol{q} = (q, q')$, $\widetilde{v}(t)$ is a signature waveform, and T and F are time and frequency spacings[1]. The prime symbol (') is used for frequency domain (FD), hereafter. A time shift of $-\frac{qT}{2}$ in the exponent in Eq. (2) is introduced so that a signal and its Fourier transform (FT) are perfectly symmetrical in terms of t_d and f_D. In this case, they are said to satisfy Time-Frequency Symmetry (TFS). Motivated by the conventional TD spread spectrum (SS) code acquisition for timing synchronization [17], FD SS codes have been introduced for frequency synchronization [18]. Transmitter and receiver are called to satisfy separable property (SP), if a delay-Doppler determination problem is factorized into two one-parameter estimations: one is for estimating f_D in TD signal, given estimated $\hat{t}_d$, and the other is for estimating t_d in FD signal, given estimated $\hat{f}_D$. The TFS has been shown to be a sufficient condition for a signal to satisfy SP [19].

The receiver consists of arrays of TD and FD correlators. These correlators exchange approximations of $\hat{f}_D$ and $\hat{t}_d$ each other and update them alternatively and iteratively [18]. Such an algorithm, referred to as a Phase Updating Loop

---

[1] A block to be processed at one time is composed of $P \cdot P'$ data.

(PUL) [19], can allow large delay and Doppler up to T and F with precision fractions of T and F. Such a large frequency deviation is beyond what the conventional PLL presumes.

A Gabor Division/Spread Spectrum System (GD/S^3) has been designed to be a tolerant communication system in a deteriorated environment with heavy Doppler as well as an inaccurate carrier frequency of a local oscillator. Applications of GD/S^3 include fundamental communication systems, such as machine-to-machine communication, in vivo communication, robot-to-robot communication, ranging, indoor communication, and sensor networks.

To discuss a multiple-target determination, we borrow an idea from code division multiple access (CDMA) philosophy. Namely, the target space is partitioned into four sub-spaces and their associated two-dimensional (2D) SS codes are assigned. Four pairs of TD and FD correlators using the assigned SS codes are introduced [20]. Each pair of correlators acquires synchronization if a termination criterion is satisfied, otherwise no target is declared.

2   Phase Distortion Caused by Data Transmission

Recently proposed Gabor Division/Spread Spectrum System (GD/S^3) is a communication system based on Gabor expansion of a signal and SS techniques. Consider a data transmission with a data symbol of address (q, q') via a channel with delay t_d and Doppler f_D. Then, a phase distortion

$$e^{j\pi(qTf_D - q'Ft_d)} \tag{3}$$

arises. Such a phase distortion is inevitable since Heisenberg's uncertainty principle says that both T and F cannot be zero. This is an important fact in any data communication. A simple answer to this problem is to compensate the phase term (3) at a transmitter or a receiver with estimates $\hat{t}_d$ and $\hat{f}_D$ of t_d and f_D. This method is referred to as an active or a passive PUL [19]. A clue, e.g., the conventional SS code acquisition technique, is, however, needed in order to obtain $\hat{t}_d$ and $\hat{f}_D$ without their prescribed information, i.e., any rough estimates.

The phase distortion Eq.(3) comes from parallelism between TD and FD signals in the sense that the role of t_D in a TD signal parallels exactly that of f_D in the FT of the TD signal, as shown in Eqs. (5) and (6). Such a signal is said to satisfy time and frequency symmetry (TFS). This situation led us to note that SS codes should be two dimensional. A signature waveform is designed using Gabor expansion in terms of chip waveform of chip address (m, m') having chip time spacing T_c and chip frequency spacing F_c. Then, the following chip-level phase distortion

$$e^{j\pi(mT_cf_D - m'F_ct_d)} \tag{4}$$

arises again at the transmitter and its compensation terms appear at the TD and FD receivers in (15) and (16) in its complicated versions. Such a chip-level compensation leads to precise estimations of t_d and f_D at chip-level and enables us to solve a multiple target problem.

2.1 Time Frequency Symmetry for Time and Frequency Synchronization

We discuss design of transmitted signals and receivers using complex baseband equivalent signals. In what follows, complex baseband equivalent signals are denoted without adding $\tilde{\ }$, unless otherwise specified.

The GD/S^3 is based on an idea that determinations of t_d and f_D are of equal importance and hence the role of t_D in the received signal parallels exactly that of f_D in the FT of the received signal. For this purpose, we slightly modify Eq. (1) and define $r^{GD}(t) = \alpha e^{j\varphi} s^{GD}(t - t_d) e^{j2\pi f_D(t - t_d/2)}$ together with $f_c = 0$ for simplicity. An extra phase $e^{j2\pi f_D(-t_d/2)}$ is needed for the received signal and its FT to be symmetric. Substituting Eq.(2) into this equation gives

$$r^{GD}(t) = \alpha e^{j\varphi} \sum_q d_q^{GD} e^{j\pi(qTf_D - q'Ft_d)} v(t - qT - t_d)$$
$$\cdot\, e^{j2\pi(q'F + f_D)(t - (qT + t_d)/2)} + \xi(t), \tag{5}$$

$$R^{GD}(f) = \alpha e^{j\varphi} \sum_q d_q^{GD} e^{j\pi(qTf_D - q'Ft_d)} V(f - q'F - f_D)$$
$$\cdot\, e^{-j2\pi(qT + t_d)(f - (q'F + f_D)/2)} + \Xi(f), \tag{6}$$

where $R^{GD}(f)$ and $\Xi(f)$ are the FTs of $r^{GD}(t)$ and $\xi(t)$. Obviously, $r^{GD}(t)$ and $R^{GD}(f)$ satisfy TFS.

2.2 Design of Signature Waveforms and Templates for GD/S^3

If Gabor expansion is used to design a transmitted signal $s(t)$, then $s(t)$ and its FT satisfy TFS condition. Let $\boldsymbol{X} = (X_0, X_1, \ldots, X_{N-1})^t$, $\boldsymbol{X'} = (X_0', X_1', \ldots, X_{N'-1}')^t$, $T_c = T/N$ and $F_c = F/N'$ be TD and FD codes [21,22], a chip duration and a chip bandwidth. Denote $\mathcal{X} = \{\boldsymbol{X}, \boldsymbol{X'}\}$. If a signature waveform $v(t)$ and its FT $V(f)$ have Gabor expansions in terms of a chip waveform $z(t)$ and its FT $Z(f)$, defined by

$$v^{GD}(t; \mathcal{X}) = \sum_{m=0}^{N-1} \sum_{m'=0}^{N'-1} X_m X_{m'}' z(t - mT_c) e^{j2\pi m' F_c(t - \frac{mT_c}{2})}, \tag{7}$$

$$V^{GD}(f; \mathcal{X}) = \sum_{m=0}^{N-1} \sum_{m'=0}^{N'-1} X_m X_{m'}' Z(f - m'F_c) e^{-j2\pi mT_c(f - \frac{m'F_c}{2})}, \tag{8}$$

then their associated received signal and its FT satisfy TFS. We refer to Eq.(2) as the first level Gabor expansion, while refer to Eqs.(7) or (8) as the second level Gabor expansion.

Recall that Gabor expansion has been often employed in signal processing and Filter Bank Multi-Carrier (FBMC) system [23]. One of the reasons why Gabor expansion is preferred is that its coefficients are easily obtained using time-frequency shifted Gabor elementary signal. On the other hand, we have given a radically new approach to the time-frequency synchronization method based on Gabor expansion, as follows.

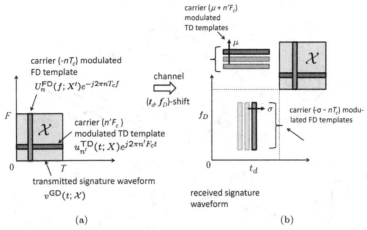

Fig. 1. (a) A transmitted signature waveform and (b) a received signature waveform in a time-frequency plane. The received signal is a (t_d, f_D)-shifted version of the transmitted signal. TD and FD templates are embedded in both signals.

A GD signature waveform and its FT are naturally decomposed, respectively,[2]

$$v^{\mathrm{GD}}(t; \mathcal{X}) = \frac{1}{\sqrt{N'}} \sum_{m'=0}^{N'-1} X'_{m'} u^{\mathrm{TD}}_{m'}(t; \boldsymbol{X}) e^{j2\pi m' F_c t}, \qquad (9)$$

$$V^{\mathrm{GD}}(f; \mathcal{X}) = \frac{1}{\sqrt{N}} \sum_{m=0}^{N-1} X_m U^{\mathrm{FD}}_m(f; \boldsymbol{X}') e^{-j2\pi m T_c f}, \qquad (10)$$

where $u^{\mathrm{TD}}_{m'}(t; \boldsymbol{X})$ and $U^{\mathrm{FD}}_m(f; \boldsymbol{X}')$ are a TD coded TD template and an FD coded FD template, defined by

$$u^{\mathrm{TD}}_{m'}(t; \boldsymbol{X}) = \frac{1}{\sqrt{N}} \sum_{m=0}^{N-1} X_m e^{-j\pi mm' T_c F_c} z(t - mT_c), \qquad (11)$$

$$U^{\mathrm{FD}}_m(f; \boldsymbol{X}') = \frac{1}{\sqrt{N'}} \sum_{m'=0}^{N'-1} X'_{m'} e^{j\pi mm' T_c F_c} Z(f - m' F_c). \qquad (12)$$

A conventional approach for estimating t_d and f_D is calculating cross-correlation between a received signal and a time-frequency shifted signature waveform and then finding its peak value. This approach requires inherently a two-dimensional brute-force detection. On the other hand, we have given a method for estimating t_d and f_D iteratively, called PUL. In each step of PUL, one-dimensional estimation of t_d or f_D is performed alternatively.

As shown in Fig. 1, decomposition of a signature waveform into multiple TD and FD templates defines their corresponding TD and FD correlators, and makes the detection of t_d and f_D more robust to time and frequency offset. A signature waveform $v^{\mathrm{GD}}(t; \mathcal{X})$ occupies a frequency bandwidth F and time duration T, while TD templates occupy F_c and T, respectively and FD templates occupy F and T_c, respectively. Generally, a wideband signal has high time resolution, and

---

[2] Obviously each equation has another decomposition [18].

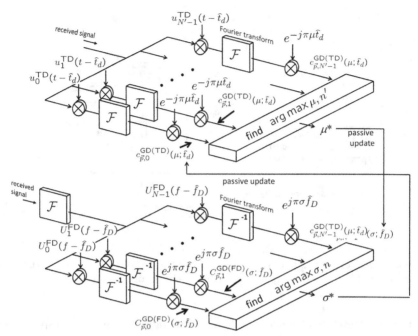

Fig. 2. TD and FD integrator arrays with $P = P' = 1$, where TD and FD integrator outputs are maximized by μ^* and σ^*, respectively. The output of TD correlator arrays, μ^*, is used to update $\hat{f}_D$ in FD integrators, and the output of FD correlator arrays, σ^*, is used to update $\hat{t}_d$ in TD integrators.

vice versa. Therefore, TD template is less sensitive to timing offset, while FD template is less sensitive to frequency offset.

Usually, a single matched filter is employed for a communication receiver that assumes carrier synchronization is already established. On the other hand, we employ both carrier μ-modulated TD integrator and delay σ-modulated FD integrator (See [24, Fig.2]) Then, the FT of the product of a received signal and a time delayed version of TD template is calculated in the TD integrator and the inverse FT of the product of the FT of the received signal and a frequency shifted version of FD template is calculated in the FD integrator (See Fig.2). The maximum value of outputs of TD and FD correlators are detected and are used to update estimations of $\hat{t}_d$ and $\hat{f}_D$. Note that TD and FD integrator arrays illustrated in the upper and lower halves of Fig. 2 have symmetric structure, where the roles of t_d and f_D are exchanged.

Template waveforms are designed so that TD-coded TD template and FD-coded FD template are symmetric with respect to FT. Thus, data symbol of data address $q = (q, q')$ is observed at the receiver with a phase distortion $e^{j\pi(qTf_D - t_dq'F)}$. This distortion increases as q and q' increase. Hence, it should be compensated at the receiver or the transmitter. Phase compensation methods for the receiver and the transmitter, called passive and active PULs have been recently proposed [19]. TD and FD correlators for passive PUL are designed, as follows:

Pattern matchings between the received signal (or its FT) and TD-coded TD template (or FD-coded FD template) for passive PUL are performed in the forms of

$$
c_{\boldsymbol{p},n'}^{\mathrm{GD(TD)}}(\mu;\hat{t}_d) = \int r^{\mathrm{GD}}(t;\mathcal{X})\overline{u}_{n'}^{\mathrm{TD}}(t-\hat{t}_d-pT;\boldsymbol{Y})
$$
$$
\times\, e^{-j(2\pi(\mu+p'F+n'F_c)(t-\frac{t_d+pT}{2})+\varphi^{\mathrm{GD(TD)}})}dt, \tag{13}
$$

$$
C_{\boldsymbol{p},n}^{\mathrm{GD(FD)}}(\sigma;\hat{f}_D) = \int R^{\mathrm{GD}}(f;\mathcal{X})\overline{U}_n^{\mathrm{FD}}(f-\hat{f}_D-p'F;\boldsymbol{Y}')
$$
$$
\times\, e^{j(2\pi(\sigma+pT+nT_c)(f-\frac{f_D+p'F}{2})+\varphi^{\mathrm{GD(FD)}})}df, \tag{14}
$$

where μ and σ are controlled parameters for guessing f_D and t_d, respectively, $\bar{}$ indicates the complex conjugate, $\varphi^{\mathrm{GD(TD)}}$ and $\varphi^{\mathrm{GD(FD)}}$ are phase terms, defined by (See [20] for their derivation)

$$
\varphi^{\mathrm{GD(TD)}} = \pi \begin{vmatrix} pT & p'F \\ \hat{t}_d & \mu \end{vmatrix} + \pi \begin{vmatrix} 0 & n'F_c \\ \hat{t}_d+pT & \mu+p'F \end{vmatrix}, \tag{15}
$$

$$
\varphi^{\mathrm{GD(FD)}} = \pi \begin{vmatrix} p'F & -pT \\ \hat{f}_D & -\sigma \end{vmatrix} + \pi \begin{vmatrix} 0 & -nT_c \\ \hat{f}_D+p'F & -\sigma-pT \end{vmatrix} \tag{16}
$$

and $u_{n'}^{\mathrm{TD}}(t;\boldsymbol{Y})$ and $U_n^{\mathrm{FD}}(f;\boldsymbol{Y}')$ are template waveforms with TD code $\boldsymbol{Y}$ for guessing $\boldsymbol{X}$ and FD code $\boldsymbol{Y}'$ for guessing $\boldsymbol{X}'$. The data address $\boldsymbol{p}=(p,p')$ and chip address n,n' of templates correspond to $\boldsymbol{q}=(q,q')$, and m,m' of the received signal, respectively.

Eqs.(13) and (14) are evaluated by Ville-Woodward's ambiguity functions [4, 5]. The ambiguity functions between $x(t)$ and $y(t)$ and their FTs, $X(f)$ and $Y(f)$, are defined by

$$
\theta_{x,y}(\tau,\nu) = \int_{-\infty}^{\infty} x(t+\frac{\tau}{2})\overline{y}(t-\frac{\tau}{2})e^{-j2\pi\nu t}dt = e^{j\pi\nu\tau}\int_{-\infty}^{\infty} x(t)\overline{y}(t-\tau)e^{-j2\pi\nu t}dt, \tag{17}
$$

$$
\theta_{X,Y}(\nu,-\tau) = \int_{-\infty}^{\infty} X(f+\frac{\nu}{2})\overline{Y}(f-\frac{\nu}{2})e^{j2\pi f\tau}df = e^{-j\pi\nu\tau}\int_{-\infty}^{\infty} X(f)\overline{Y}(f-\nu)e^{j2\pi\tau f}df. \tag{18}
$$

These functions are used in the form of controlled carrier modulated correlators. The main terms of the two arguments are described by

$$
\tau_0^{\mathrm{GD}}(\sigma) = (p-q)T+\sigma-t_d, \qquad \nu_0^{\mathrm{GD}}(\mu) = (p'-q')F+\mu-f_D. \tag{19}
$$

That is, we get

$$c_{\boldsymbol{p},n'}^{\mathrm{GD(TD)}}(\mu;\hat{t}_d) = \alpha e^{j\varphi} \sum_{\boldsymbol{q}} d_{\boldsymbol{q}}^{\mathrm{GD}} e^{+j\pi(\delta(\hat{t}_d,\mu)+n'F_c\tau_0^{\mathrm{GD}}(\hat{t}_d))}$$

$$\cdot \frac{1}{\sqrt{N'}} \sum_{m'=0}^{N'-1} X'_{m'} e^{j\pi m' F_c \tau_0^{\mathrm{GD}}(\hat{t}_d)} \cdot \left\{ \frac{1}{N} \sum_{m=0}^{N-1} \sum_{n=0}^{N-1} W_c^{\frac{m'n}{2}} W_c^{-\frac{n'm}{2}} X_m \overline{Y}_n \right.$$

$$\left. \cdot e^{-j\pi(m+n)T_c\nu_0^{\mathrm{GD}}(\mu)} \theta_{zz}(\tau_0^{\mathrm{GD}}(\hat{t}_d)+(n-m)T_c,\nu_0^{\mathrm{GD}}(\mu)+(n'-m')F_c) \right\}, \qquad (20)$$

$$C_{\boldsymbol{p},n}^{\mathrm{GD(FD)}}(\sigma;\hat{f}_D) = \alpha e^{j\varphi} \sum_{\boldsymbol{q}} d_{\boldsymbol{q}}^{\mathrm{GD}} e^{j\pi(\Delta(\sigma,\hat{f}_D)-nT_c\nu_0^{\mathrm{GD}}(\hat{f}_D))}$$

$$\cdot \frac{1}{\sqrt{N}} \sum_{m=0}^{N-1} X_m e^{-j\pi m T_c \nu_0^{\mathrm{GD}}(\hat{f}_D)} \left\{ \frac{1}{N'} \sum_{m'=0}^{N'-1} \sum_{n'=0}^{N'-1} W_c^{\frac{m'n}{2}} W_c^{-\frac{n'm}{2}} X'_{m'} \overline{Y}'_{n'} \right.$$

$$\left. \cdot e^{j\pi(m'+n')F_c\tau_0^{\mathrm{GD}}(\sigma)} \theta_{ZZ}(\nu_0^{\mathrm{GD}}(\hat{f}_D)+(n'-m')F_c,-\tau_0^{\mathrm{GD}}(\sigma)-(n-m)T_c) \right\}, \qquad (21)$$

where $W_c = e^{-j2\pi T_c F_c}$, and

$$\delta(\hat{t}_d,\mu) = -(qp'-q'p)TF + (q+p)T(f_D-\mu)$$
$$+ (q'+p')F(t_d-\hat{t}_d) + (f_D\hat{t}_d - \mu t_d). \qquad (22)$$

$$\Delta(\sigma,\hat{f}_D) = -(qp'-q'p)TF + (q+p)T(f_D-\hat{f}_D)$$
$$+ (q'+p')F(t_d-\sigma) + (f_D\sigma - \hat{f}_D t_d). \qquad (23)$$

The last terms of (22), i.e., $(f_D\hat{t}_d - \mu t_d)$, as well as a product of twiddle factors $W_c^{\frac{m'n}{2}} W_c^{-\frac{n'm}{2}}$, shows that f_D and t_d are not separable. Nevertheless, if a Gaussian chip waveform with the exponential decayness of their ambiguity functions is employed, $|\tau_0^{\mathrm{GD}}(\hat{t}_d)| < T_c$ and $|\nu_0^{\mathrm{GD}}(\hat{f}_D)| < F_c$ are satisfied after a few times iteration of PUL, as shown below. If the two parameters t_d and f_D are estimated by TD and FD integrators with TFS structure separately and cooperatively, then such a pair of integrator arrays is said to satisfy separable property (SP).

2.3   Gaussian Case

Gaussian waveforms have their ambiguity functions

$$\theta_{gg}(\tau,\nu) = \theta_{GG}(\nu,-\tau) = \exp\left(-\frac{\tau^2}{2s_t^2}\right) \cdot \exp\left(-\frac{\nu^2}{2s_f^2}\right), \qquad (24)$$

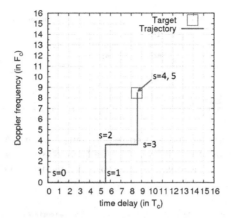

Fig. 3. A trajectory for estimating a time delay and a Doppler frequency in a target space, using FD-coded FD correlators and TD-coded TD correlators (Figs. 4 and 5), where $t_d \simeq 8.55$, $f_D \simeq 8.45$, and SNR is -10dB

that satisfy SP, where $s_t = 1/(2\pi s_f)$, $g(t)$ and $G(f)$ are a Gaussian elementary signal and its FT. Then we get

$$c_{p,n'}^{GD(TD)}(\mu; \hat{t}_d) = \alpha e^{j\varphi} \sum_q d_q^{GD} \cdot e^{j\pi(\delta(\hat{t}_d, \mu) + n' F_c \tau_0^{GD}(\hat{t}_d))} \frac{1}{\sqrt{N'}} \sum_{m'=0}^{N'-1} X'_{m'} e^{+j\pi m' F_c \tau_0^{GD}(\hat{t}_d)}$$

$$\cdot \theta_{zz}(0, \nu_0^{GD}(\mu) + (n' - m')F_c) \left\{ \frac{1}{N} \sum_{m=0}^{N-1} \sum_{n=0}^{N-1} W_c^{\frac{m'n}{2}} W_c^{-\frac{n'm}{2}} X_m \overline{Y}_n \right.$$

$$\left. \cdot e^{-j\pi(m+n)T_c \nu_0^{GD}(\mu)} \theta_{zz}(\tau_0^{GD}(\hat{t}_d) + (n-m)T_c, 0) \right\}, \tag{25}$$

$$C_{p,n}^{GD(FD)}(\sigma; \hat{f}_D) = \alpha e^{j\varphi} \sum_q d_q^{GD} e^{j\pi(\Delta(\sigma, \hat{f}_D) - nT_c \nu_0^{GD}(\hat{f}_D))} \frac{1}{\sqrt{N}} \sum_{m=0}^{N-1} X_m e^{-j\pi m T_c \nu_0^{GD}(\hat{f}_D)}$$

$$\cdot \theta_{ZZ}(0, -\tau_0^{GD}(\sigma) - (n-m)T_c) \left\{ \frac{1}{N'} \sum_{m'=0}^{N'-1} \sum_{n'=0}^{N'-1} W_c^{\frac{m'n}{2}} W_c^{-\frac{n'm}{2}} X'_{m'} \overline{Y}'_{n'} \right.$$

$$\left. \cdot e^{j\pi(m'+n')F_c \tau_0^{GD}(\sigma)} \theta_{ZZ}(\nu_0^{GD}(\hat{f}_D) + (m' - n')F_c, 0) \right\}. \tag{26}$$

Eqs. (25) and (26) show that parameters μ and σ are adjusted such that $m' = n'$ and $m = n$ hold.

3 Phase Updating Loop (PUL)

A time delay and a Doppler shift are estimated iteratively and alternatively. Let $\hat{t}_{d,s}$ and $\hat{f}_{D,s}$ be estimations of the time delay and Doppler shift at the s-th stage. Initial values $\hat{t}_{d,0}$ and $\hat{f}_{D,0}$ are chosen arbitrarily. Define

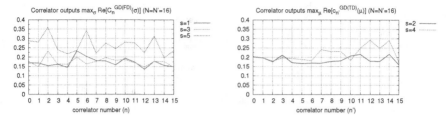

Fig. 4. The real parts of FD and TD correlator outputs with $N = N' = 16$. These values are relatively small at $s = 1, 2$ but gradually increase. At $s = 5$, the real part of FD correlator outputs take large values, and correct time-frequency synchronization is established.

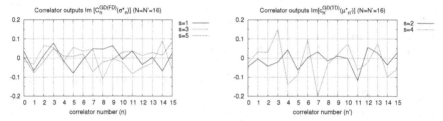

Fig. 5. The imaginary parts of FD and TD correlator outputs with $N = N' = 16$. Note that when synchronization is established at $s = 5$, the real parts of FD correlator outputs for $n = 2$ and $n = 6$ takes large values, while their imaginary parts are close to zero.

$$(\mu^*, n'^*) = \arg \max_{(\mu, n')} \Re[c_{\boldsymbol{p},n'}^{\mathrm{GD(TD)}}(\mu; \hat{t}_{d,s})], \text{ if } s \text{ is odd}, \tag{27}$$

$$(\sigma^*, n^*) = \arg \max_{(\sigma, n)} \Re[C_{\boldsymbol{p},n}^{\mathrm{GD(FD)}}(\sigma; \hat{f}_{D,s})], \text{ if } s \text{ is even}. \tag{28}$$

We select μ^* and σ^* to be the candidates of $\hat{f}_{D,s+1}$ and $\hat{t}_{d,s+1}$, respectively. The estimation procedure is terminated, if $|\hat{t}_{d,s+1} - \hat{t}_{d,s}| < \frac{T_c}{2}$ and $|\hat{f}_{D,s+1} - \hat{f}_{D,s}| < \frac{F_c}{2}$ are satisfied.

Suppose that the receiver is almost synchronized at the chip level and assume $\boldsymbol{q} = \boldsymbol{p}$, $m = n$ and $m' = n'$. Then, Eqs. (25) and (26) are simplified and the real parts of the TD and FD integrators are given by

$$\Re[c_{\boldsymbol{p},n'}^{\mathrm{GD(TD)}}(\mu; \hat{t}_d)] = \frac{\alpha}{\sqrt{N}} X'_{n'} \cos\left(\varphi + \pi(\delta(\hat{t}_d, \mu) + 2n' F_c \tau_0^{\mathrm{GD}}(\hat{t}_d))\right)$$
$$\cdot \mathrm{sinc}((\mu - f_D)T) \theta_{gg}(\tau_0^{\mathrm{GD}}(\hat{t}_d), \nu_0^{\mathrm{GD}}(\mu)) \tag{29}$$

$$\Re[C_{\boldsymbol{p},n}^{\mathrm{GD(FD)}}(\sigma; \hat{f}_D)] = \frac{\alpha}{\sqrt{N}} X_n \cos\left(\varphi + \pi(\Delta(\sigma, \hat{f}_D) - 2n T_c \nu_0^{\mathrm{GD}}(\hat{f}_D))\right)$$
$$\cdot \mathrm{sinc}((\sigma - t_d)F) \cdot \theta_{GG}(\nu_0^{\mathrm{GD}}(\hat{f}_D), -\tau_0^{\mathrm{GD}}(\sigma)). \tag{30}$$

Replacing the cosine functions in Eqs.(29) and (30) by sine functions gives the imaginary parts of TD and FD integrators. These equations show that although chip-level quasi-synchronization is assumed, there exist phase terms, i.e., $\varphi + \pi(\delta(\hat{t}_d, \mu) + 2n'T_c\nu_0^{\mathrm{GD}}(\mu))$ and $\varphi + \pi(\Delta(\sigma, \hat{f}_D) - 2nT_c\nu_0^{\mathrm{GD}}(\hat{f}_D))$. Maximization of the real parts of TD and FD integrator outputs makes the phase terms to be zero. This situation is the same as carrier synchronization in a super-heterodyne receiver [3].

Simulation results for a passive PUL with $N = N' = 16$ are shown in Figs. 3, 4 and 5. Started from $(\hat{t}_{d,0}, \hat{f}_{D,0}) = (0,0)$, the proposed methods successfully gives the correct synchronization after 5 iterations, under the condition that SNR is -10dB. In Fig. 4, real parts of the N' TD and N FD correlator outputs of the same instance as Fig. 3 are shown for $s = 1, 2, \ldots, 5$. These figures show that the real parts of the correlator outputs are gradually increased. Fig. 5 shows the imaginary parts of the N' TD and N FD correlator outputs are shown. It is shown that imaginary parts of FD correlator outputs for $n = 2, 6$ take very small absolute values, when their real parts are maximized at $s = 5$.

4   Code Division Multiple Target (CDMT)

In order to detect multiple delay-Doppler targets, we borrow an idea from code division multiple access (CDMA) philosophy.

A whole acceptable delay and Doppler space $[0, T) \times [0, F)$ is divided into four sub-spaces, i.e., $\mathcal{R}_1 = [0, T/2) \times [0, F/2)$, $\mathcal{R}_2 = [0, T/2) \times [F/2, F)$, $\mathcal{R}_3 = [T/2, T) \times [0, F/2)$, and $\mathcal{R}_4 = [T/2, T) \times [F/2, F)$. We attach 2D SS codes $\mathcal{X} = \{\boldsymbol{X}, \boldsymbol{X'}\}$, $\mathcal{Y} = \{\boldsymbol{Y}, \boldsymbol{Y'}\}$, $\mathcal{Z} = \{\boldsymbol{Z}, \boldsymbol{Z'}\}$, and $\mathcal{W} = \{\boldsymbol{W}, \boldsymbol{W'}\}$ to $\mathcal{R}_1$, $\mathcal{R}_2$, $\mathcal{R}_3$, and $\mathcal{R}_4$, respectively (See Fig. 6). Then, the chip addresses for $\mathcal{X}$, $\mathcal{Y}$, $\mathcal{Z}$, and $\mathcal{W}$ are given by

$$\mathcal{M}_1 = \{(m, m') | 0 \le m \le \tfrac{N}{2} - 1, 0 \le m' \le \tfrac{N'}{2} - 1\}, \tag{31}$$

$$\mathcal{M}_2 = \{(m, m') | 0 \le m \le \tfrac{N}{2} - 1, \tfrac{N'}{2} \le m' \le N' - 1\}, \tag{32}$$

$$\mathcal{M}_3 = \{(m, m') | \tfrac{N}{2} \le m \le N - 1, 0 \le m' \le \tfrac{N'}{2} - 1\}, \tag{33}$$

$$\mathcal{M}_4 = \{(m, m') | \tfrac{N}{2} \le m \le N - 1, \tfrac{N'}{2} \le m' \le N' - 1\}. \tag{34}$$

Then, GD signature waveforms for the 2D SS codes are defined by

$$v^{(i)}(t; \mathcal{X}^{(i)}) = \sum_{(m, m') \in \mathcal{M}_i} X_m^{(i)} X_{m'}^{\prime(i)} z(t - mT_c) e^{j2\pi m' F_c(t - mT_c/2)}, \tag{35}$$

where $\mathcal{X}^{(1)}$, $\mathcal{X}^{(2)}$, $\mathcal{X}^{(3)}$, and $\mathcal{X}^{(4)}$ correspond to $\mathcal{X}$, $\mathcal{Y}$, $\mathcal{Z}$, and $\mathcal{W}$. Define a transmitted signal with four codes as

$$s^{\mathrm{GDM}}(t) = \sum_{i=1}^{4} \sum_q d_q^{\mathrm{GD}} v^{(i)}(t - qT; \mathcal{X}^{(i)}) e^{j2\pi q' F(t - qT/2)}. \tag{36}$$

Eq.(36) can be regarded as a signal in code division multiple-access (CDMA) system. We assume $P = P' = 1$ and $d_q^{\mathrm{GD}} = 1$ in a synchronization mode.

Let us denote a transmitted signal and its associated received signal by $s^{\mathrm{GDM}}(t)$ and $r^{\mathrm{GDM}}(t)$, respectively. The FT of $r^{\mathrm{GDM}}(t)$ is denoted by $R^{\mathrm{GDM}}(f)$. We define four pairs of TD and FD integrator arrays, each correlator employs TD code

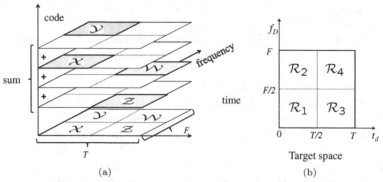

Fig. 6. SS code assignment for code division multiple-target (CDMT). SS codes $\mathcal{X}$, $\mathcal{Y}$, $\mathcal{Z}$, and $\mathcal{W}$, are, respectively, assigned to $\mathcal{R}_1$, $\mathcal{R}_2$, $\mathcal{R}_3$, and $\mathcal{R}_4$.

$\boldsymbol{X}^{(i)}$ and FD code $\boldsymbol{X}'^{(i)}$. Replacing $r^{\mathrm{GD}}(t; \mathcal{X})$ and $\boldsymbol{Y}$ in the right hand side (rhs) of Eq.(13) by $r^{\mathrm{GDM}}(t)$ and $\boldsymbol{X}^{(i)}$ defines TD integrators and replacing $R^{\mathrm{GD}}(f; \mathcal{X})$ and $\boldsymbol{Y}'$ in the rhs of Eq.(14) by $R^{\mathrm{GDM}}(f)$ and $\boldsymbol{X}'^{(i)}$ defines FD integrators.

For $\mathcal{X}$, pattern matching with template waveforms $u^{\mathrm{TD}}(t; \boldsymbol{X})$ and $U^{\mathrm{FD}}(f; \boldsymbol{X}')$ are performed only for $\mu \in [0, F/2)$, and $\sigma \in [0, T/2)$. For $\mathcal{Y} = \{\boldsymbol{Y}, \boldsymbol{Y}'\}$, pattern matching with template $u^{\mathrm{TD}}(t; \boldsymbol{Y})$ and $U^{\mathrm{FD}}(f; \boldsymbol{Y}')$ are performed only for $\mu \in [F/2, F)$, and $\sigma \in [0, T/2)$, and so on.

5   Performance of Multiple Target Detection

Because the acceptable target space is divided into four sub-spaces, the proposed method may detect multiple targets $(t_{d,i}, f_{D,i})$s. Let us replace the channel model in Eq.(1) by

$$r(t) = \sum_{i=1}^{N_{\mathrm{path}}} \alpha_i s(t - t_{d,i}) e^{j2\pi f_{D,i}(t - t_{d,i}/2)} + \xi(t), \tag{37}$$

where N_{path} is the number of paths.

Numerical simulation is executed for a four-path model[3] with equivalent path attenuation, i.e., $\alpha_i = 1$ for $i = 1, \ldots, 4$. $t_{d,i}$ and $f_{D,i}$ are randomly generated and they are uniformly distributed in $[0, T)$ and $[0, F)$. Simulation results are shown in Fig. 7 under the assumption that no prescribed knowledge about $t_{d,i}$ and $f_{D,i}$ is available, where $N = N' = 16$ and SNR is 10 dB. For each codes, four trajectories with different initial values are depicted. In Fig. 7 (a), there exist two targets in $\mathcal{R}_3$ and no target in $\mathcal{R}_2$. It is observed that one trajectory

---

[3] If the number of targets, N_{path}, are more than four, we choose N and N' to be linearly proportional to N_{path} and increase the number of disjoint sub-spaces.

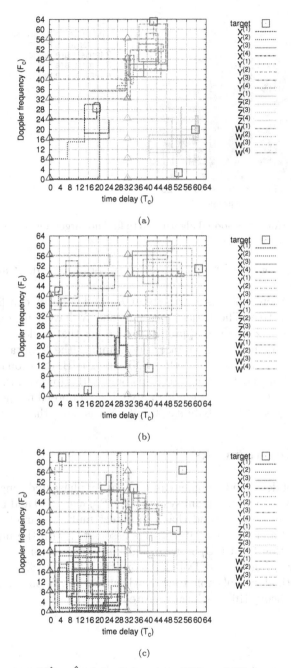

Fig. 7. Trajectories of $(\hat{t}_{d,s}, \hat{f}_{D,s})$ for four pairs of TD and FD integrator arrays in the target space, where the superscript $^{(i)}$ for the code X, Y, Z, and W suggests that the different initial values are used. Targets are expressed by symbols $\square$ and four initial values for each code are expressed by $\triangle$. In (a) and (b), four targets are found, while in (c) only two targets are found.

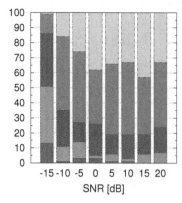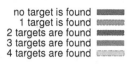

Fig. 8. Percentage for the proposed algorithms to find no target, one target, two targets, three targets, and four targets

for code Z goes to one target, while three trajectories for code Z approaches to the other target.

In Fig. 7 (c), there exist three targets in $\mathcal{R}_4$ and code W can find only one target among the tree. The trajectories for code X have long tail, while the trajectories for code Z seem to approach to a target that is close to $\mathcal{R}_3$.

Fig. 8 shows how many targets are found among the four targets by PUL with SNR from -15 dB to 20 dB. When SNR is -15 dB, the probability for the proposed algorithm to detect four targets is only 0.01. However, the probability to detect four targets increases for a high SNR. The proposed method can detect three or four targets with probability 80% if SNR is more than 5 dB.

6   Concluding Remarks

Determination of delay and Doppler can be done by phase updating loop (PUL) in Gabor division/spread spectrum system (GD/S^3) using TD and FD correlator arrays. We have given a method that can detect multiple targets, where multiple pairs of TD and FD correlator arrays associated with the multiple codes are used. Simulation for a GD/S^3 with multiple codes has shown that we can detect four pairs of delay and Doppler more than 25%, if SNR is more than 0dB. Such a method is applicable to channel estimation. Importance of Gabor's communication theory [16] has been revisited.

References

1. Molisch, A.F.: Wireless Communications, 2nd edn. Wiley (2010)
2. Gitlin, R.D., Hayes, J.F., Weinstein, S.B.: Data Communication Principles. Kluwer Academic Plenum Publishers (1992)
3. Couch, L.W.: Digital and Analog Communication Systems, 7th edn. Prentice Hall (2006)

4. Ville, J.: Théorie et applications de la notion de signal analytique. Câbles et Transmission (2), 61–74 (1948)
5. Woodward, P.M.: Probability and Information Theory, with Applications to Radar. McGraw-Hill, New York (1953)
6. Levanon, N., Mozeson, E.: Radar Signals. John Wiley & Sons (2004)
7. Antonio, G.S., Fuhrmann, D.R., Robey, F.C.: MIMO radar ambiguity functions. IEEE J. Sel. Topics Signal Process. 1, 167–177 (2007)
8. Blahut, R.E.: Theory of remote Image Formation. Cambridge University Press (2004)
9. Yao, K., Lorenzelli, F., Chen, C.E.: Detection and Estimation for Communication and Radar Systems. Cambridge Univ. Press, Cambridge (2013)
10. Morelli, M., Kuo, C.-C.J., Pun, M.-O.: Synchronization techniques for orthogonal frequency division multiple access (OFDMA): A tutorial review. Proc. of the IEEE 95(7), 1394–1427 (2007)
11. Li, X., Rueetschi, A., Eldar, Y.C., Scaglione, A.: GPS signal acquisition via compressive multichannel sampling. Physical Communication 5, 173–184 (2012)
12. Stojanovic, M.: Low complexity OFDM detector for underwater acoustic channels. In: OCEANS 2006, pp. 1–6 (2006)
13. Herman, M.A., Strohmer, T.: High-resolution radar via compressed sensing. IEEE Trans. Signal Process. 57(6), 2275–2284 (2009)
14. Bajwa, W.U., Gedalyahu, K., Eldar, Y.C.: Identification of parametric underspread linear systems and super-resolution radar. IEEE Trans. Signal Process. 59(6), 2548–2561 (2011)
15. Blu, T., Dragotti, P.-L., Vetterli, M., Marziliano, P., Coulot, L.: Sparse sampling of signal innovations. IEEE Signal Process. Mag. 31–40 (March 2008)
16. Gabor, D.: Theory of communication. J. Inst. Electr. Eng. 93, 429–457 (1946)
17. Madhow, U., Pursley, M.: Acquisition in direct-sequence spread-spectrum communication networks: An asymptotic analysis. IEEE Trans. Inf. Theory 39(3), 903–912 (1993)
18. Kohda, T., Jitsumatsu, Y., Aihara, K.: Frequency-division spread-spectrum makes frequency synchronisation easy. In: Proc. IEEE Globecom 2012, pp. 3976–3982 (December 2012)
19. Kohda, T., Jitsumatsu, Y., Aihara, K.: Separability of time-frequency synchronization. In: Proc. Int. Radar Symp., pp. 964–969 (June 2013)
20. Kohda, T., Jitsumatsu, Y., Aihara, K.: PLL-free receiver for Gabor division/spread spectrum system. In: Proc. 9th IEEE Int. Conf. Wireless and Mobile Computing, Networking and Commun. (WiMob 2013), pp. 662–669 (2013)
21. Caldwell, R., Anpalagan, A.: Adaptive subcarrier allocation in synchronous reverse links of a multicarrier CDMA system with time and frequency spreading. IEEE Trans. Vehicular Tech. 57(3), 1494–1501 (2008)
22. You, C.W., Hong, D.S.: Multicarrier CDMA systems using time-domain and frequency-domain spreading codes. IEEE Trans. Commun. 51(1), 17–21 (2003)
23. Farhang-Boroujeny, B.: OFDM versus filter bank multicarrier. IEEE Signal Processing, 92–112 (May 2011)
24. Jitsumatsu, Y., Kohda, T., Aihara, K.: Spread spectrum-based cooperative and individual time-frequency synchronization. In: Proc. 10th Int. Symp. Wireless Commun. Syst., pp. 497–501 (2013)

A Real-Time Medium Access Protocol Supporting Dynamic Spectrum Allocation in Industrial Networks

Magnus Jonsson, Kristina Kunert, and Urban Bilstrup

CERES – Centre for Research on Embedded Systems, Halmstad University,
Box 823, SE-30118 Halmstad, Sweden
{Magnus.Jonsson,Kristina.Kunert,Urban.Bilstrup}@hh.se

Abstract. Cognitive radio with spectrum sensing and spectrum reuse has great opportunities for industrial networking. Adapting to the current interference situation and utilising the available frequencies in an effective manner can greatly improve the data delivery capabilities. At the same time, real-time demands must be met. In this paper, we present a medium access control protocol supporting dynamic spectrum allocation as done in cognitive radio networks, providing deterministic medium access for heterogeneous traffic. The possibility of spectrum sensing in the nodes opens up for the possibility of increasing successful data transmissions, and a real-time analysis framework with three formalized constraints to be tested provides support for guaranteed timely treatment of hard real-time traffic. The real-time analysis framework includes a new type of delay check that more exactly bounds the delay compared to earlier work. Simulation experiments and performance comparisons are provided.

Keywords: Real-Time Guarantees, Medium Access Control, Cognitive radio.

1 Introduction

Industrial communication systems often have to work in an environment where other networks or radiation create different levels of interference for the data traffic. To improve the situation, cognitive radio networks [1-2] offer great potential. They enable dynamic spectrum access by, e.g., sensing channel characteristics and channel usage to adapt transmission parameters to the current channel availability and channel quality. Networks with spectrum reuse have already been targeted in the standardization through the work on IEEE 802.22 [2]. The standard describes a network where secondary users can utilize frequency channels not currently in use by their primary users (licensed TV broadcasting). Even though the same type of channel reuse can be used in industrial networks [3], the great potential for cognitive radio in an industrial context, in our opinion, lies in the adaptation based on the current channel quality of different available frequencies [4-5]. Spectrum sensing in an industrial context has also been addressed in, e.g., [6-7].

We present a real-time medium access control protocol for a cognitive radio network which provides deterministic medium access for heterogeneous traffic and supports dynamic spectrum allocation. The medium access is scheduled according to

M. Jonsson et al. (Eds.): MACOM 2013, LNCS 8310, pp. 54–69, 2013.

the earliest deadline first (EDF) algorithm. A real-time analysis is used as an admission control tool in order to only admit traffic that will not jeopardize any deadline.

Cognitive radio systems are a hot research topic and a number of MAC (Medium Access Control) protocols targeting real-time traffic support have been presented. However, none of the reviewed protocols can provide the deterministic medium access necessary for real-time applications as found in, e.g., industrial control systems. In [8], the authors target Quality of Service (QoS) support only indirectly by striving to protect the QoS of the primary users. The QoS-aware MAC protocol presented in [9] cannot provide any delay bound guarantees due to its random access nature. Moreover, it only supports a limited number of traffic classes and does not include deadline-aware scheduling. In [10], a collision-free MAC protocol considering QoS demands is presented, but without a delay analysis to state delay bound guarantees. QoS support for cognitive radio systems is also discussed in [11], but without specifying a specific MAC protocol providing delay bound support. A framework to support both real-time and non-real-time traffic is introduced in [12], but no methods to calculate delay bounds are presented. More MAC protocols in general for cognitive radio systems can be found in, e.g., [13]. In [14] the authors proposed a method for hard scheduling of the unifying slot assignment protocol (USAP) based on virtual circuits, but the analysis framework is based on capacity bounds instead of deadline bounds.

Our main contributions in this paper are

1. a deterministic MAC protocol supporting spectrum-aware cognitive radio and heterogeneous real-time traffic handling for industrial applications (presented earlier in a work-in-progress paper [15]),
2. a real-time analysis framework, including three constraints to be fulfilled, able to guarantee real-time demands of hard real-time traffic,
3. a more exact delay analysis, as part of the real-time analysis framework, that can guarantee more real-time traffic,
4. a new constraint check, also part of the real-time analysis framework, that is introduced due to the limited size of control packets,
5. a performance evaluation of the medium access protocol through simulation, and
6. a comparison of the new analysis method with the one presented previously [15].

The remaining paper is structured as follows. Section 2 describes the system architecture assumed, followed by the protocol specification in Section 3. The timing and real-time analysis framework is presented in Section 4, while performance evaluations are presented in Section 5. Section 6 concludes the paper.

2 System Model

The target network is a single-hop network with all of the nodes being in each other's transmission range. One node acts as a control node taking responsibility for scheduling and coordination of which radio frequencies to use.

In cognitive radio networks the available network capacity depends on the existence of other networks using the same frequency bands. Therefore, all nodes are equipped with radio sensing equipment and the control node collects sensing information, i.e., information about the different available frequencies, as, e.g., experienced bit error rate or load on a specific frequency. The control node uses this information when scheduling packets and frequencies, and distributes to the remaining nodes not only the schedule, but also information on the frequency spectrum to use. Each node in the network has three queues dedicated to hard real-time (HRT), soft real-time (SRT), and non-real-time (NRT) traffic, respectively (Fig. 1). Packets are sorted in deadline-order using EDF scheduling in the HRT and the SRT queue, i.e., the packet with the shortest deadline is at the head of the respective queue. As non-real-time traffic is assumed to have no deadline, this queue is sorted according to the first come first serve algorithm (FCFS). Strict priority ordering is used in the multiplexing between the queues, i.e., all packets in the HRT queue are treated prior to those in the SRT queue, and those in the NRT queue are only treated if both the HRT and the SRT queue are empty.

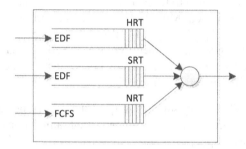

Fig. 1. Node architecture

3 Protocol Specification

Cognitive radio networks need flexible MAC protocols that are able to adapt to the changing radio environment. Other interfering networks lead to different frequencies being available and therefore any MAC protocol needs to support dynamic spectrum allocation. The available network capacity is divided between hard real-time traffic on one hand and soft and non-real-time traffic on the other hand. This division is done in a way that hard real-time traffic is guaranteed an experienced minimum bit rate (R_{HRT}). R_{HRT} is a system parameter normally chosen according to $R_{HRT} \leq R_{Min}$, where R_{Min} is the minimum available physical bit rate expected at any given point in time. The remaining network capacity is dedicated for soft real-time and non-real-time traffic in order to not starve these traffic classes and provide a certain degree of fairness in the network.

As mentioned above, the network has one node acting as a control node, responsible to collect all the nodes' spectrum sensing information, schedule the traffic, and broadcast the schedule and spectrum allocation to the rest of the network. The access to the network is cyclic and divided into superframes (Fig. 2). All nodes are synchronized on reception of the feedback from the control node. In the start of a superframe of length T_{cycle} each node will sense the available spectrum for the length of T_{sense}. During the following control phase ($T_{control}$), each node has an individual control slot during which it broadcasts the result of its spectrum sensing, plus information about the β first packets (referred to as data packets) in its local HRT EDF queue. In case the HRT EDF queue contains less than β data packets, the remaining space in the control packet is filled with information about the first packets in the SRT queue. Only if information about all packets in the HRT and SRT queue can be sent, the node will add information about packets in the NRT queue to the control packet until the maximum amount of information is reached (i.e., a maximum of β transmission requests). If, e.g., each request consists of 16 bits, ten bits can express the deadline, while six bits can express the destination address of the packet the request relates to. The six bit address can, in that case, address up to 64 nodes. If an underlying standard with longer addresses is used, each node can have a table to translate the six bit address to, e.g., a 48 bit MAC address. Since we target real-time systems for which predictability is important, those tables can be assumed to be known at system start-up. The control packets can potentially also be used to efficiently carry short messages for services like process synchronization [16]. The data transmission requests, gathered from the control packets during the collection phase, are stored in a global EDF queue in the control node. During $T_{feedback}$, the control node will schedule transmission requests globally in the same order as in the end nodes, i.e., according to EDF or FCFS within each traffic class and strict priority between the classes, and then broadcast the schedule to the nodes. Together with the schedule, information on the frequency to be used by all nodes during the current superframe is included. $T_{feedback}$ includes time for the nodes to tune to the right frequency (or frequencies if, e.g., OFDM is used) according to the spectrum information sent out by the control node. The remaining time of the superframe (T_{data}) is time-slotted according to the schedule sent out by the control node. T_{data} can be calculated straight forward as follows.

$$T_{data} = T_{cycle} - T_{sense} - T_{control} - T_{feedback} \tag{1}$$

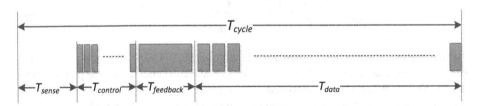

Fig. 2. Superframe structure

It is important to avoid inconsistency in the scheduling result among the nodes. A node is therefore not allowed to initiate a new transmission during an on-going superframe if its control packet during this superframe is lost. Concerning the reliability of data messages, we have developed a framework combining a retransmission scheme with real-time support [17-19]. The framework has also been adapted for IEEE 802.15.4 in a multichannel context [20]. An adaptation for the here described protocol is possible, but outside the scope of this paper.

4   Timing and Real-Time Analysis

In order to be able to guarantee that the deadlines of the hard real-time traffic are met, a real-time timing and scheduling analysis is necessary. This analysis will be able to provide the necessary guarantees under the assumption that traffic characteristics are specified and followed by the nodes.

The hard real-time traffic in the network is specified in the form of logical real-time channels (RT channels) which are traffic flows denoted as τ_i with $1 \leq i \leq Q$, where Q defines the number of RT channels. The RT channels are specified by the following parameters: sending node $m_{s,i}$, receiving node $m_{d,i}$, period P_i, message length L_i, and end-to-end delay bound D_i. Each RT channel τ_i can therefore be defined completely by the following expression: $\tau_i = \{m_{s,i}, m_{d,i}, P_i, L_i, D_i\}$.

Messages sent over the network are divided into packets. The maximum total transmission time $T_{x\_tot,i}$ of one message belonging to τ_i, i.e., the total time the physical channel is occupied, is calculated in the following way:

$$T_{x\_tot,i} = \left\lceil \frac{L_i}{L_{data}} \right\rceil \cdot T_{packet} \qquad (2)$$

L_{data} denotes the maximum amount of pure data (payload) per packet, and T_{packet} is the maximum duration of a data packet (slot) plus one interframe space (T_{IFS}), i.e.,

$$T_{packet} = \frac{L_{data} + L_{header}}{R_{Min}} + T_{IFS} \qquad (3)$$

where L_{header} is the length of the header per packet. The transmission time of a data message can then be defined as

$$T_{x\_tot,i} = \left\lceil \frac{L_i}{L_{data}} \right\rceil \cdot \left(\frac{L_{data} + L_{header}}{R_{Min}} + T_{IFS} \right) \qquad (4)$$

The queuing discipline assumed for the data packets is EDF, i.e., the packets are sorted in the queue according to their absolute deadlines (generation time plus relative deadline). Deadlines are not restricted to be equal to the periods, but arbitrary deadlines, i.e., shorter than, equal to, or longer than the periods, are supported.

As the real-time scheduling analysis only considers delay introduced by queuing, plus the total transmission time $T_{x\_tot,i}$ of a message, all other delays need to be excluded before further analysis. The maximum queuing delay, d_i, can be isolated by subtracting all other delays from the relative deadline D_i, resulting in the following maximum queuing delay (and new relative deadline):

$$d_i = D_i - T_{cycle} - T_{feedback} - T_{control} \qquad (5)$$

The worst case scenario reflected in the equation happens if the packet arrives in the node queue just a fraction too late for the node to be able to include its information in the next control packet. This will lead to the data packet having to wait one complete cycle time, plus additional time during the control and the feedback phase until the next data phase starts before it can be sent. For the worst case delay analysis, furthermore, the worst case position of the control packet is assumed, i.e., it is send first of all control packets during the control phase. Relaxing this assumption, taking into account the actual position of the control packet, would make it possible to improve the analysis by making it less pessimistic. Anyway, no blocking time for a lower-priority packet has to be subtracted from the end-to-end delay bound of the data packet under consideration, as the control node schedules all of T_{data} at the same time.

The real-time scheduling analysis is used to check if a traffic allocation over the network is feasible, i.e., it checks if all messages belonging to the scheduled RT channels will meet their deadlines. The first of three conditions to be checked is link utilization. It is a necessary, but not sufficient (as the deadlines of any RT channel are not restricted to be equal to the periods of that channel), condition that the utilization U_{HRT} by the allocated HRT traffic over the network does not exceed its allocated maximum utilization U_{HRT_Max}. The formal demand is:

$$U_{HRT} \leq U_{HRT\_Max} \tag{6}$$

The utilization U_{HRT} of periodic hard real-time traffic can be calculated as follows:

$$U_{HRT} = \sum_{i=1}^{Q} \left(\frac{T_{x\_tot,i}}{P_i} \right) \tag{7}$$

while the maximum possible utilization U_{HRT_Max} by HRT traffic is given by

$$U_{HRT\_Max} = \frac{R_{HRT}}{R_{Min}} \cdot \frac{T_{data} - T_{block}}{T_{cycle}} \tag{8}$$

where T_{block} is the maximum transmission time of one data packet (including the necessary preceding interframe space). This blocking time has to be taken into consideration because of the case when the remaining time of T_{data} is just a fraction too short to send a further (maximum sized) data packet. T_{block} is given by

$$T_{block} = \frac{L_{data} + L_{header}}{R_{Min}} + T_{IFS} \tag{9}$$

A second constraint has to be fulfilled in the real-time scheduling analysis in order to ensure that the workload on the network at no time instance will be higher than allowed, so as to meet the deadlines for the allocated traffic. For the description of this second part of the feasibility check, a number of concepts, originating from the area of real-time scheduling, have to be introduced. Firstly, the hyperperiod, HP, of periodic traffic is the least common multiple of all periods of the RT channels, i.e., the interval starting when the periods of all traffic flows start at the same time and ending when they do so again. Secondly, the analysis uses the concept of busy periods, BP, which are any intervals within an HP when the link is busy. Additionally, we need the workload function, $h(t)$, which measures the traffic demand at any point in time in the network. Originally, this function was designed for the control of the processor demand in a real-time system, but due to the assumption of EDF scheduling, this analysis can be adapted for analysing traffic scheduling in a network [21]. Generally speaking, $h(t)$ is the sum of the transmission times of all data packets for all message instances of all RT channels that have an absolute deadline that is less than or equal to a point in time t, and where t is the number of time units elapsed since the beginning of HP. This synchronous traffic pattern where all RT channels' periods start at the same time is the worst case in terms of workload, leading to the worst case queuing delay for the data packets pertaining to those RT channels [22-24]. $h(t)$ is calculated as:

$$h(t) = \sum_{i \in [1,Q], d_i \leq t} \left(1 + \left\lfloor \frac{t - d_i}{P_i} \right\rfloor \right) \cdot T_{x\_tot,i} \qquad (10)$$

The summation only includes terms for which the value of t is equal or higher than the value of the corresponding relative deadline. The second constraint, introduced in [22-23] and generalized in [24], was added in order to be able to ensure the continued feasibility of the traffic allocation even for the case when a new traffic flow is added. The original constraint (to be modified below) demands that:

$$h(t) \leq t \quad \forall t \geq 0 \qquad (11)$$

In our case, transmissions cannot occur all the time due to the sensing phase, the control phase, etc. After the worst-case delay described above, the data phase starts and the total guaranteed time $g(t)$ available for transmission up until time t can be calculated as

$$g(t) = \left\lfloor \frac{t}{T_{cycle}} \right\rfloor \cdot (T_{data} - T_{block}) + \min \left(T_{data} - T_{block}; \mathrm{mod}\left(t; T_{cycle} \right) \right) \qquad (12)$$

The first part of the equation delivers the possible transmission time contributed by an integer number of whole superframes, while the second part contributes with the corresponding time for the last but not fully passed superframe. The start of a superframe, i.e., $t = 0$, in this context actually occurs when the data phase starts since delays compensating for the sensing, control, and feedback time have already been subtracted from the end-to-end delay bound in order to isolate the queuing deadline, d_i. In other words, as we in Eq. 5 derives the pure queuing deadline by subtracting other delays, we can assume that $t = 0$ when the data phase starts, i.e., when we can start sending queued packets. The original constraint is thereby modified to the following demand:

$$h(t) \le g(t) \quad \forall t \ge 0 \tag{13}$$

Unfortunately, the constraint stated in Eq. 13 suffers from a high degree of computational complexity, but [25] presents a way of reducing the time and memory complexity by limiting the number of time instances for which $h(t)$ has to be checked to a sufficient subset. It is possible to reduce the number of instances of evaluation to those of absolute message deadlines during an interval upper-bounded by BP_1, the first busy period in the first hyperperiod of the schedule where all periods start at time zero, i.e.,

$$t \in \bigcup_{i=1}^{Q} \{m \cdot P_i + d_i : m = 0,1,2...\} \tag{14}$$

where

$$t \in [1; BP_1] \tag{15}$$

A third constraint is introduced by the use of control packets. The length of a control packet will limit the amount of data packets about which control information can be sent to the control node. The condition on the control packet is therefore that there has to be enough space in the control packets to be able to inform about possible queued hard real-time packets. So the following must be true for all i, $1 \le i \le M$, where M is the number of end nodes in the network:

$$\beta \ge \sum_{j=1}^{Q_i} \left\lceil \frac{T_{cycle}}{P_j} \right\rceil \cdot \left\lceil \frac{L_j}{L_{data}} \right\rceil \tag{16}$$

where β is (as stated earlier) the number of data packets a control packet can carry information about, and Q_i is the number of RT channels with node $m_{s,i}$ as their source node. In Eq. 16, the summation contains only RT channels from one specific node $m_{s,i}$ at a time.

When assuming a maximum of S packets during the data phase and S is given by

$$S = \left\lfloor \frac{T_{data}}{T_{x,min}} \right\rfloor , \tag{17}$$

denoting the number of minimum-sized data packets fitting in the data phase, and $T_{x,min}$ being the length of a minimum-sized data packet, it is sufficient that the following inequality holds:

$$\beta \ge S . \tag{18}$$

The reason is that even in the worst case, i.e., when one node has all S packets that are to be scheduled first by the control node scheduler, this node can still send information about all of them in one single control packet.

Only in the case when all three constraints (utilization, workload, and control packets) are fulfilled, a feasible traffic scheduling can be guaranteed, i.e., only then will it be possible to guarantee that no deadlines will be missed.

In the runtime implementation of this schedulability test the three constraints are checked every time a new RT channel is added in order to guarantee the requested delay bounds for both the new and the existing RT channels. As new RT channels are not expected to be requested frequently, the computational demands of this admission control will not be very high, and any of the nodes might be responsible for it and be chosen as the control node in the network. If all RT channels are known at the design stage or system start-up of the network, the analysis can be made offline instead.

5   Performance Analysis

In order to analyse the behaviour and show the performance of the studied network, we have conducted simulation experiments using MATLAB. We have simulated the network both with hard real-time traffic, including the real-time analysis, and with soft real-time traffic, i.e., injecting traffic without the use of the real-time analysis. We have studied throughput, average delay and deadline miss ratio. Moreover, we have compared the real-time analysis, in terms of reachable utilization for hard real-time traffic, with the analysis presented earlier in [15].

5.1   Simulation Assumptions

We assume a single-hop network with $M = 20$ nodes, where one node is acting as the protocol control node. Several of the network parameters have values inspired by the IEEE 802.11b standard, as described below. The minimum physical bit rate allocated for hard real-time traffic, R_{HRT}, is assumed to be equal to the minimum bit rate R_{Min} available in low-bandwidth situations (according to the spectrum sensing). We assume the minimum bit rate to be 11 Mbit/s, i.e., $R_{HRT} = R_{Min} = 11$ Mbit/s. The propagation delay is assumed to be negligible.

The length of the sensing phase is assumed to be $T_{sense} = 2$ ms. The duration of a control packet is set to 196 μs, corresponding to 320 bits excluding preamble, header, and interframe spacing. The total duration of the control phase is therefore:

$$T_{control} = 20 \cdot 196 = 3920 \text{ μs} . \tag{18}$$

The maximum number of packets covered by one control packet is assumed to be $\beta = 20$. The duration of the feedback phase, including time for the control node to do the traffic scheduling, is set to $T_{feedback} = 1$ ms, while the whole superframe duration is set to $T_{cycle} = 30$ ms.

The traffic over the network belongs to one of three traffic classes and the parameters for all RT channels are chosen from these with even random distribution. The three traffic classes have periods of 50 ms, 100 ms, and 200 ms, with the deadlines in all traffic classes being equal to the periods. The periods of the different traffic flows are not synchronized in the simulations. Instead, each traffic flow starts with an offset from the starting time, randomly generated with even distribution between zero and its period. Independent of the traffic class, a packet with duration of $T_{x\_tot,i} = 200$ µs is generated at the start of each period of an RT channel. The 200 µs correspond to a 45 Byte (360 bit) packet excluding preamble, header, and interframe spacing.

5.2   Hard Real-Time Traffic

Fig. 3 shows the throughput when simulating only hard real-time traffic. After the generation of about 200 RT channels, some of the RT channels are starting to be rejected by the real-time analysis in the admission control. Each simulation point is run ten times for the duration of ten hyperperiods.

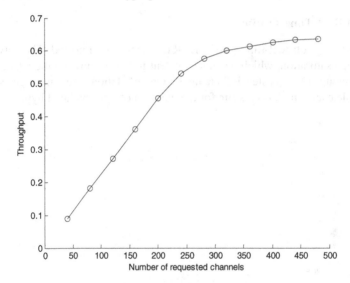

Fig. 3. Throughput for the case with hard real-time traffic

Since the delay bounds are guaranteed, the shape of the average delay curve (Fig. 4) is given. The average delay is significantly lower than the delay bounds specified for the traffic classes (50 ms, 100 ms, and 200 ms). This is also not surprising since the worst-case delay analysed in the real-time analysis constitutes a case not always happening. The deadline miss ratio has also been measured, but is always zero as expected when using the real-time analysis. The curve is therefore omitted.

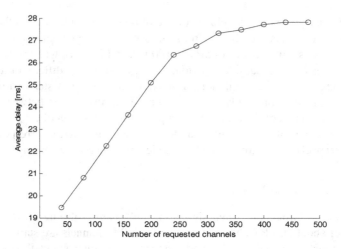

Fig. 4. Average delay for the case with hard real-time traffic

5.3   Soft Real-Time Traffic

When simulating soft real-time traffic, no RT channels are rejected. The network can thereby reach saturation, which becomes evident in Fig. 5 showing the average delay. For each amount of requested RT channels, ten simulations are run to get smoother curves, while each simulation is run for the duration of ten simulated hyperperiods.

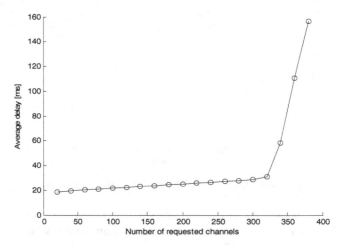

Fig. 5. Average delay for the case with soft real-time traffic

The throughput is plotted in Fig. 6. A throughput of about 75% is reached before saturation. Compared to numerous other networks this is very high, which shows that the control overhead in the network is well invested, not only supporting spectrum reuse but also efficient scheduling.

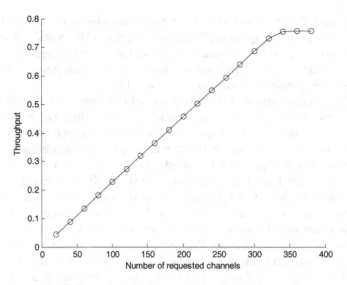

Fig. 6. Throughput for the case with soft real-time traffic

Fig. 7 shows the deadline miss ratio, where again the bottleneck is evident. Deadlines are missed first at (or near) the saturation point.

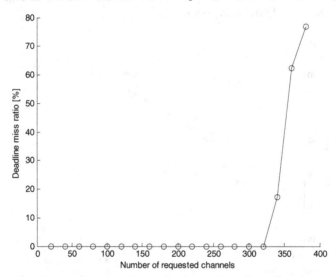

Fig. 7. Deadline miss ratio for the case with soft real-time traffic

5.4 Real-Time Analysis Comparison

As mentioned above, we have compared the presented real-time analysis with the analysis proposed in [15], which was based on the concept of experienced bit rate. The experienced bit rate was scaled as seen in [26], compensating for the fact that parts of the superframe are not available for the transmission of data packets. This was done by using the average available network capacity in the workload analysis. In the current paper, the workload function is checked more exactly against the specific parts of the superframe that have passed. This results in a less pessimistic analysis, able to potentially guarantee more hard real-time traffic.

Fig. 8 shows a comparison of the here proposed real-time analysis with the previous one in terms of utilization of accepted hard real-time traffic. The behaviour when the curves separate (at about 175 requested RT channels) is explained by the fact that the previous method cannot accept traffic with tough delay requirements. With an even higher amount of requested RT channels, though, enough RT channels with less strict delay demands have been requested to reach utilization closer to the new method. In order to avoid this behaviour during this evaluation, we restrict the RT channel generation to only one traffic class, in this case with period and delay bound set to 50 ms (otherwise the same simulation parameters are kept). As seen in Fig. 9, the performance difference between the two methods now is much larger. The performance is compared in terms of total achievable utilization for hard real-time traffic, for a few different cases in Table 1. The number of queued packets a control packet can carry information about is assumed to be unlimited in order to instead focus on the difference of the two methods in checking the workload. This, in combination with only having a single traffic class, eliminates the randomness. The parameters are otherwise the same as explained above. As seen, an improvement as high as 31.6% has been observed for shorter delay bounds.

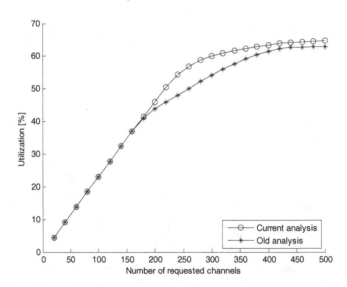

Fig. 8. Utilization comparison of the new and old real-time analysis

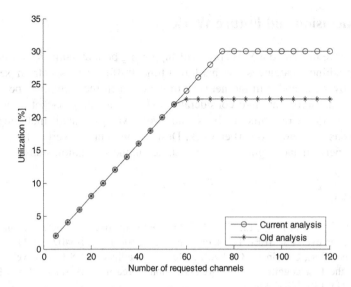

Fig. 9. Utilization comparison of the new and old real-time analysis with a single traffic class

Table 1. Comparison of achievable utilization for hard real-time traffic

Period and deadline	Old analysis	Current analysis	Improvement
40 ms	16.9%	22.2%	31.6%
50 ms	22.8%	30.0%	31.6%
60 ms	31.7%	38.0%	20.0%
70 ms	38.0%	39.7%	4.5%
80 ms	42.8%	47.3%	10.5%
90 ms	46.7%	50.7%	8.6%
100 ms	49.6%	50.8%	2.4%
110 ms	52.0%	55.3%	6.3%
118 ms	53.6%	58.1%	8.5%
120 ms	54.0%	57.2%	5.9%
125 ms	54.9%	54.9%	0.0%
130 ms	55.7%	56.6%	1.7%
140 ms	57.1%	59.7%	4.5%
150 ms	58.4%	60.9%	4.3%
160 ms	59.5%	60.4%	1.5%
200 ms	62.9%	64.7%	2.9%

6   Conclusion and Future Work

In this paper we presented a MAC protocol supporting both dynamic spectrum allocation and deadline guarantees for hard real-time traffic. The spectrum sensing is
distributed over the nodes in the network to better catch the available spectrum and
taking these measurements into consideration when scheduling packet transmissions
over the network. A real-time analysis framework was presented, including several
novel methods compared to earlier work. Despite the control overhead, the network
shows good performance figures, as demonstrated in the simulation study.

References

1. Liang, Y.-C., Chen, K.-C., Li, G.Y., Mähönen, P.: Cognitive radio networks and communications: an overview. IEEE Trans. on Veh. Techn. 60(7), 3386–3407 (2011)
2. Stevenson, C.R., Chouinard, G., Lei, Z., Hu, W., Shellhammer, S.J., Caldwell, W.: IEEE
   802.22: the first cognitive radio wireless regional area network standard. IEEE Comm.
   Mag. 47(1), 130–138 (2009)
3. Cavalcanti, D., Das, S., Wang, J., Challapali, K.: Cognitive radio based wireless sensor
   networks. In: Proc. of 17th International Conference on Computer Communications and
   Networks (ICCCN 2008), St. Thomas, U.S. Virgin Islands, August 3-7 (2008)
4. Block, D., Meier, U.: Wireless deterministic medium access: a novel concept using cognitive radio. In: The Third International Conference on Advances in Cognitive Radio
   (COCORA 2013), Venice, Italy, April 21-26, pp. 35–38 (2013)
5. Vitturi, S., Seno, L., Tramarin, F., Bertocco, M.: On the rate adaptation techniques of IEEE
   802.11 networks for industrial applications. IEEE Transactions on Industrial Informatics 9(1), 198–208 (2013)
6. Ahmad, K., Meier, U., Kwasnicka, H., Pape, A., Griese, B.: A cognitive radio approach to
   realize coexistence optimized wireless automation systems. In: Proc. 14th IEEE International Conference on Emerging Technologies & Factory Automation (ETFA 2009), Mal-
   lorca, Spain, September 22-26 (2009)
7. Tytgat, L., Barrie, M., Goncalves, V., Yaron, O., Moerman, I., Demeester, P., Pollin, S.,
   Ballon, P., Delaere, S.: Techno-economical viability of cognitive solutions for a factory
   scenario. In: Proc. IEEE Symp. on New Frontiers in Dyn. Spectr. Acc. Netw. 2011 (DyS-
   PAN 2011), pp. 254–264 (May 2011)
8. Yao, Y., Feng, Z., Li, W., Qian, Y.: Dynamic spectrum access with QoS guarantee for
   wireless networks: a Markov approach. In: GLOBECOM 2010, Miami, FL, USA (December 2010)
9. Cai, L.X., Li, Y., Shen, X., Mark, J.W., Zhao, D.: Distributed QoS-aware MAC for multimedia over cognitive radio networks. In: GLOBECOM 2010, Miami, FL, USA (December
   2010)
10. Passiatore, C., Camarda, P.: A MAC protocol for cognitive radio wireless ad hoc networks.
    In: Sacchi, C., Bellalta, B., Vinel, A., Schlegel, C., Granelli, F., Zhang, Y. (eds.) MACOM
    2011. LNCS, vol. 6886, pp. 1–12. Springer, Heidelberg (2011)
11. Willkomm, D., Wolisz, A.: Efficient QoS support for secondary users in cognitive radio
    systems. IEEE Wirel. Comm. 17(4), 16–23 (2010)
12. Alshamrani, A., Shen, X., Xie, L.-L.: QoS provisioning for heterogeneous services in co-
    operative cognitive networks. IEEE J. on Sel. Areas in Comm. 29(4), 819–830 (2011)

13. Cormio, C., Chowdhury, K.R.: A survey on MAC protocols for cognitive radio networks. Ad Hoc Netw. 7(7), 1315–1329 (2009)
14. Perumal, S., Tabatabaee, V., Baras, J.S., Graff, C.J., Yee, D.G.: Modeling and sensitivity analysis of reservation based usap hard scheduling unicast traffic in manets. In: Military Communications Conference, MILCOM 2009 (October 2009)
15. Kunert, K., Jonsson, M., Bilstrup, U.: Deterministic real-time medium access for cognitive industrial radio networks. In: Proc. of the 9th IEEE International Workshop on Factory Communication Systems (WFCS 2012), Lemgo/Detmold, Germany, May 21-24 (2012)
16. Jonsson, M., Bergenhem, C., Olsson, J.: Fiber-ribbon ring network with services for parallel processing and distributed real-time systems. In: Proc. ISCA 12th International Conference on Parallel and Distributed Computing Systems (PDCS 1999), Fort Lauderdale, FL, USA, August 18-20, pp. 94–101 (1999)
17. Jonsson, M., Kunert, K.: Towards reliable wireless industrial communication with real-time guarantees. IEEE Trans. on Ind. Inf. 5(4), 429–442 (2009)
18. Kunert, K., Uhlemann, E., Jonsson, M.: Predictable Real-Time Communications with Improved Reliability for IEEE 802.15.4 Based Industrial Networks. In: Proc. 8th IEEE Int. Works. on Factory Comm. Syst. (WFCS 2010), Nancy, France, pp. 13–22 (May 2010)
19. Jonsson, M., Kunert, K.: Reliable hard real-time communication in industrial and embedded systems. In: Proc. 3rd IEEE Int. Symp. on Ind. Emb. Syst. (SIES 2008), Montpellier, France, pp. 184–191 (June 2008)
20. Kunert, K., Jonsson, M., Uhlemann, E.: Exploiting time and frequency diversity in IEEE 802.15.4 industrial networks for enhanced reliability and throughput. In: Proc. 15th IEEE Int. Conf. on Emerging Techn. and Factory Automation (ETFA 2010), Bilbao, Spain (September 2010)
21. Hoang, H., Jonsson, M.: Switched real-time Ethernet in industrial applications - deadline partitioning. In: 9th Asia-Pacific Conf. on Comm. (APCC 2003), Penang, Malaysia, vol. 1, pp. 76–81 (September 2003)
22. Baruah, S.K., Mok, A.K., Rosier, L.E.: Preemptively scheduling hard-real-time sporadic tasks on one processor. In: Proc. 11th Real-Time Syst. Symp. (RTSS 1990), pp. 182–190 (December 1990)
23. Baruah, S.K., Rosier, L.E., Howell, R.R.: Algorithms and complexity concerning the preemptive scheduling of periodic, real-time tasks on one processor. Real-Time Syst. 2(4), 301–324 (1990)
24. Spuri, M.: Analysis of deadline scheduled real-time systems, Tech. Rep. 2772, INRIA, France (1996)
25. Stankovic, J.A., Spuri, M., Ramamritham, K., Buttazzo, G.C.: Deadline scheduling for real-time systems - EDF and related algorithms. Kluwer Academic Publishers, Boston (1998)
26. Böhm, A., Jonsson, M.: Supporting real-time data traffic in safety-critical vehicle-to-infrastructure communication. In: The 2nd IEEE LCN Workshop On User MObility and VEhicular Networks (ON-MOVE), Montreal, Canada, October 14, pp. 614–621 (2008)

CSMA/CA Bottleneck Remediation
in Saturation Mode with New Backoff Strategy

Baher Mawlawi[1,2,3] and Jean-Baptiste Doré[1]

[1] CEA-Leti Minatec, 17 rue des Martyrs, 38054 Grenoble Cedex 9, France
baher.mawlawi@cea.fr jean-baptiste.dore@cea.fr
[2] University of Lyon, INRIA, Villeurbanne, France
[3] INSA-Lyon, CITI-INRIA, F-69621, Villeurbanne, France

Abstract. Many modern wireless networks integrate carrier sense multiple access/collision avoidance (CSMA/CA) with exponential backoff as medium access control (MAC) technique. In order to decrease the MAC overhead and the collision probability, we propose in this paper a new backoff strategy leading to better saturation throughput and access delay performance comparing to the classical protocol. We investigate the CSMA/CA with RTS/CTS technique, and we show that our strategy reaches better saturation throughput and access delay especially in dense networks. This proposed strategy distributes users over all the backoff stages to solve the bottleneck problem present in the first backoff stage. Finally, we analyze our strategy and we compare it to the classical one modeled by Markov chain. Analytical and simulation results show the improvment in term of saturation throughput. Cumulative density function (CDF) of the access delay illustrates the important gain obtained by the proposed strategy.

Keywords: Carrier sense multiple access/collision avoidance (CSMA /CA), Markov chain, delay, throughput, backoff algorithm.

1 Introduction

The design of wireless networks for local area communication attracted much of interest [1]. Carrier Sense Multiple Access/Collision Avoidance (CSMA/CA) protocols rely on a decentralized random packet transmission for the efficient use of shared medium. The key features of CSMA/CA is that each link with a pair of transmitter and receiver first senses the medium and transmits a packet only if the channel is sensed idle. Due to its simple and distributed nature, it has been considered as one of the most practical MAC protocols for wireless network. It has been adopted for instance for Wireless Local Area Networks (WLANs) through study group 802.11 [2] and for Wireless Sensor Networks (WSNs) through 802.15.4 [3]. This family of random access protocols is also a good candidate for future communication systems such as cognitive radio [4], Machine to Machine (M2M) wireless networks and so on.

M. Jonsson et al. (Eds.): MACOM 2013, LNCS 8310, pp. 70–81, 2013.

Many previous works try to improve the throughput performance by attempting to optimize the contention window [5] [6] [7], but they are based on the IEEE 802.11 backoff strategy.

In [8], the throughput and the average access delay for different backoff algorithms were studied by simulation only. In the classical CSMA/CA protocol with 802.11 backoff strategy modeled by Bianchi, it's clearly seen that the first state is the bottleneck of the system, especially in charged mode. In order to improve the throughput and the system delay we propose and develop in this paper a mathematical model for a new backoff strategy based on Markov chain and we analytically prove that the outcome of the new strategy is better than the classical one in terms of saturation throughput and statistical access delay.

The paper is outlined as follows. We briefly review in Section 2 the RTS/CTS mechanisms of CSMA/CA protocol. In Section 3 we explain the proposed backoff strategy and we give a throughput analytical model. Section 4 presents the numerical results of the proposed protocol and a comparision with the classical protocol. Finally, Section 5 is reserved for conclusion.

2   CSMA/CA Protocol MAC Layer

In order to describe the CSMA/CA protocol, we propose to explain the well known 802.11 CSMA/CA MAC layer. The basic medium access mechanism of IEEE 802.11 is DCF (Distributed Coordination Function) which uses CSMA/CA algorithm to serve shared medium access. It contains two different variants of access method, the basic access method and the optional channel access method with *request-to-send* (RTS) and *clear-to-send* (CTS) exchange. As the latter variant introduces more efficient performance in term of average throughput [9] and solves the hidden node problem [10], CSMA/CA with RTS/CTS will be investigated in this paper. Let's consider a network with many terminals and one access point. If the channel is busy for the transmitters, each one chooses randomly a backoff time (measured in time slots) in the interval $[0, CW)$ where CW is the *contention window*. As long as the channel is sensed idle for a DIFS, i.e. *distributed inter-frame space* time, the timer (backoff) is decreased by one. When the channel is busy the timer counter is blocked and it resumes when the channel is idle again for at least a DIFS period. CW is an integer between CW_{min} and CW_{max}. After each unsuccessful transmission, CW is doubled up to the maximum value equal to $CW_{max}+1$. The source transmits an RTS frame when the backoff reaches zero and wait for transmission permission (CTS) from the potential receiver before sending the current data packet. All stations located in the sender's range that hear the RTS packet should update their NAVs (Network Allocation vector) and defer their transmissions for the duration specified by the RTS. By this strategy, the transmission of data packets and the corresponding ACK can proceed without interference from other nodes. In addition, whenever erroneous frame is detected by a node, it defers its transmission by a fixed duration indicated by EIFS, i.e., *extended inter-frame space* time. The contention window is initialized to CW_{min} (minimum contention window). Dense networks

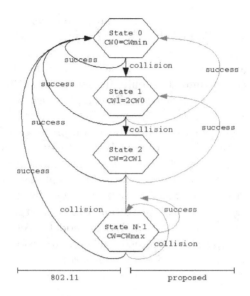

Fig. 1. 802.11 and proposed backoff strategy

cause collisions between transmitters. Each station involved in the collision double the size of its contention window. In case of a successful transmission, the transmitter re-initialize its contention window by CW_{min}.

3   Proposed Backoff Algorithm Description

3.1   Description

As explained in Section 2, when a station transmits successfully it returns directly to the first backoff stage. This fact introduces a high collision probablity as well as an enormous additive transmission delay due to the high number of users in the same backoff stage ($m = 1$). This situation is seen as bottleneck problem. The proposed CSMA/CA is quite similar to the IEEE 802.11 protocol (Section 2), the main difference remains in case of a successful (i.e. collision-free) transmission, the transmitting station reduces the value of its contention window by half, so as to keep its contention window at least equal to CW_{min} (see Figure 1).

3.2   System Model

In this section we will give the model, the analytical calculation of saturation throughput for the proposed CSMA/CA backoff strategy. We compute the probability of a packet transmission failure due to collision by assuming the following hypothesis [11]:

- No hidden terminal and capture effect.
- Failed transmissions only occur as a consequence of collision.

- All stations are saturated, always having packets to send.
- For any given station, the probability of collision, p, is constant and independent of the station's collision history of the station and all other stations.
- The probability of collision does not depend on the backoff stage at which the transmission is made.
- All users have same bitrates and same amount of time to transmit.

Using the Bianchi's model described in [9] [12] we model the proposed protocol by a Markov chain of $m + 1$ backoff stages as illustrated Figure 2. Each stage of the Markov chain modelled the backoff counter. The number of states per stage is equal to the maximum authorized value of the backoff counter, i.e CW_i. It should be mentioned that we use notations described in [9], i.e $CW_i = 2^i(CW_{min} + 1)$.

When a collision occurs a transition from stage i to $(i + 1)$ is considered and a random backoff will be chosen between 0 and CW_i-1 with probability of $\frac{p}{CW_i}$. A successful transmission is modelled by a transition from stage $(i + 1)$ to i and a random backoff will be chosen between 0 and CW_{i-1}-1 with probability of $\frac{1-p}{CW_{i-1}}$.

Each state of this Markov process is represented by $\{s(t), b(t)\}$, where $b(t)$ is the stochastic process representing the backoff time counter for a given station and $s(t)$ is the stochastic process representing the backoff stage $(0, 1, ...m)$ of the station at time t [9]. A discrete and integer time scale is adopted where $t,(t + 1)$ stands for the beginning of two consecutive slot times.

We define p as the probability that, in a slot time, at least one of the $N - 1$ remaining stations transmits. This probability can be expressed by:

$$p = 1 - (1 - \pi)^{(N-1)} \tag{1}$$

Where π is the probability that a station transmits a packet. It can be written by:

$$\pi = \sum_{i=0}^{m} b_{i,0} \tag{2}$$

Where $b_{i,k} = \lim_{t \to \infty} P\{s(t) = i, b(t) = k\}, i \in (0, m), k \in (0, CW_i - 1)$ is the stationary distribution of the chain. Only $b(i, 0)$ are considered because a transmission occurs when the backoff time counter is equal to zero. By considering the proposed Markov chain, $b_{i,0}$ can be expressed as a function of p:

$$\begin{cases} b_{i,0} = (\frac{p}{1-p})^i b_{0,0} \ 0 < i \le m \\ b_{i,k} = \frac{CW_i - k}{CW_i} b_{i,0} \ 0 < i \le m, \qquad 0 \le k \le CW_i - 1 \end{cases} \tag{3}$$

It should be noticed that this expression is different from the one expressed in [9], due to the proposed backoff strategy. By imposing the classical normalization condition and considering Equation 3, $b_{0,0}$ can be expressed as a function of p:

$$1 = \sum_{i=0}^{m} \sum_{k=0}^{CW_i-1} b_{i,k}$$

$$= \frac{b_{0,0}}{2} \left(W_{min} + 1 + W_{min} \frac{(1-p)^m - (2p)^m}{(1-3p)(1-p)^{m-1}} \right. \tag{4}$$

$$\left. + \frac{(1-p)^m - p^m}{(1-2p)(1-p)^{m-1}} \right)$$

Where $W_{min} = CW_{min} - 1$. Finally, combining equations (2),(3), and (4), the channel access probability π is equal to:

$$\pi = \sum_{i=0}^{m} b_{i,0}$$

$$= \sum_{i=0}^{m} \left(\frac{p}{1-p} \right)^i b_{0,0} \tag{5}$$

$$= b_{0,0} \frac{(1-p)^m - p^m}{(1-2p)(1-p)^{m-1}}$$

This two equations, (1) and (5), form a system of two nonlinear equations that has a unique solution and can be solved numerically for the values of p and π.

The saturation throughput, which is the average information payload in a slot time over the average duration of a slot time, can be expressed using the classical expression [9]:

$$\tau = \frac{E[Payload\ information\ transmitted\ in\ a\ slot\ time]}{E[Duration\ of\ slot\ time]}$$

$$= \frac{P_s P_{tr} L}{P_s P_{tr} T_s + P_{tr}(1 - P_s)T_c + (1 - P_{tr})T_{id}} \tag{6}$$

where $P_{tr} = 1 - (1 - \pi)^N$ is the probability that there is at least one transmission in the considered slot time; L is the average packet payload size; T_s is the average time needed to transmit a packet of size L (including the inter-frame spacing periods [12]); $P_s = \frac{N\pi(1-\pi)^{N-1}}{1-(1-\pi)^N}$ is the probability of a successful transmission; T_{id} is the duration of the idle period (a single slot time); and T_c is the average time spent in the collision. T_c and T_s can be calculated for RTS/CTS transmission mode with [9]:

$$\begin{cases} T_s = RTS + SIFS + \sigma + CTS + SIFS + \sigma + H + L \\ \quad + SIFS + \sigma + ACK + DIFS + \sigma \\ T_c = RTS + DIFS + \sigma \end{cases} \tag{7}$$

where H, L, and ACK are the transmission times needed to send the packet header, the payload, and the acknowledgment, respectively. σ is the propagation delay.

4 Numerical Results

In this Section we study the validity, the saturation throughput and the delay of the analytical proposed model. The system of two nonlinear equations (1) and (5) is solved numerically. The protocol and channel parameters adopted are those specified in Table 4. However analysis and results can be extended to others PHY layers. The minimal contention window (W_{min}) has been chosen constant and equal to 16.

Table 1. PHY layer parameters

Packet payload	8184 bits
MAC header	272 bits
PHY header	128 bits
ACK length	112 bits + PHY header
RTS length	160 bits + PHY header
CTS length	112 bits + PHY header
Channel Bit Rate	1 Mbit/s
Propagation Delay	1 μs
SIFS	28 μs
Slot Time	50 μs
DIFS	128 μs

4.1 Validation of Analytical Results

In order to validate the analytical model, the proposed backoff strategy is simulated for various number of mobile stations. Saturation throughput is computed for 2 different maximum backoff stages ($m = 3$ and $m = 7$). Figure 3 illustrates the relative error. The difference between the analytical and the simulated model is negligeable and it is due to the solve function tolerance as well as the finite number of iteration considered in the simulation.

4.2 System Performance

In this Section, we study the performance of the proposed backoff strategy, so we compute the saturation throughput (bits/sec) vs the number of mobile stations for the RTS/CTS mode. RTS/CTS transmission mode is considered as it avoids the collision between the long data packets especially for high number of mobile stations. Figures 4 and 5 show that the saturation throughput in the proposed strategy is better than the saturation throughput in the classical CSMA/CA protocol with 802.11 backoff strategy for RTS/CTS mechanism, and especially in the cases of large CW_{max} (big m) independently from the number of mobile stations.

For example, in the proposed protocol and for $CW_{max} = 511$ ($m = 5$) we can achieve better saturation throughput than the 802.11 protocol with $CW_{max} = 2047$ ($m = 7$).

Numerical results show, as expected and due to lower probability of collision between transmitters, that the throughput increase when the number of states become higher. This fact is due to the distribution of all users within different backoff states, instead to be all located in the first state (bottleneck of classical 802.11 protocol). Note that we don't take into consideration the retransmission limit and the maximum backoff stage as defined by the IEEE standard specification [13]. It should be mentioned that 802.11 strategy has better performance for large number of users and $m = 3$ and it is due to the lack of spatial degree of liberty.

4.3   Statistical Delay Study

Many previous works [8, 14–16] evaluates the system performance in term of delay by computing or simulating the average access delay. Since the average access delay isn't always a sufficient metric especially in VoIP applications, we go forward to simulate the cumulative density function (CDF) of the access delay. Figure 6 represents the CDF of the access delay for $m = 3$. It's seen clearly from Figure 6 that the delay of the proposed strategy is less than the classical one especially in charged mode (large number of mobile stations). It is due to the fact that users are distributed over all the stages instead to be located in the bottleneck ($m = 1$). Also, the proposed backoff strategy is much more robust with high states number (big m) thanks to the offered spatial liberty. Tables 2 and 3 give different delay values for some CDF with an idea about the gain introduced by our strategy. For instance, 99% of packets are transmitted with at most 17.6 ms (resp 13.9 ms) by the classical IEEE backoff while they are sent with at most 15.5 ms (resp 12.5 ms) by our proposed backoff strategy for $m = 3$ (resp $m = 7$).

Table 2. Delay (ms) and gain (%) values in both backoff strategies for many CDF values with $m = 3$

CDF	Proposed Backoff (ms)	IEEE Backoff (ms)	Gain (%)
99%	15.5	17.6	11.93
98%	14.5	16.4	11.58
95%	13.3	14.6	8.90
90%	12.4	13.4	7.46

Table 3. Delay (ms) and gain (%) values in both backoff strategies for many CDF values with $m = 7$

CDF	Proposed Backoff (ms)	IEEE Backoff (ms)	Gain (%)
99%	12.5	13.9	10.07
98%	12.0	13.2	9.09
95%	11.4	12.3	7.32
90%	10.9	11.5	5.22

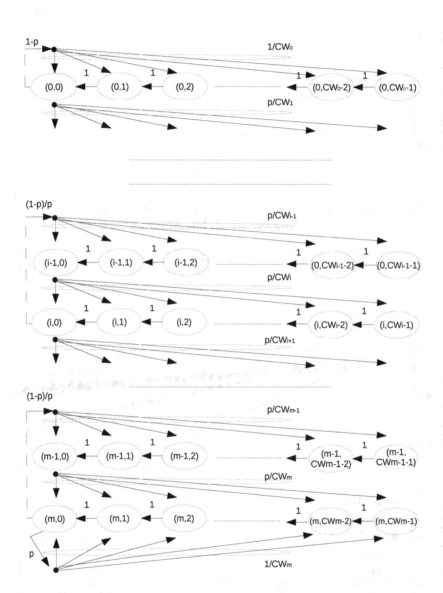

Fig. 2. Markov chain model of backoff window size in proposed CSMA/CA

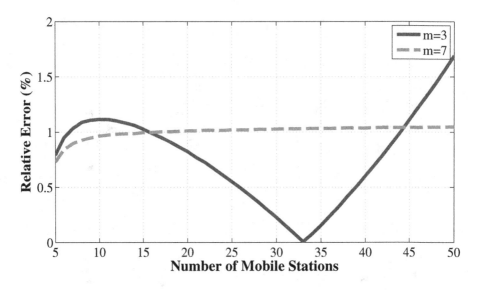

Fig. 3. Relative error vs number of mobile stations

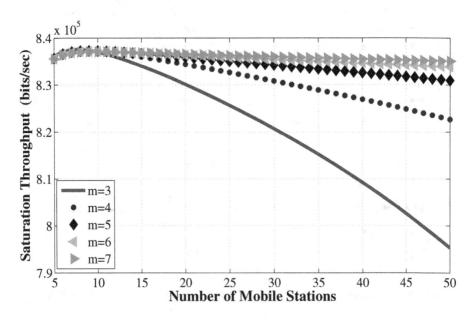

Fig. 4. Saturation throughput for proposed strategy with RTS/CTS transmission

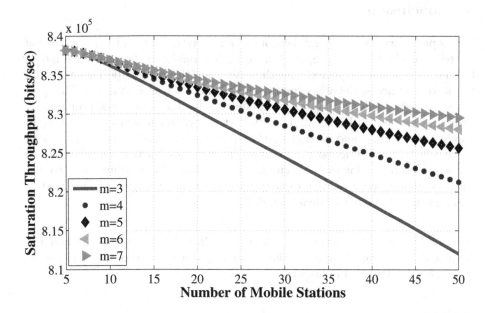

Fig. 5. Saturation throughput for classical 802.11 FH with RTS/CTS transmission

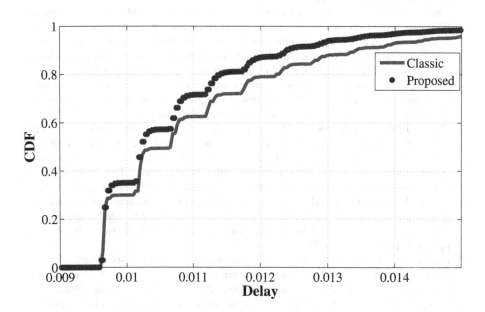

Fig. 6. CDF of access delay for $m = 3$ with 50 mobile stations. Delay is expressed in second

5   Conclusion

In this paper, we proposed and developped an analytical model for a new backoff strategy for CSMA/CA-CTS/RTS protocol. We validated the analytical model by simulations and we proved that the saturation throughput performance and the statistical access delay are improved especially in loaded systems. This proposed strategy could be a good candidate to solve the bottleneck problem existing in the classical IEEE 802.11 backoff strategy. Our model assumes a finite number of terminals and ideal channel conditions. The model is suited for both Basic and RTS/CTS access mechanisms. To conclude, in this contribution we proposed a solution for the bottleneck problem, but still as future work to discuss the improvement relative to adaptive minimum contention window and to find an original manner to deal with different users bitrates.

Acknowledgment. Authors wish to thank Prof. Jean-Marie Gorce and Dr. Nikolai Lebedev for their discussions and important remarks given following their intensive review for this work.

References

1. Pahlavan, K., Levesque, A.: Wireless data communications. Proceedings of the IEEE 82(9), 1398–1430 (1994)
2. Draft standard for information technology–telecommunications and information exchange between systems–local and metropolitan area networks–specific requirements–part 11: Wireless lan medium access control (mac) and physical layer (phy) specifications. Amendment 3: 3650-3700 mhz operation in usa (amendment to ieee 802.11-2007), IEEE Unapproved Draft Std P802.11y_D7.0 (2007)
3. "Ieee tg 15.4, part 15.4: wireless medium access control (mac) and physical layer (phy) specifications for low rate wireless personal area network (lr-wpans), ieee-sa standard board," IEEE standard for Information Technology, (2) (2006)
4. Chong, J.W., Sung, Y., Sung, D.K.: Rawpeach: Multiband csma/ca-based cognitive radio networks. Journal of Communications and Networks 11(2), 175–186 (2009)
5. Yun, J., Bahk, S.: Parallel contention algorithm with csma/ca for ofdm based high speed wireless lans. In: 14th IEEE Proceedings on Personal, Indoor and Mobile Radio Communications, PIMRC 2003, vol. 3, pp. 2581–2585 (September 2003)
6. Xu, Y., Huang, M., Lin, M., Zheng, Y.: A self-adaptive minimum contention window adjusting backoff algorithm in ieee 802.11 dcf. In: 2012 2nd International Conference on Consumer Electronics, Communications and Networks (CECNet), pp. 1577–1582 (April 2012)
7. Ru-yan, W., Da-peng, W., Mian, W.: Contention awared adaptive backoff mechanism in ieee 802.11 wireless lan. In: International Conference on Computational Intelligence and Software Engineering, CiSE 2009, pp. 1–4 (December 2009)
8. Kang, S.-W., Cha, J.-R., Kim, J.-H.: A novel estimation-based backoff algorithm in the IEEE 802.11 based wireless network. In: 2010 7th IEEE Consumer Communications and Networking Conference (CCNC), pp. 1–5 (January 2010)
9. Manshaei, M.H., Hubaux, J.-P.: Performance analysis of the IEEE 802.11 distributed coordination function: Bianchi model (March 2007)

10. Tobagi, F., Kleinrock, L.: Packet switching in radio channels: Part ii–the hidden terminal problem in carrier sense multiple-access and the busy-tone solution. IEEE Transactions on Communications 23(12), 1417–1433 (1975)
11. Fang, M.: Power evaluation and performance enhancement of csma/ca based wlans. Masters Thesis, Hamilton Institute (June 2010)
12. Bianchi, G.: Performance analysis of the ieee 802.11 distributed coordination function. IEEE Journal on Selected Areas in Communications 18(3), 535–547 (2000)
13. IEEE standard for information technology-telecommunications and information exchange between systems-local and metropolitan area networks-specific requirements-part 11: Wireless lan medium access control (mac) and physical layer (phy) specifications, ANSI/IEEE Std 802.11, 1999 Edition (R2003), pp. i–513 (2003)
14. Chong, J.W., Sung, D.K., Sung, Y.: Cross-layer performance analysis for csma/ca protocols: Impact of imperfect sensing. IEEE Transactions on Vehicular Technology 59(3), 1100–1108 (2010)
15. Kwon, H., Seo, H., Kim, S., Lee, B.G.: Generalized csma/ca for ofdma systems: protocol design, throughput analysis, and implementation issues. IEEE Transactions on Wireless Communications 8(8), 4176–4187 (2009)
16. Chong, J.W., Sung, Y., Sung, D.K.: Analysis of csma/ca systems under carrier sensing error: Throughput, delay and sensitivity. In: IEEE Global Telecommunications Conference, IEEE GLOBECOM 2008, pp. 1–6, November 30-December 4 (2008)

Prototyping Distributed Collision-Free MAC Protocols for WLANs in Real Hardware

Luis Sanabria-Russo, Jaume Barcelo, and Boris Bellalta

Universitat Pompeu Fabra
Carrer de Tànger 122 − 150, 08018 Barcelona, Spain
{luis.sanabria,jaume.barcelo,boris.bellalta}@upf.edu

Abstract. Carrier Sense Multiple Access with Enhanced Collision Avoidance (CSMA/ECA) is a totally distributed, collision-free MAC protocol for IEEE 802.11 WLANs. It is capable of achieving greater throughput than the MAC protocol used in the current standard, called Carrier Sense Multiple Access with Collision Avoidance (CSMA/CA), by means of picking a deterministic backoff after successful transmissions. This work is the first implementation of the main concept behind CSMA/ECA on real hardware. Experimental results confirm the advantages of CSMA/ECA over CSMA/CA in terms of throughput and set the ground for its complete prototyping on real hardware using Open-FWWF.

Keywords: OpenFWWF, WMP, MAC, Collision-free, CSMA/ECA.

1 Introduction

Even-though the IEEE 802.11 set of WLAN standards define the procedures to guarantee effective communication among hosts, the implementation part is the task of manufacturers. This means that *how* the standard is implemented vary from vendor to vendor and explains why firmware is closely related to the underlying hardware. Current efforts both from the industry and the open source community (as in the case of MadWiFi [1] driver and OpenFWWF [2,3] firmware), had created the opportunity to prototype and test new MAC protocols proposals on cheap commodity hardware.

A simple, totally-distributed MAC protocol for WLANs called Carrier Sense Multiple Access with Enhanced Collision Avoidance (CSMA/ECA) proposed in [4] provides an increase in the achieved throughput for contending stations by eliminating collisions. To achieve that, CSMA/ECA requires modifications to the contention mechanism of the current standard, Carrier Sense Multiple Access with Collision Avoidance (CSMA/CA); which is a very time-sensitive task handled at firmware level.

By modifying some functions of the open sourced OpenFWWF firmware, this work presents the first implementation and performance tests results of CSMA/ECA in real hardware.

M. Jonsson et al. (Eds.): MACOM 2013, LNCS 8310, pp. 82–87, 2013.

2 Prototyping CSMA/ECA

CSMA/ECA builds a collision-free schedule in WLANs by instructing contenders to pick a deterministic backoff, $B_d = CW_{min}/2$, after successful transmissions (where CW_{min} is the minimum contention window with typical value of 16) instead of a random backoff as in CSMA/CA (see Figure 1). Further modifications [5] allowed CSMA/ECA to increase the number of contenders able to maintain the collision-free schedule.

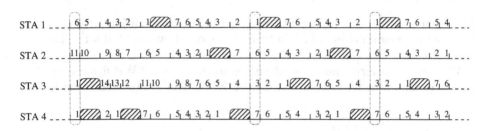

Fig. 1. CSMA/ECA example in saturation

In Figure 1, each station (STA) generates a random backoff at startup. The first outline indicates that at least two of the generated backoff values are the same and stations will consequently collide. On the other hand, successful stations will generate a deterministic backoff (7 slots in the case of the example in Figure 1) and effectively avoid collisions with other successful stations in future cycles, achieving a collision-free schedule.

In order to make an initial prototype of CSMA/ECA, the firmware was modified to execute a procedure which is very similar to the proposed protocol in saturated conditions. This implementation will be called CSMA/ECA$_{test}$ to distinguish it from CSMA/ECA [5]:

1. When a packet arrives at a previously empty MAC queue, a CSMA/ECA$_{test}$ node generates a deterministic backoff, $B_d = CW_{min}/2$. Where CW_{min} is the minimum Contention Window.
2. Each passing empty slot decrements B_d in one. When the backoff expires ($B_d = 0$), the node will attempt transmission.
3. If an ACKowledgement (ACK) from the receiver is received, and if there are other packets in the MAC queue, CSMA/ECA$_{test}$ instructs the node to pick a deterministic backoff, $B_d = CW_{min}/2$ (goes back to Step 1).
4. If no ACK is received, a collision is assumed. This causes CSMA/ECA$_{test}$ nodes to handle the collision as in CSMA/CA:
   - The node's backoff stage $k \in [0, m]$ is incremented in one ($k = k + 1$, where m is its maximum value, usually 5).
   - It generates a random backoff, $B \in [0, CW(k)]$. Where $CW(k) = 2^k CW_{min}$ is the Contention Window at backoff stage k.

- The node keeps decrementing the random backoff after each passing empty slot until it expires ($B = 0$). Then it will attempt transmission and go back to Step 3 or 4 depending on the result of the attempt.

The prototyped CSMA/ECA$_{test}$ difers from what is shown in Figure 1 in not picking a random backoff when a packet arrives at a previously empty MAC queue.

Modifying the Wireless Card's Firmware

The open source OpenFWWF firmware is used in combination with the b43 Linux wireless card driver, which in turn is supported by a limited set of Broadcom cards [6].

We have performed simple modifications to the OpenFWWF firmware to be able to evaluate the performance of CSMA/ECA$_{test}$ in a saturated scenario [7].

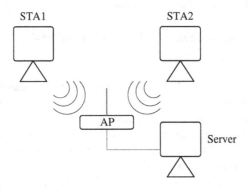

Fig. 2. Test setup

Testing Scenario

A simple testing scenario was built in order to check whether the modifications performed matched the expected CSMA/ECA$_{test}$ behaviour. This was composed of two Ubuntu 8.10 PCs with Broadcom BCM4318 cards running OpenFWWF firmware as WLAN STAtions (STA): STA1 with Intel Pentium 4 3 GHz and 768 MB of RAM; and STA2 with Intel Core 2 Quad 2.66 GHz and 3 GB of RAM, both connected to a Linksys WAG354G Access Point (AP). To make performance tests, Iperf [8] tool generates 1470 bytes UDP datagrams at 65 Mbps from both STAs to a Server wired to the AP using Ethernet, effectively saturating each STA. At the Server, Wireshark [9] captures all packets from the STAs. Figure 2 provides an overview of the testing scenario.

Two tests were performed, the first tries to reveal evidence of the deterministic backoff counter, while the second aims at looking at the achieved throughput.

2.1   Results

Figures 3 and 4 show a random set of a hundred server-received packets from STAs running CSMA/CA and CSMA/ECA$_{test}$, respectively.

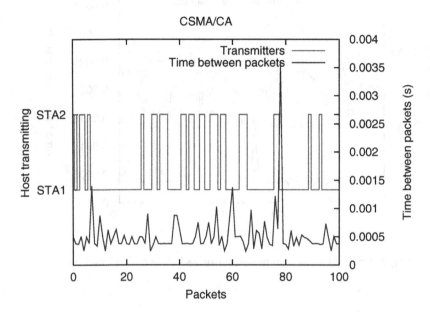

Fig. 3. CSMA/CA transmission turns between STA1 and STA2

Backoff Mechanism. CSMA/CA's randomized backoff mechanism can be appreciated in Figure 3, where the "Transmitters" line shows how the transmitter of a given packet could be either of the contending stations. Whereas in CSMA/ECA$_{test}$ (Figure 4), transmitters almost alternate transmissions.

Time between Packets

From the "Time between packets" curve, we can appreciate that with CSMA/CA the average time between two consecutive packets (seen from the channel perspective) is greater than with CSMA/ECA$_{test}$. This is due to the random backoff time of CSMA/CA, which is prone to collisions, and to retransmission attempts; whereas for CSMA/ECA$_{test}$ contenders this backoff is fixed after successful transmissions, originating a collision-free schedule.

Throughput. Because CSMA/ECA$_{test}$ stations successfully transmit packets more frequently and are less prone to collisions, their achieved throughput is higher than CSMA/CA stations. Figure 5 evidenced this effect by displaying the average throughput achieved by each station while attempting to transmit generic UDP packets generated at 65 Mbps to the Server.

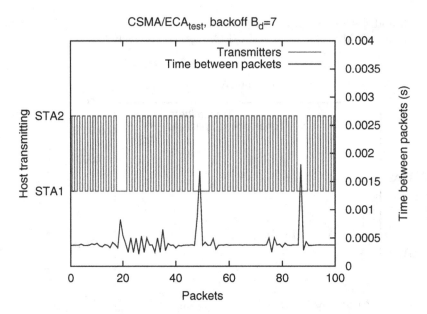

Fig. 4. CSMA/ECA$_{test}$ transmission turns between STA1 and STA2

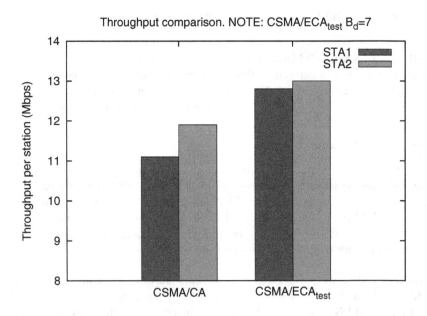

Fig. 5. Throughput

3 Conclusion

OpenFWWF is an open alternative for researchers wanting to test new MAC protocols in realistic conditions. In this document CSMA/ECA is described and evaluated with encouraging results.

The benefits in throughput experienced with Carrier Sense Multiple Access with Enhanced Collision Avoidance (CSMA/ECA) are the result of the construction of a collision-free schedule. Results from these tests show evidence of an effective modification of CSMA/CA's backoff mechanism alongside with the throughput increase of CSMA/ECA.

This is the first real hardware implementation of CSMA/ECA. Further work involves the design of more accurate testing scenarios, better data gathering techniques and the extension of CSMA/ECA to work with more contenders [5].

All the details and necessary steps to reproduce the results presented in this work are available in a technical report [7].

Acknowledgements. The authors would like to thank the editors and the anonymous reviewers for their valuable feedbacks in improving the paper. This work was partially supported by the Spanish and the Catalan governments, through the projects CISNETS (TEC2012-32354) and AGAUR SGR2009-617, respectively.

References

1. The MADWifi Project: Multiband Atheros Driver for Wireless Fidelity. Webpage (2013)
2. Gringoli, F., Nava, L.: Open Firmware for WiFi Networks,
   http://www.ing.unibs.it/openfwwf/ (webpage accessed July 2013)
3. Tinnirello, I., Bianchi, G., Gallo, P., Garlisi, D., Giuliano, F., Gringoli, F.: Wireless MAC processors: Programming MAC protocols on commodity Hardware. In: 2012 Proceedings IEEE INFOCOM, pp. 1269–1277 (2012)
4. Barcelo, J., Bellalta, B., Cano, C., Oliver, M.: Learning-BEB: Avoiding Collisions in WLAN. In: Eunice (2008)
5. Sanabria-Russo, L., Faridi, A., Bellalta, B., Barceló, J., Oliver, M.: Future Evolution of CSMA Protocols for the IEEE 802.11 Standard. In: 2nd IEEE Workshop on Telecommunications Standards: From Research to Standards, Budapest, Hungary (2013)
6. Linux Wireless: b43 and b43legacy,
   http://wireless.kernel.org/en/users/Drivers/b43 (webpage accessed July 2013)
7. Sanabria-Russo, L.: Report: Prototyping Collision-Free MAC Protocols in Real Hardware. Webpage (2013), http://luissanabria.me/written/beca-test1.pdf
8. Tirumala, A., Qin, F., Dugan, J., Ferguson, J., Gibbs, K.: Iperf: The TCP/UDP bandwidth measurement tool (2005), http://dast.nlanr.net/Projects
9. Combs, G., et al.: Wireshark (2007)

Performance Analysis of Cooperative Cognitive Distributed MAC Protocol with Full Duplex Links

Senthilmurugan S. and T.G. Venkatesh

Department of Electrical Engineering
Indian Institute of Technology - Madras
Chennai - 600036, India
{ee12s070,tgvenky}@ee.iitm.ac.in

Abstract. Recent advancements in Full Duplex (FD) wireless system opens up many research opportunities in the Medium Access Control (MAC) layer. In this paper, we propose Cooperative Cognitive Distributed MAC (CCD-MAC) protocol in which the FD Secondary User (SU) will help Primary User (PU) by relaying PU's packet when the primary link quality is bad. We consider two-state primary link quality model with fixed Average Non-Fade Duration for 'Good' state followed by exponentially distributed fading duration for 'Bad' state. When the PU is idle, SUs use p-persistent CSMA protocol for channel access. An analytical model has been developed for the proposed protocol. Using our model, throughput of secondary network and the delay experienced by PU's packet are calculated. The validity of the analytical work is supported with simulation results.

Keywords: Wireless Network, Full Duplex link, Cognitive Relay, Cooperative Medium Access Control.

1 Introduction

Wireless spectrum scarcity has paved the way for development of cognitive networks where unlicensed users try to access the spectrum when it is not being used by licensed user [1],[2]. International standardization of Cognitive Radio Networks (CRN) by the agencies like IEEE, ETSI, ITU, ETSI are detailed in [3]. In CRN's terminology, licensed users are called as Primary Users (PU) where as unlicensed users are termed as Secondary Users (SU). The design and performance analysis of Medium Access Control (MAC) protocols for CRN is an important research issue. An exhaustive literature survey of existing cognitive MAC protocol with variations like centralization /decentralization of SUs, single /multiple channels, slotted /unslotted systems, synchronous /asynchronous PU-SU systems are discussed in [4],[5] and [6].

In wireless communication, the term 'Full Duplex' system means that wireless nodes are capable of transmitting their own signal and receiving another signal in the same frequency band and at the same time. Around 2010, Sachin et.al

M. Jonsson et al. (Eds.): MACOM 2013, LNCS 8310, pp. 88–99, 2013.
© Springer International Publishing Switzerland 2013

[7] demonstrated the practical implementation of full duplex system on Software Defined Radio (SDR) platforms like WARP [8] and USRP boards [9]. To achieve FD capability, they adopted both antenna cancellation and digital cancellation techniques. They also discussed MAC layer's performance improvement in WLAN using Contraflow generalized FD MAC from Microsoft.

In this work, we consider three scenarios based on the primary link quality and the degree of co-operation between SUs and PU. Here, the term 'primary link' means the channel between primary transmitter and primary receiver. In first scenario, the primary link is always assumed to be good and hence there is no need for co-operation between SUs and PU. SUs will access the channel whenever channel is free from PU. This is similar to the existing CRN MAC protocols discussed in literature [6]. Two sub-cases based on whether SUs have Half /Full duplex capabilities are also analyzed for this scenario. In second scenario, we will consider the case where primary link can become bad. There is no co-operation between PU and SUs and hence PU will not be able to transmit its packet till primary link returns back to good state. During this time, the spectrum will be available for secondary network. Third scenario considers the same assumptions as in the second scenario that the primary link can go bad. In this scenario, we propose co-operative cognitive distributed MAC protocol where SU is used to relay PU's packet whenever the primary link is bad. For the proposed protocol, we develop an analytical model to calculate the throughput of secondary network and the delay experienced by PU's packets.

Some cooperative models have already been proposed for Half-Duplex (HD) system in which SU acts as relay when the primary link goes bad [10],[11]. In [10], the authors have implemented their proposed MAC protocol in SDR test-bed where Access Point (AP) does co-ordination among SUs and PU. The authors of [11] have proposed a centralized scheme in which SUs assist PU by adopting amplify-and-forward TDMA protocol and analyzed it using M/G/1 preemptive priority queuing model. Our work varies significantly from these two works in the following manner. Our proposed CCD-MAC is distributed in nature with no requirment for centralised co-ordinator. Whenever secondary network senses free channel, SUs will use p-persistent CSMA for accessing it. We analysed our proposed protocol using renewal theory and queueing models.

The rest of the paper is organized as follows: Section 2 describes system model and assumptions made in our work. The first scenario described above is detailed in Section 3 followed by the study of second scenario in Section 4. In Section 5, we elaborate our CCD-MAC protocol used in the third scenario. The throughput of secondary network and the delay experienced by PU's packet in CCD-MAC protocol are calculated using analytical model. Simulation of all three scenarios are carried out and their results are compared with the analytical model in Section 6.

2 System Model

2.1 Arrival Model

We consider single primary transmitter - receiver pair with a transmission channel. The packet arrival for PU is modeled as Poisson process with rate λ. Let L_p be the packet length of PU. All SUs are slot synchronized with each other and are not synchronized with PU.

Let N_s be the number of secondary transmitter - receiver pair and L_s be the packet length of secondary users. SUs are time slotted with unit slot time. We assume SUs operate under saturated condition. Each SU senses the channel with probability P_a at the beginning of every slot. If the channel is sensed free, all SUs who have participated in sensing will transmit their packets. We assume that the SUs will not make any sensing errors. For simplicity, the data rate of a channel is taken as $R_c = 1$ data unit / time unit and hence L_s is the time units to transmit SU's packet.

2.2 Channel Quality Model

The primary link is modeled as a two state system with 'Good' state if the channel is in non-fade condition and 'Bad' state for channel in fading condition. We model the channel as an alternation of 'Good' state with fixed non-fade duration of $\overline{T_{nf}}$ and 'Bad' state with exponentially distributed fade duration with mean $\overline{T_f}$. Paper [12] shows that the above model closely captures the features of Rayleigh fading channel model. The probability that the primary link is in 'Good' state at an arbitrary time is given as [12]

$$P_g = \overline{T_{nf}}/(\overline{T_{nf}} + \overline{T_f}) \tag{1}$$

The fixed non-fade duration, $\overline{T_{nf}}$, is assumed to be much larger when compared to PU's packet transmission time. However we assume that the secondary - primary links and the secondary -secondary links are always good because SUs use cognitive radio which has many flexibilities like changing transmit power, implementing different detection techniques based on the SNR values,etc.

2.3 Secondary User Behavior

When the PU's buffer is empty, the channel will be accessed by SUs using the slotted p-persistent CSMA protocol. The throughput calculation of the secondary network will vary based on SUs HD/FD capabilities:

Only two slots are wasted by FD-SUs in collision where as L_s slots are wasted by HD-SUs. When the SUs are FD capable, they can detect collision even when they are transmitting and hence they can stop transmission immediately. This will also limits the maximum interference of two slots to PU if SUs are FD capable. We assume that the primary user is tolerable to SUs interference as $L_p >> L_s$

3 p - persistent CSMA CRN MAC Protocol

3.1 Renewal Model

In our first scenario, the primary link is always in 'Good' state, hence there is no need of SU's co-operation. The channel will be free whenever PU's queue is empty. The time duration of PU's queue being empty (Free period) and non-empty (Busy Period) can be modeled using Renewal theory. The renewal points are taken as those instances at which the arrival of PU's packet occurs when the PU's queue is empty.

A typical renewal interval is explained as follows: Let us assume that the PU's queue is empty. The arrival of the first packet to an empty queue marks the beginning of the renewal interval. While the packet get served, more packets can arrive which will be served in FCFS discipline. Recursively this may lead to build-up of the queue. When the queue becomes empty, the arrival of the first packet marks the starting of the next renewal cycle.

Since the packet arrivals of PU is Poisson, the time duration of the first arrival after PU's queue becoming empty follows exponential distribution with mean 1 / λ. Thus, the expected free period $E(F)$ will be

$$E(F) = 1/\lambda \tag{2}$$

Similarly, the expected busy period $E(B)$ of a renewal interval is calculated using M/D/1 queueing model for PU. The expected service time of the PU's packet is $E(S) = L_p$. Thus, the utilization factor ρ of M/D/1 queue is given by

$$\rho = \lambda E(S) = E(B)/(E(F) + E(B))$$

$$E(B) = \frac{\rho}{(1-\rho)\lambda} = \frac{L_p}{(1 - \lambda L_p)} \tag{3}$$

3.2 Throughput Calculation of Secondary Network in Channel Free Condition

Whenever the channel is free from PU, SUs will go for p-persistent CSMA protocol with probability P_a. The probability of only one SU transmission in a slot (P_{st}) and the probability of collision (P_c) of SUs can be calculated as:

$$P(\ 1\ SU\ transmits) \equiv P_{st} = N_s P_a (1 - P_a)^{N_s - 1}$$

$$P(\ No\ SU\ transmits) \equiv P_i = (1 - P_a)^{N_s}$$

$$P_c = 1 - P_{st} - P_i$$

Once a SU successfully starts transmission in a slot, other SUs will not transmit their data in remaining $(L_s - 1)$ slots as they sense channel to be busy. However, the PU can start transmission at any time and this may result in loss of packet for SU. The probability of SU's transmission not interfering with PU (P_{ss}) and the probability of SU's transmission interfering with PU (P_{sc}) are calculated as follows:

Let X be a random variable that denotes the time interval between the time instant at which SU starts transmission and the time instant at which PU interferes. As a result of the memory-less property of PU's exponential inter-packet arrival time, X will also be exponentially distributed with parameter λ. For interference-free transmission, the random variable X has to be greater than L_s.

$$P(X > L_s \mid 1 \ SU \ transmits) = \int_{t=L_s}^{\infty} \lambda e^{-\lambda t} \, dt = e^{-\lambda L_s}$$

Thus, the probability of successful transmission of SU without interfering with PU (P_{ss}) is given as

$$P_{ss} = P_{st} P(X > L_s \mid 1 \ SU \ transmits) = N_s P_a (1 - P_a)^{N_s - 1} e^{-\lambda L_s}$$

$$P_{sc} = P_{st} P(X < L_s \mid 1 \ SU \ transmits) = N_s P_a (1 - P_a)^{N_s - 1} (1 - e^{-\lambda L_s}) \quad (4)$$

Given a SU's transmission encounters an interference with the PU, the expected number of slots that are transmitted by SU before the interference can be calculated using the following fact: PU's interference occurs if PU's packet arrives during an on-going transmission of SU. Conditioned on one arrival of PU's packet in the interval $(0, L_s)$, the arrival instance is uniformly distributed in $(0, L_s)$ for Poisson arrival process [13]. Hence, the expected number of slots transmitted by the SU before interfering with PU is given by $E(N_I) = L_s/2$.

Whenever there is a collision among SUs, L_s slots are wasted in HD-SU network while it is only two slots for the FD-SUs network. Thus, the throughput of HD-SU network given that the channel is free from PU denoted by $\tau_{s,HD-CSMA}$ is calculated as follows:

$$\tau_{s,HD-CSMA} = \frac{L_s P_{ss}}{L_s P_{ss} + 1 P_i + L_s P_c + \frac{L_s}{2} P_{sc}} \quad (5)$$

Similarly, the throughput of FD-SU network given that channel is free from PU , $\tau_{s,FD-CSMA}$ is given as

$$\tau_{s,FD-CSMA} = \frac{L_s P_{ss}}{L_s P_{ss} + 1 P_i + 2 P_c + \frac{L_s}{2} P_{sc}} \quad (6)$$

Note that in the above Equations 5 and 6, the contribution of the term $(L_s P_{sc})/2$ occurs only at the end of channel free period. Similarly, the term $L_s P_{ss}$ is conditioned by the fact that there is no PU interference.

3.3   Overall Throughput of Secondary Network

The overall throughput of secondary network for the p-persistent CSMA CRN MAC protocol in both HD/FD cases are given by:

$$\tau_{s,HD/FD} = \frac{E(F)}{E(F) + E(B)} \ \tau_{s,HD/FD-CSMA} \tag{7}$$

where $E(F)$ and $E(B)$ are given in Equations 2 and 3 respectively. The factor $E(F)/(E(F) + E(B))$ accounts for the fact that SUs implement p-persistent CRN CSMA only during the PU's queue being empty.

3.4   Delay Experienced by PU Packets

The mean delay experienced by the PU packet $E(D)$ is calculated using M/D/1 queueing model as follows: $E(D) = E(S) + W_q$ where W_q is the waiting time of PU packet in the queue [13].

$$E(D) = L_p + \frac{\lambda E(S^2)}{2(1 - \rho)} = L_p + \frac{\lambda L_p^2}{2(1 - \lambda L_p)} \tag{8}$$

4   Non-cooperative CRN MAC Protocol

For second scenario, the primary link quality is modeled as detailed in Section 2.2 and there are no co-operation between PU and SUs. The primary link quality can either be in 'Good' state with probability P_g calculated in Equation 1 or in 'Bad' state with probability $1 - P_g$. Whenever the primary link is not good, PU cannot start transmission and has to wait till the primary link returns to 'Good' state. Here, the term 'non-cooperation' means that SUs will not participate in relaying PU's packet.

In general a PU which starts transmission with the primary link quality in 'Good' state might finishes the transmission in 'Bad' state. However the probability of occurence of this event can be made as small as desired by conservatively fixing the PU's transmission policy (threshold level for distinguishing between 'Good' and 'Bad' state).

In this non-cooperative scenario, the channel will be free not only when PU's queue is empty but also when the primary link quality is in the 'Bad' state. Thus, FD-SUs implement the p-persistent CSMA protocol whenever the channel is free from PU. The overall throughput of secondary network is calculated by finding the fraction of time the channel is free from PU in a renewal interval and multiplying it with $\tau_{s,FD-CSMA}$ which is same as Equation 6 derived in Section 3.

As in the Section 3,the renewal points for this scenario are also taken as the first arrival of PU's packet when PU's queue is empty. The overall throughput of secondary network and the delay experienced by PU packets are obtained through simulation and are plotted in Section 6 to compare with other scenarios.

5 Proposed Cooperative Cognitive Distributed MAC Protocol (CCD-MAC)

In our proposed Cooperative Cognitive Distributed MAC (CCD-MAC) protocol, the primary link quality is modeled as in Section 2.2. However when the primary link quality is 'Bad', the primary transmitter randomly selects one of the FD-SUs and informs its decision to SUs on the dedicated control channel. Following this, the primary transmitter transmits its packet which is relayed by the selected SU to the primary receiver with negligible delay (as compared to L_s) as they are full-duplex capable. Since the selected SU has helped PU by relaying, the channel is reserved for the transmission of its packet. Similar to other scenarios, FD-SUs will implement p-persistent CSMA protocol for transmitting their data when PU's queue is empty.

5.1 Algorithm in CCD-MAC Protocol

The algorithm followed in our proposed CCD-MAC protocol is given below:

> **if** *PU has non-empty queue* **then**
> > Check Primary link quality;
> > **if** *Primary link is in 'Good' state* **then**
> > > PU transmits the data ;
> >
> > **else**
> > > PU randomly selects one SU;
> > > PU inform its selection to SUs on the dedicated control channel;
> > > Selected SU relays PU's data followed by its data;
> >
> > **end**
>
> **else**
> > SUs follow p-persistent CSMA to access the spectrum;
>
> **end**

Algorithm 1: Algorithm for CCD-MAC protocol

5.2 Renewal Model

Similar to earlier scenarios, the time duration of channel being free and channel being busy is modeled using Renewal theory with renewal point as the first arrival of PU's packet which sees empty PU queue. As mentioned in the Section 3, the expected free period of channel in the renewal interval is given by $E(F) = 1/\lambda$.

When the PU has data, the channel will be occupied depending up on the channel condition and SUs. Let L be the time taken to serve a PU's packet

$$L = \begin{cases} L_{oh} + L_p + L_s & w.p \ (1 - P_g) \\ L_p & w.p \ P_g \end{cases}$$

where P_g is the probability of primary link being good and L_{oh} be the overhead i.e. the number of slots used by PU for broadcasting its decision to secondary network.

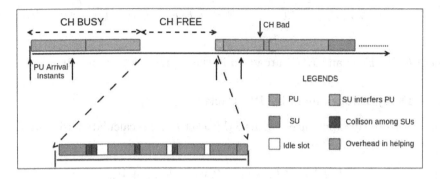

Fig. 1. Typical PU and SUs interaction in CCD-MAC protocol

The expected busy time $E(B)$ of the channel in a renewal interval is calculated using M/G/1 queuing model as follows: The expected service time of PU packet $E(S)$ is

$$E(S) = P_g L_p + (1 - P_g)(L_p + L_s + L_{oh}) \qquad (9)$$

Since $\rho = \lambda E(S) = E(B)/(E(B) + E(F))$ holds good,

$$E(B) = \frac{\rho}{(1 - \rho)\lambda} = \frac{L_p + (1 - P_g)(L_s + L_{oh})}{1 - \lambda[L_p + (1 - P_g)(L_s + L_{oh})]} \qquad (10)$$

5.3 Overall Throughput of Secondary Network

The expected number of PU packet transmissions $E(N)$ in a busy period of a renewal cycle is calculated as

$$E(N) = E(B)/E(S) \qquad (11)$$

where $E(S)$ and $E(B)$ are given in Equations 9 and 10 respectively. Thus, the throughput of secondary network by helping PU is given by

$$\tau_{s,Busy} = \frac{E(B)}{E(B) + E(F)} \frac{(1 - P_g)L_s E(N)}{E(B)} \qquad (12)$$

Note that out of $E(N)$ packets transmitted by PU in a busy period, $(1 - P_g)E(N)$ packets get transmitted with the help of SU. As a result of helping PU, the SU will get $(1 - P_g)E(N)L_s$ time units out of $E(B)$ time units for its own packet transmission. Similarly, the throughput of secondary network by accessing PU-free channel is given as

$$\tau_{s,Free} = \frac{E(F)}{E(B) + E(F)} \tau_{s,FD-CSMA} \qquad (13)$$

where $\tau_{s,FD-CSMA}$ is same as in Equation 6. Thus, the overall throughput of secondary network denoted by $\tau_{s,FD} = \tau_{s,Free} + \tau_{s,Busy}$ is calculated as

$$\tau_{s,FD} = \frac{E(B)}{E(B)+E(F)} \frac{(1-P_g)L_s}{E(S)} + \frac{E(F)}{E(B)+E(F)} \frac{L_sP_{ss}}{L_sP_s + 1P_e + 2P_c + \frac{L_s}{2}P_{sc}}$$

$$(14)$$

where $E(F)$, $E(S)$ and $E(B)$ are given in the Equations 2, 9 and 10.

5.4   Delay Experienced by PU Packets

The average delay experienced by the PU packet $E(D)$ is calculated using M/G/1 queueing model as follows:

$$E(D) = P_gL_p + (1-P_g)(L_{oh}+L_p) + W_q$$

where the delay due to transmission of SU's packet is captured in the waiting time of PU's packet in queue W_q. Since the SU relays PU's packet before transmitting its packet, L_s is not included in the first part of an equation.

$$E(D) = P_gL_p + (1-P_g)(L_{oh}+L_p) + \frac{\lambda E(S^2)}{2(1-\rho)} \qquad (15)$$

where $E(S)$ is given in the Equation 9 and $E(S^2)$ can also be calculated as

$$E(S^2) = P_gL_p{}^2 + (1-P_g)(L_{oh}+L_p+L_s)^2$$

6   Simulation Results

Extensive discrete time simulation of all three scenarios have been carried out using MATLAB® to validate analytical models. The throughput of the secondary network and the mean delay experienced by PU's packet are obtained.

In simulation, the throughput of secondary network is calculated as the long run fraction of time the SUs packet is successfully transmitted in total simulation time. The PU's packet arrival is modeled as Poisson process and all SUs are assumed to be in the saturated condition.

In first scenario ,where the primary link is always 'Good', the secondary network implements p-persistent CSMA CRN for accessing the free spectrum. The two sub-cases (i) HD-SUs and (ii) FD-SUs in this scenario are simulated and their throughput's are plotted against P_a of SUs along with their analytical result in figure 2. An improvement in the throughput of secondary network by FD-SUs when compared to HD-SUs is observed from figure 3.

In the non-cooperative scenario, the primary link quality is simulated as detailed in Section 2.2. The average non-fade duration $\overline{T_{nf}}$ is fixed and then the average fade duration $\overline{T_f}$ is calculated using Equation 1 for given P_g value. The exponential random number generator with the mean $\overline{T_f}$ is used for generating random fading duration. The throughput of non-cooperative scenario is plotted along with CCD-MAC protocol in figure 5.

The proposed CCD-MAC protocol is also simulated in MATLAB and the normalized throughput is plotted against P_a along with the theoretical value in

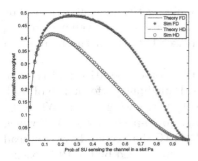

Fig. 2. The throughput of the secondary network for first scenario against P_a for HD-SUs and FD-SUs (Params: $N_s = 3$, $L_p = 40$, $L_s = 10$, $\lambda = 1/100$)

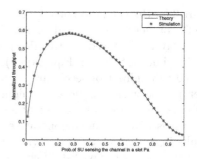

Fig. 3. The throughput of the secondary network for CCD-MAC against P_a (simulation and theory) (Params: $N_s = 3$, $L_p = 20$, $L_s = 5$, $\lambda = 1/100$, $P_g = 0.8$)

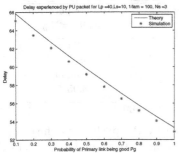

Fig. 4. The delay experienced by PU packet (in time units) for CCD-MAC protocol against P_g (Params: $L_p = 40$, $L_s = 10$, $N_s = 3$, $\lambda = 1/100$)

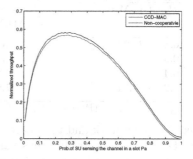

Fig. 5. The throughput of secondary network for Non-cooperative and CCD-MAC against P_a (Params: $N_s = 3$, $L_p = 20$, $L_s = 5$, $\lambda = 1/100$, $P_g = 0.8$)

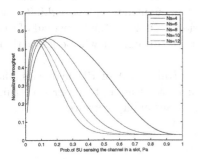

Fig. 6. The throughput of the secondary network of CCD-MAC protocol against P_a for different values of N_s (Params: $P_g = 0.4$, $L_p = 20$, $L_s = 5$, $\lambda = 1/100$)

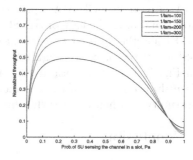

Fig. 7. The throughput of the secondary network of CCD-MAC protocol against P_a for different values of λ (Params: $P_g = 0.4$, $L_p = 40$, $L_s = 10$, $\lambda = 1/100$)

figure 3 for the validation of analytical model. Similarly, the delay experienced by the PU packet is also plotted against P_g values in figure 4. As P_g value decreases, the delay experienced by the PU packet increases because of the increase in service time $E(S)$ (as in Equation 9).

The throughput of secondary network for the Non-cooperative and the Cooperative scenario are plotted in figure 5. The throughput performance of both these scenarios are close to each other because of the following reason. When the channel is bad, the non-cooperative SUs will go for p-persistent CSMA which results in contention overhead whereas in CCD-MAC,the SU will have overhead of relaying the PU's packet. However, the delay experienced by the PU's packet in Non-cooperative scenario is greater than the CCD-MAC protocol as tabulated in Table 1. From figures 2, 3 and 4, one can observe that the throughput

Table 1. Delay experienced by PU packet

P_g	CCD-MAC	Non-cooperative ADF $= 3L_p$	Non-cooperative ADF $=2L_p$
0.8	22.94	35.48	32.09
0.6	23.53	66.30	51.91
0.4	24.11	4.81e4	196.30
0.2	24.74	7.91e5	3.95e5

(Params: $L_p = 20$, $L_s = 10$, $1/\lambda = 100$)

of secondary network and the dealy experienced by PU packet matches closely with their simulation results thus validating the analytical model. Henceforth, the analytical model is used to investigate the performance of CCD-MAC for different parameter settings.

Fig. 6 shows the normalized throughput of CCD-MAC with peaks at different P_a values for different N_s. Because of the full-duplex nature of SUs in CCD-MAC, very little time is wasted in idle and collision state. Therefore, the optimal P_a value which maximizes the throughput occurs at $P_a^* \approx 1/N_s$ as p-persistent CSMA is used in CCD-MAC protocol. This phenomenon is also exhibited in figures 2 and 3. In the case of HD-SUs, collision occupies L_s slots instead of two slots. Hence, the optimal P_a that maximizes the throughput will be lesser than FD-SUs network as seen in figure 2.

In Fig. 7, it can be noticed that as the arrival rate λ of PU increases, the PU's utilization factor of the channel also increases leading to lesser spectrum opportunity and hence lesser the throughput of secondary network.

7   Conclusion

In this paper, we have proposed a cooperative MAC protocol for the distributed cognitive radio network where full-duplex SUs assist PU's packet transmission when the primary link is bad. An analytical model was developed for the proposed CCD-MAC protocol using simple renewal theoretic concepts to calculate the throughput of saturated secondary network. Using the same model, the delay experienced by PU packets is also computed.

References

1. Song, M., Xin, C., Zhao, C.Y., Cheng, X.: Dynamic Spectrum Access: From Cognitive Radio to Network Radio. IEEE Wireless Comm. Magazine, 23–29 (February 2012)
2. Geirhofer, S., Tong, L., Sadler, B.M.: Dynamic Spectrum Access in the Time Domain: Modeling and Exploiting White Space. IEEE Comm. Magazine, 66–72 (May 2007)
3. Filin, S., Harada, H., Murakami, H., Ishizu, K.: International Standardization of Cognitive Radio Systems. IEEE Comm. Magazine, 82–89 (March 2011)
4. Liang, Y.C., Chen, K.C., Li, G.Y., Mahonen, P.: Cognitive Radio Networking and Communications - An Overview. IEEE Trans. on Vehicular Technology 60(7), 3386–3407 (2011)
5. Ren, P., Wang, Y., Du, Q., Xu, J.: A survey on dynamic spectrum access protocols for distributed cognitive wireless networks. EURASIP Journal on Wireless Communication and Networking 2012(1), 60 (2012)
6. Cormio, C., Chowdhury, K.R.: A survey on MAC protocols for cognitive radio networks. Ad Hoc Networks 7(7), 1315–1329 (2009)
7. Jain, M., Choi, J.I., Kim, T., Bharadia, D., Seth, S., Srinivasan, K., Levis, P., Katti, S., Sinha, P.: Practical, real-time, full duplex wireless. In: Proc. of the 17th Annual Intl. Conf. on Mobile Computing and Networking, MobiCom 2011, p. 301 (2011)
8. Rice University WARP Project, http://warp.rice.edu
9. Universal Software Radio Peripheral (USRP), Ettus Research LLC, http://www.ettus.com
10. Jia, J., Zhang, J., Zhang, Q.: Cooperative Relay for Cognitive Radio Networks. In: IEEE INFOCOM 2009 - The 28th Conference on Computer Communications, vol. 1, pp. 2304–2312 (April 2009)
11. Zhang, C., Wang, X., Li, J.: Cooperative Cognitive Radio with Priority Queueing Analysis. In: 2009 IEEE Intl. Conf. on Communications, pp. 1–5 (June 2009)
12. Ashraf, M., Jayasuriya, A., Perreau, S.: Channel MAC Protocol for Opportunistic Communication in Ad Hoc Wireless Networks. EURASIP Journal on Advances in Signal Processing, 2009(1), id. 368209 (2009)
13. Kulkarni, V.G.: Modeling and Analysis of Stochastic Systems. Chapman & Hall (1995)

Large-Scale Femtocell Network Deployment and Measurements

Miika Kankare, Ari Asp, Yaroslav Sydorov, Jarno Niemelä, and Mikko Valkama

Department of Electronics and Communications Engineering,
Tampere University of Technology, P.O. Box 692 FI-33101 Tampere Finland

Abstract. Modern, advanced mobile radio networks have billions of users and an increasing amount is using the mobile networks indoors. Smartphones are designed for data consumption and thus the demand is for higher and higher throughput rates. At the same time the users and operators of mobile radio networks encounter difficulties with coverage gaps, especially indoors. Femtocells are a new concept that aims for ease of use, low cost and high performance in providing coverage and capacity for indoor users. This paper presents measurement results for an arbitrary, large-scale, indoor femtocell deployment. The measurements revealed clear promise in the technology, but at the same time difficulties with interference in such a high density femtocell environment. Power management is increasingly important in femtocell deployments as the placement is uncontrolled by the operator. Femtocell network parameters and density have a clear impact on the performance.

1 Introduction

With the advent of more advanced mobile radio networks, the amount of cellular network users has been climbing from the first cellular phone call in 1973 [1] to an estimated 6.8 billion in 2013 [2]. Among the plurality of standardized technologies available, the *3rd Generation* (3G) networks are increasing popularity [3]. 3G and especially the newer *4th Generation* (4G) technologies are well equipped for data transfers with throughputs reaching from 384 kbps to even beyond 100 Mbps [4].

Recently an increasing demand for higher and higher throughput rates has been the trend due to the popularity of so called smartphones. Total global mobile data traffic was *885 petabytes* per month in 2012, of which smartphones generated an astounding 92% [5]. Some predictions are showing 60% of the data traffic will be generated indoors in 2013 [6] and the percentage rising to 75% in 2015 [7].

In addition to the increasing capacity demand, operators are facing coverage problems due to a variety of reasons. Currently energy efficient housing is causing additional indoor coverage problems. In Europe the legislative changes by the European Union have made it mandatory for new housing to reach a zero-energy status [8]. Instinctively, new materials and manufacturing processes are needed to produce low-energy and passive apartments. According to multiple reports [9,10] and research [11], the new materials are very efficient in blocking *Radio Frequency*

M. Jonsson et al. (Eds.): MACOM 2013, LNCS 8310, pp. 100–112, 2013.

(RF) signals. Recent measurements have shown that, e.g., double-glazed, energy-efficient windows can attenuate the signal by 20 dB in the 2 GHz frequency range [12]. The signal attenuation of construction materials has been researched earlier [13] with models on the attenuation properties of different materials being outlined in multiple separate studies [14]-[19]

Coverage gaps and blocked signals are instinctively an annoyance to the users and might also be fatal as the emergency services cannot be reached. Thus it is extremely important to find a working solution for indoor coverage issues, in addition to providing sufficient capacity for the users. Indoor problems have multiple solutions ranging from *Distributed Antenna Systems* (DAS) and repeaters to picocells. But such solutions are inevitably expensive and require time-consuming design and maintenance. [20].

Femtocells are a concept that grants the quality, capacity and coverage improvements of cell densification without the need for adding expensive macrocell sites. The deployment of the devices in the home of the users leads to a smaller distance between the transmitter and the receiver. A closer proximity allows for a smaller transmit power while providing the equipment with a better *Signal-to-Interference-plus-Noise Ratio* (SINR). Providing indoor users with service originating from indoors has also the benefit of releasing the macrocell resources to others. In the femtocell concept, the end user provides needed backhaul and electricity, leaving the operator in charge of femtocell device IP connectivity to the core network and potential updates to the technology. By just comparing expenses, the femtocells are a promising alternative: the operating expenses range from $60,000 per year for macrocells to $200 per year for femtocell deployments [21]. [22]

The deployment of femtocells is not strictly controlled by the operators which might lead to large savings, but at the same time will provide additional challenges in spectrum allocation and RF performance [22]. Earlier research has identified RF interference as a key limiting factor in femtocell deployments [23]-[28]. The interference problems can be divided in to three categories when femtocells are deployed in the vicinity of existing macrocells: macrocell-to-femtocell, femtocell-to-macrocell and femtocell-to-femtocell interference [22].

In a recent study of femtocell-to-macrocell interference the conclusion was that as long as the macrocell's signal level is better than that of the femtocell, the macro performance will not be deteriorated due to the deployment of a femtocell [29]. The same study concludes that when the femtocell is indoors and not close to the macrocell centre it is unlikely to degrade the performance of the outlying macrocell [29]. Others note that a large-scale femtocell deployment can severely impact the use of the macrocell, especially when the two deployments operate on the same channel the coverage holes can reach a 31 m in size [30]. With an adjacent channel operation the effect is less severe and the coverage holes reach approximately 5.5 m in size [30].

The purpose of this paper is to provide large-scale empirical results regarding an arbitrary, residential femtocell deployment. The empirical measurements are concerned with femtocell-to-femtocell interference and done strive to answer the questions regarding basic functionality and RF performance in interference limited situations caused by end users placing the femtocell devices arbitrarily in a residential building. Extensive measurements with varying femtocell densities and transmission powers are reported and analyzed. Based on the obtained results, the density and DL transmission powers have a great impact on the performance. Transmission power control is important in femtocell deployments, as the interference from other co-channel femtocells largely defines the performance of one cell.

The rest of this paper is organized as follows: Section 2 provides details of the conducted measurements. The results of the measurement campaign are presented in Section 3 while the final conclusions are available in Section 4.

2   Measurement Campaign

2.1   Measurement Location

The building selected for the measurement campaign was an old structure built in 1966. Thus, the building did not represent a modern energy efficient apartment building and approximations and estimations had to be made to generalize the measurement results. The location was very close to a macrocell base station, which in turn provided more than sufficient coverage to the measurement building causing additional challenges in trying to fit the measurement results to a common femtocell use case. In addition to the actual RF measurements on the femtocells, some reference measurements were carried out to help achieve this. Multiple measurement scenarios were devised for the campaign. Results were gathered when the interfering *Femto Access Points* (FAP) were placed in the adjacent corridor, another building and another floor. This paper concentrates on and only presents the results from the worst case scenario with all FAPs in the same corridor.

The building and it's approximate scale is visible in the blueprint shown in Figure 1. The distance between the two wings of the building was approximately 80m. The rooms of the building were small and simple. Depending on the corridor, there were some 16 rooms per corridor. If all were to be populated with femtocells, the density would have been far greater than in a common femtocell deployment. The first step in the measurement process was to deploy the femtocells to the rooms of the building. For each of the measurement scenario, rooms were selected arbitrarily based on access and *Asynchronous Digital Subscriber Line* (ADSL) connectivity limitations. The femtocell devices were placed approximately at table level at the window of each room. After the placement of the equipment a rough plan of a measurement route was devised for each scenario.

2.2   Measurement Scenarios and Parameters

In most cases the functionality of the network was tested with a *Universal Mobile Telecommunications System* (UMTS) R99 voice call. A call was initiated using a Nokia C5-03 with the Nemo Handy software. The *User Equipment* (UE) was

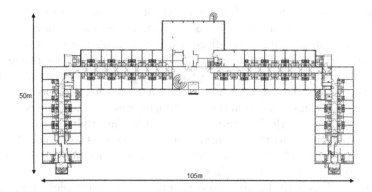

Fig. 1. The blueprint of the measurement location's ground floor

in connected mode during the measurements. Idle mode was in use periodically after handovers. The measurements were done without locking the UE to one channel or scrambling code. This ensured real world behaviour with handovers and cell selections. A normal cell selection was not always possible, as the signal level of the outdoor cell was sufficiently high. This limitation was counteracted manually: after a handover to the macrocell, the ongoing voice call was aborted and a scrambling code lock initiated to ensure a connection through the to-be-measured femtocell.

Multi Radio Access Bearer (MultiRAB) tests were done similarly. In addition to the voice call a *High Speed Downlink Packet Access* (HSDPA) data transfer over *HyperText Transfer Protocol* (HTTP) and a delay test using *Internet Control Message Protocol* (ICMP) *ping* were initiated. For this purpose a script for the Nemo Handy was created.

Several parameters were recorded with the measurement software and these parameters plotted in graphs for analysis of the effects of added interference resulting from different amounts of cells with certain network parameters. Depending on measurement type, the selected parameters differed. The recorded parameters were E_c/N_o, *Received Signal Code Power* (RSCP), *Tx power*, *Pilot Bit Bit Error Ratio* (BER) and *Number of UL/DL power up/down commands*, *High Speed Shared Control Channel* (HS-SCCH) *usage*, *Application throughput* and *Channel Quality Indicator* (CQI). The last three were needed for the MultiRAB tests.

E_c/N_o was probably one of the most important and thoroughly analyzed parameter. It is the received energy per chip divided by the wideband power density, or the ratio of RSCP and *Received Signal Strength Indicator* (RSSI) as shown in Equation (1). It is a good indicator of interference.

$$E_c/N_o = \frac{RSCP}{RSSI} \qquad (1)$$

The measurements were at first concentrated on testing different deployment scenarios with different amounts of femtocells to ascertain the effect of added interference on one particular cell and its sole voice call user. The scenarios were designed to correspond with real world deployment setups. Primarily the tests concentrated on investigating the effect of different transmission powers on the devices. 10 dBm was the default maximum transmission power for the femtocell devices, tests with 0 dBm and with a variable power between -14 and 0 dBm were conducted as well. Naturally, one factor that was changed was the amount of cells. In the measurement scenario with all femtocells in the same corridor the amounts were 1, 5 and 10. The values presented in the results of this paper are solely from the same corridor scenario, but measurements were also done with the interfering femtocells in the second floor, adjacent corridor and across the yard in the other wing of the building.

To ensure a high correlation with a normal residential deployment, the devices were configured to use closed access mode. Closed access is the probable state when the consumer equipment is concerned. Access will be provided to family members and neighbours' access will be denied. Handovers will not work between femtocell access points in closed mode, even if access restrictions are lifted. However, handovers to the macrocell are possible, and were possible during the measurement campaign as well. Since the femtocells are not in the neighbour lists of the surrounding macrocells, handovers did not work from the macro- to the femtocells.

The parameters of the live macrocell network were not disclosed, but affect the femtocells as well in the form of cell selection and potential interference. In this case, the macrocell used a different frequency than the femtocells. Also, the carriers were not close to the ones used in the femtocells. Thus *Inter Carrier Interference* (ICI) from the outlying macrocell was minimal.

To determine the attenuation of the walls between the apartments, measurements with a Rohde & Schwarz FSL spectrum analyzer and two A-INFOMW JXTXLB-880-NF antennas were conducted. The measurements consisted of a non-attenuated signal level measurement in the corridor and another measurement with a wall between the antennas. Both measurements used the same antenna height and separation distance. By also measuring the size of the apartments and the corridor, an approximation of how the apartments correspond to regular apartments in regular buildings was formulated. Femtocell deployment is most likely to occur in modern buildings with high outdoor-to-indoor attenuation for the macro cells' signal level. Prior to the measurement campaign the attenuation of the building structure was also measured.

3   Measurement Results

Handovers to the *Global System for Mobile Communications* (GSM) and UMTS macrocell networks worked well during the whole measurement campaign. A small number of dropped calls was encountered, but the total amount was insignificant when compared to the number of test runs. Due to the limitations of the equipment, the actual rate of dropped calls could not be determined. The handover process can be configured to rely on measured E_c/N_o, RSCP or UE Tx power according to the 3GPP specifications. In the measurements only E_c/N_o based handovers were used.

As reference measurements a series of RF measurements similar to the ones performed using the femtocells were first done to determine the levels of the surrounding macrocell network and outdoor-to-indoor attenuation. The averages from these measurements were -72 dBm for both 2100 MHz UMTS and 900 MHz GSM, with the attenuation being approximately 10 – 12 dB. The vicinity of the macrocell provided clear boundaries for the femtocell cells, as inter-frequency handovers to the macro showed when the interference from the nearby femtocells grew too high.

The intervening gypsum walls of two rooms were approximately 150 mm and measured for attenuation with a spectrum analyzer and two antennas, resulting in a 2 to 4 dB attenuation in the frequency band used by the femtocells. This is in line with the measurements done by NIST, where a drywall was determined to attenuate 0.03 dB/mm at 2 GHz [13] which amounts to 4.5 dB with the 150 mm wall. Based on the attenuation of the walls and the size of the rooms, approximately four of the measurement building's rooms represent one regular larger apartment.

The RSCP stayed reasonably high for all of the measurement scenarios. This is due to the measurements being done on a relatively small geographical area and the maximum distance of the UE from the femtocell device being under 100m at all times in all scenarios. Due to interference and the following handovers the effective maximum distance was much lower than this. The handover point was reached in some tens of meters or less. The distribution of the measured RSCP values from the same corridor scenario are shown in Figure 2. A high percentage of extremely good values can be seen, this is due to the close proximity to the measured femtocell device. With one femtocell, and thus no interference caused by other cells, the RSCP values reach lower. This clearly indicates the effect of added interference on the size of the cell.

The effect of interference in terms of the E_c/N_0 value is visible in Figure 3. The unloaded neighbouring cells had a visible effect on the measured radio parameters as seen in the average E_c/N_0 values. There is an approximately 2 dB change when changing the amount of femtocells from 1 to 5 and further to 10.

All femtocell amounts have high E_c/N_0 values, over -4 dB, and even with 10 femtocells the median is close to -5 dB. This is partly due to the measurement route which began and ended very close to the femtocell. However, it should be noted, that 10% of samples with 10 femtocells are under -17 dB while for 5 and 1 femtocells the values are -12 dB and -5 dB, respectively. The distribution for E_c/N_0 and other measured parameters with 10 dBm DL transmit power are available in Table 1. For voice calls the E_c/N_0 can be quite low before breakage is noticed, according to the 3GPP specifications an acceptable quality is reached with a 1% *Block Error Ratio* (BLER) [31]. In a reasonably static channel, such as the one in the measurements, this BLER can be achieved with a -16.6 dB E_c/I_{or} [31]. Anything over this value is acceptable in a UMTS network. Thus,

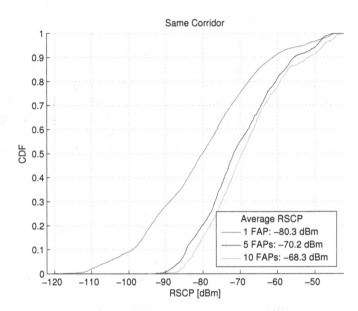

Fig. 2. RSCP distribution for voice call for 10 dBm transmit power and 2 scrambling codes in the same corridor

the situation in the measurements was not dire, but the values are lower 10% of time with 10 femtocells in the same corridor.

The effect of added interference is directly visible in the BER of the pilot signal as well, as can be seen in Figure 4. The averages give a good idea of the effect, being under 1% for 1 femtocell and rising to 1.7% for 5 and 3.8% for 10 femtocells. For the maximum amount of used femtocells, the distribution shows 10% of the BER values being over 6%.

Partly due to the mentioned close proximity in the beginning and end of the measurement routines, it seems that a too high transmit power is used for DL in most cases. The number of power down commands decreases as more interference is introduced, but does not reach the optimal situation of a 50% / 50% split. In UL the power dynamics are much wider, reaching from +24 dBm to -50 dBm, and the ratio between the power adjustment commands seemed to be in balance with a slight deviation seen in the case of 10 femtocells.

The effect of *Co-Channel Interference* (CCI) caused by other femtocells was clearly visible for R99 voice call. For the MultiRAB measurements the CCI effect was similarly clear, if not even more noticeable. The average throughput is almost halved when comparing the case of 1 femtocell with the maximal interference of 9 neighbouring femtocells as shown in Table 3. The average values remain rather low for all femtocell amounts, considering the UE should support 10.2 Mbps rates. Maximum experienced throughput was, with 1 femtocell, close to 6 Mbps, which is better but still far from the theoretical limit UE category 9 specifications. With 10 femtocells 40% of time the throughput was lower than 1 Mbps. The freezing affected the delays noticeably, as the maximum measured

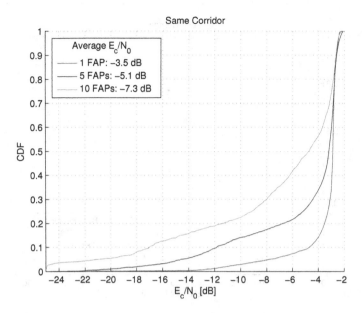

Fig. 3. E_c/N_0 distribution for voice call for 10 dBm transmit power and 2 scrambling codes in the same corridor

delays reached as high as 12000 ms. Median round-trip times are in the vicinity of an acceptable 130 ms, but averages rose to 200 ms for 5 femtocells and 387 ms for the maximum amount of 10 femtocells. For 10 femtocells the delay was over 700 ms 10% of the time.

Low transmission rates are partly caused by the inefficient usage of available resources. HS-SCCH usage was on average only 59% with 1 femtocell and decreased further to 57.7% with 5 femtocells and 44.6% with 10 femtocells. Even with only 1 femtocell under 80% of the capacity was utilized for 90% of time. CQI on the other hand was good during the tests. The best CQI value, 30, was reported with over 45% probability for 1 and 5 femtocells and over 40% for 10 femtocells. With all femtocell amounts CQI values under 25 had probability of under 3%.

One way of countering the effect of interference is to lower DL transmission powers. The measurement campaign clearly showed that at least in this deployment the maximum power of 10 dBm was way too high as can be seen in the improvement of performance as presented in Table 2. To determine an optimal femtocell transmission power for most situations, the tests were run with three different power parameters. The configured power is the maximum power, and could be lower and varying in time. In the measurements, the transmission powers of the other femtocells were lower than the specified maximum due to the low number of transmitted channels without load.

For 10 femtocells, the average values for RSCP with the different transmission powers were: -68.3 dBm for 10 dBm, -76.3 for 0 dBm and -75.5 dBm. For pilot

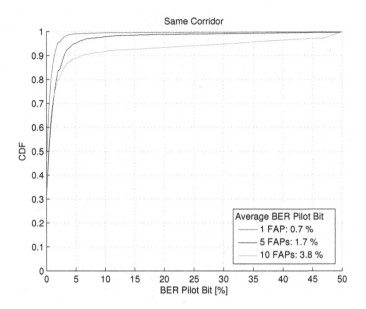

Fig. 4. Pilot BER distribution for voice call for 10 dBm transmit power and 2 scrambling codes in the same corridor

BER 3.8%, 1.4% and 1.6%, while E_c/N_0 averaged at -7.3 dB, -5.8 dB and -5.3 dB, respectively. The difference between the full power of 10 dBm and 0 dBm is clear, but the varying power between -14 and 0 dBm does not seem to be working as well as it should. The difference between 0 dBm and variable power

Table 1. Results of the same corridor scenario for voice call with 10 dBm

Parameter	CDF	1 femtocell	5 femtocells	10 femtocells
RSCP [dBm]	10%	-99.1	-84.5	-81.9
	50%	-80.1	-71.8	-69.6
	90%	-61.1	-55.5	-51.7
E_c/N_0 [dB]	10%	-4.7	-11.9	-17.1
	50%	-2.9	-3.2	-4.8
	90%	-2.6	-2.6	-2.7
Pilot BER [%]	10%	n/a	n/a	n/a
	50%	0.1	0.45	0.4
	90%	1.4	3.1	6.3
Tx Power [dBm]	10%	-48.0	n/a	n/a
	50%	-32.0	-39.0	-41.5
	90%	-13.5	-26.0	-28.0

Table 2. Results of the same corridor scenario for voice call with 10 cells and different DL powers

Parameter	CDF	10 dBm	0 dBm	-14 – 0 dBm
	10%	-81.9	-89.0	-86.9
RSCP [dBm]	50%	-69.55	-76.5	-75.8
	90%	-51.7	-63.8	-63.2
	10%	-17.1	-11.5	-10.6
E_c/N_0 [dB]	50%	-4.8	-4.0	-3.6
	90%	-2.7	-2.8	-2.7
	10%	n/a	n/a	n/a
Pilot BER [%]	50%	0.4	0.3	0.2
	90%	6.3	2.6	2.7
	10%	n/a	n/a	n/a
Tx Power [dBm]	50%	-41.5	-45.5	-44.2
	90%	-28.0	-32	-32.5

is minor, so it could be argued that even with variable power the femtocells select the used power when starting and then use it statically. The behaviour of the variable power algorithm was not disclosed and is dependent on the implementation. It is clear however, that modifying the parameters and especially lowering the maximum output power of the femtocells has a positive effect on the performance.

The gathered results for the different parameters are presented in Table 1, Table 2 and Table 3. The values are given as cumulative distribution percentages for different femtocell amounts.

Table 3. Results of the same corridor scenario for MultiRAB with 10 dBm

Parameter	CDF	1 femtocell	5 femtocells	10 femtocells
	10%	1.6	0.8	0.1
Throughput [Mbps]	50%	3.1	2.6	1.6
	90%	4.6	4.2	3.8
	10%	n/a	n/a	n/a
Round Trip Time [ms]	50%	127	129	130
	90%	152	292	760
	10%	34.5	6.0	0.8
HS-SCCH Usage [%]	50%	61.0	61.0	49.0
	90%	80.0	93.0	84.0

4   Conclusion and Discussion

This paper provided practical large-scale measurement results to determine potential caveats in an uncontrolled residential femtocell deployment. In addition the goal was to find out the differences in performance between distinct femtocell parameters, especially femtocell density and DL transmit power. Based on the approximation of four of the measurement building's rooms representing one regular larger apartment and the overall measurement results, it is clear that one femtocell per apartment is feasible. During all of the measurement scenarios it became clear that the cell size of the measured femtocell is defined by the amount of interference. The minimum of RSCP and the maximum of Tx power were never reached. The handovers were done based on the E_c/N_0 which became worse due to the added interference and handovers done long before the cell edge was reached. E_c/N_0 might not be the optimal parameter for handovers, as the RSCP values were sufficient in most cases.

In the same corridor scenario the cell size was largely unaffected after a certain amount of interfering femtocells were added. As an example, the difference between the average RSCP and Tx power values between 5 and 10 femtocells in the same corridor scenario was only slight. This means only that the interfering femtocells close to the measured femtocell are the defining factor in interference, and the femtocells further away have only a limited effect.

Measurements were performed with different maximum DL transmission powers. The default value of 10 dBm proved to be too high at least for the measurement location, this was especially noted when observing the E_c/N_0 values. The E_c/N_0 was lower than 3GPP performance requirements for voice calls 10% of time. In a building with higher wall attenuation the outcome might differ. In the measurements however, lowering the power to 0 dBm showed clear improvement in the overall interference level, while the cell size actually grew. This could be counter-intuitive, but the results showed that with lower DL power the UE was able to go further from the femtocell. Using such automatic power determination might be the best option, but it is unclear whether the femtocell changes the power during operation, or defines it statically from within the given limits. The results seem to point to the latter, which would render such variable power scheme less useful. So, as with all UMTS based systems that are interference limited, the power control is important in femtocell deployments as well.

Although the femtocell concept has its limitations, it certainly shows promising attributes and is a suitable technology for extending coverage and capacity. Femtocell deployment is designed to be very flexible, giving the end-user the freedom and responsibility of installation. This flexibility is the source of cost-effectiveness and performance, but can also be problematic. During the measurement campaign problems and non-optimal performance was encountered, but most of these can be solved by better design and implementation. Overall, the femtocells are very usable now and most certainly in the future, but still require work to reach their maximum potential.

References

1. Teixeira, T.: Meet marty cooper - the inventor of the mobile phone. BBC News (April 2010) (accessed: March 24, 2013)
2. International Telecommunication Union: The world in 2013: Ict facts and figures (February 2013) (accessed: March 23, 2013)
3. Cellular News: A billion 3g/umts mobile connections, confirms umts forum (January 2012) (accessed: November 28, 2012)
4. Sauter, M.: From GSM to LTE: An Introduction to Mobile Networks and Mobile Broadband. John Wiley & Sons Ltd. (2011)
5. Cisco: Cisco visual networking index: Global mobile data cisco visual networking index: Global mobile data traffic forecast update, 2012–2017 (February 2013)
6. Informa Telecoms & Media: Mobile broadband access at home (August 2008)
7. Analysys Mason: Wireless network traffic 2008–2015: forecasts and analysis (2009)
8. Directive 2010/31/eu of the European parliament and of the council. Official Journal of the European Union (May 2010)
9. Aamulehti: Uusien talojen ongelma: Kännykkä ei toimi sisällä - työryhmä käy pulman kimppuun (September 2012) (accessed: March 24, 2013) (in Finnish)
10. Yle: Energiapihit ikkunat katkaisivat kännykkäyhteydet (January 2012) (in Finnish) (accessed: March 24, 2013)
11. Asp, A., Sydorov, Y., Valkama, M., Niemelä, J.: Radio signal propagation and attenuation measurements for modern residential buildings. In: GC 2012 Workshop: The 4th IEEE International Workshop on Heterogeneous and Small Cell Networks. IEEE (2012)
12. Knauer, N., Doelecke, H., O'Leary, P.: Outdoor-indoor wireless sensor communications in a modern building management system. In: 4th Workshop on Wireless Sensor Networks (2008)
13. National Institute of Standards and Technology: Electromagnetic signal attenuation in construction materials. Technical Report NISTIR 6055, United States Department of Commerce Technology Administration National Institute of Standards and Technology (1997)
14. Stavrou, S., Saunders, S.R.: Factors influencing outdoor to indoor radio wave propagation. In: 12th ICAP International Conference on Antennas and Propagation (2003)
15. Stavrou, S., Saunders, S.R.: Review of constitutive parameters of building materials. In: 12th ICAP International Conference on Antennas and Propagation (2003)
16. Aguirre, S., Loew, L.H., Leo, Y.: Radio propagation into buildings at 912, 1920, and 5990 mhz using microcells. In: 3rd Annual Universal Personal Communications Conference (1994)
17. Turkmani, A.M.D., de Toledo, A.F.: Modelling of radio transmissions into and within multistorey buildings at 900,1800 and 2300 mhz. In: Speech and Vision Proceedings, IEEE Communications (1993)
18. Hoppe, R., Wölfle, G., Landstorfer, F.M.: Measurement of building penetration loss and propagation models for radio transmission into buildings. In: 50th Vehicular Technology Conference. IEEE (1999)
19. Turkmani, A.M.D., Parson, J.D., Lewis, D.G.: Measurement of building penetration loss on radio signals at 441,900 and 1400mhz. Journal of the Institution of Electronic and Radio Engineer (1988)
20. Zhang, J., de la Roche, G.: Femtocells: Technologies and Deployment. John Wiley & Sons Ltd. (2010)

21. Analysys Mason: Picocells and femtocells: Will indoor base-stations transform the telecoms industry?
22. Chandrasekar, V., Andrews, J.G., Gatherer, A.: Femtocell networks: a survey. IEEE Communications Magazine 46, 59–67 (2008)
23. Chowdhury, M., Ryu, W., Rhee, E., Jang, Y.M.: Handover between macrocell and femtocell for umts based networks. In: Advanced Communication Technology, vol. 1. IEEE (2009)
24. Maqbool, M., Lalam, M., Lestable, T.: Comparison of femto cell deployment models for an interference avoidance technique. In: Future Network Mobile Summit. IEEE (2011)
25. Wang, H., Zhao, M., Reed, M.: Outage analysis for wcdma femtocell with uplink attenuation. In: GLlobecom Workshops. IEEE (2010)
26. Chu, F.S., Chen, K.C.: Mitigation of macro-femto co-channel interference by spatial channel separation. In: Vehicular Technology Conference. IEEE (2011)
27. Alexiou, A., Bouras, C., Kokkinos, V., Kontodimas, K., Papazois, A.: Interference behavior of integrated femto and macrocell environments. In: Wireless Days. IEEE (2011)
28. Mukherjee, S.: Analysis of ue outage probability and macrocellular traffic offloading for wcdma macro network with femto overlay under closed and open access. In: IEEE International Conference on Communications. IEEE (2011)
29. Jorgensen, N., Isotalo, T., Pedersen, K., Mogensen, P.: Joint macro and femto field performance and interference measurements. In: Vehicular Technology Conference. IEEE (2012)
30. Espino, J., Markendahl, J.: Analysis of macro - femtocell interference and implications for spectrum allocation. IEEE (2009)
31. Holma, H., Toskala, A.: WCDMA for UMTS: HSPA Evolution and LTE, 4th edn. John Wiley & Sons Ltd. (2007)

Empirical Study on Local Similarity of Spectrum Occupancy in the 2.4 GHz ISM Band

Till Wollenberg and Andreas Dähn

University of Rostock, Rostock, Germany
{till.wollenberg,andreas.daehn}@uni-rostock.de

Abstract. The 2.4 GHz frequency band is used by various devices, including WiFi, microwave ovens and Bluetooth. For WiFi devices, it is desirable to have information about occupancy of the spectrum available to select optimal channels and to predict link performance. As only few devices are capable of acquiring such information, devices may share it. However, using these information only makes sense if the measurements are made by a device that is nearby. In this paper, we suggest using information about present WiFi devices to assess proximity. We present the design and results of an extensive indoor study carried out to assess locality of spectrum occupancy and usefulness of the described nearness measure.

Keywords: 802.11, Wireless LAN, Spectrum occupancy, Measurement, Similarity measures.

1 Introduction and Background

In this paper, we focus on spectrum occupancy in the 2.40–2.48 GHz frequency band. While this band was initially reserved for industrial, scientific, and medical applications (ISM), it is today also widely used for various communication electronics. Operating a device in this band usually does not require a license. However, devices have to accept any interference caused by other users. In most countries, the maximum *effective radiated power* (ERP) is limited which in turn limits typical communication ranges.

Due to the high number of active communication devices, the 2.4 GHz ISM band is often found to be crowded especially in densely populated areas. Popular spectrum users are IEEE 802.11 Wireless LAN (WiFi), Bluetooth, IEEE 802.15.4 (Zigbee), cordless phones, baby-phones, video transmitters, remotes, and microwave ovens [6].

Our focus is on WiFi and we therefore categorize spectrum users as either *WiFi* or *non-WiFi* throughout this paper. The 802.11 standard employs a *Carrier Sense Multiple Access* channel access method with *Collision Avoidance* (CSMA/CA). WiFi devices determine channel availability logically from received transmissions (network allocation vector, NAV) and physically by *Channel Clear Assessment* (CCA). This way, different WiFi stations share the medium fairly and reduce the probability of collisions.

M. Jonsson et al. (Eds.): MACOM 2013, LNCS 8310, pp. 113–127, 2013.

Non-WiFi devices normally cannot decode WiFi transmissions and many non-WiFi devices start transmitting regardless of channel availability. With increasing activity of non-WiFi devices not only the channel time available to WiFi devices is reduced but also the probability of collisions is significantly increased [5]. Both effects will lead to decreased performance on upper network layers. WiFi transmissions from other (third party) stations being undecodable due to low signal level and transmissions on adjacent channels may cause similar effects [10].

To capture both spectrum use caused by WiFi and by non-WiFi devices, observing WiFi transmission is not sufficient, but we need to perform measurements on the *radio frequency* (RF) level instead. By using a spectrum analyzer, we are able to measure the power level within narrow portions (frequency bins) of the entire 2.4 GHz ISM band. Subsequently, we apply a threshold to the measured power level and consider the corresponding frequency bin as "busy" if the threshold is exceeded and "idle" otherwise. We repeat this process over the entire band and within an arbitrary time window and eventually compute the average duty cycle for each frequency bin. In this paper, we refer to this array of duty cycles as *spectrum occupancy*.

Knowledge of the current spectrum occupancy can be employed by WiFi devices in various ways:

- Selecting an optimal channel for establishing an off-channel peer to peer link[1]

- Automatically selecting a channel for an access point (during set-up phase and optional periodically during run-time)

- Estimating performance of a WiFi link from both signal constellation [2] and channel occupancy [1] for cross-layer optimization (e. g. adjust VOIP jitter buffer size, set quantization level for video compression)

- Assessing general feasibility of network transactions (e. g. postpone an automatic software update) based on current channel conditions

Unfortunately, only very few of the currently available WiFi hardware supports spectrum measurements. While such measurement capabilities can be added at reasonable cost [7], it is unlikely to find this feature in a majority of devices any time soon because of cost, energy, and space constraints.

Due to the limited transmission power in the 2.4 GHz band, spectrum occupancy is normally a local phenomenon, especially in indoor scenarios, i. e. devices being in the same room will usually detect a similar spectrum occupancy. This effect can be exploited to share spectrum occupancy information between devices that are capable of spectrum measurement and devices which are not. However, the crucial point is that a device lacking measurement capabilities needs to assess if it is *arbitrarily close* to a particular device which offers to share spectrum occupancy information.

---

[1] i. e. Tunneled Direct Link Setup (TDLS), see [4].

2   Problem

We can generalize the problem of sharing spectrum occupancy information as follows. We have two WiFi devices. One of them is able to measure spectrum occupancy and is willing to share this information with other devices. The other device lacks spectrum measurement capabilities and wants to re-use spectrum occupancy information offered by the first device. Therefore, it needs to assess whether the other device's information is applicable to it, i. e. it needs to quantify the probability of having similar spectrum occupancy conditions.

An obvious approach to this problem would be to use existing localization technologies and to assume applicability of the other device's spectrum occupancy information if the distance between both devices is sufficiently low. However, this approach is likely to fail because:

- Positioning services such as *Global Positioning System* (GPS) or *WiFi Positioning Systems* (WPS) are not always available, especially indoors.

- The position information retrieved through GPS or WPS is usually not accurate enough for using it in the aforementioned way (again, especially indoors).

- It is unlikely that low (Euclidean) distance generally implies similar spectrum occupancy situations.

For understanding the last point, we can imagine two WiFi devices being 2 m apart from each other. When both devices are in the same room and no obstacles are in between, the signal attenuation (free space loss) is almost negligible. Thus, the probability of having a similar spectrum occupancy situation is high. However, if both devices are 2 m apart with a 30 cm wall from reinforced concrete in between, signal propagation in the 2.4 GHz range will be attenuated markedly. As a result, both devices may have largely unrelated spectrum occupancy measurements.

To overcome this problem, we propose a different measure to assess locality based on receiving transmissions from other (third party) WiFi devices. The approach is grounded on the rationale that two devices with similar receiving conditions will both have similar spectrum occupancy measurements and a similar set of other WiFi devices from which they are able to receive and decode transmissions.

In this way, the first WiFi device offers spectrum occupancy information along with the set of observed devices (*observation set*) to the second device. If the second device detects a high similarity between the received set and its own set of observed devices, then it may incorporate the received spectrum occupancy information. To increase the accuracy, the observation set may be attributed with information about signal level, device role (access point, client), or the time passed since last received frame.

An different, naïve approach to this problem would be the idea of both devices trying to establish a direct connection between each other in order to assess whether they are close to each other or not. Unfortunately, this method would be limited by several factors. First, the two devices might have a different channel hopping sequence or might be bound to different channels. Also, direct communication might be prevented if both devices belong to different administrative domains, i. e. two WiFi devices being associated to different WiFi networks. Finally, if no direct communication is necessary, then spectrum occupancy information could be relayed between devices in a store-and-forward approach. This way, the two devices do not need to be present at the very same time.

In order to assess the feasibility of the approach we designed an experiment which is described in the following sections.

3   Methods

We conducted an experiment in order to evaluate the relationship between similarity of spectrum occupancy and similarity of observed WiFi nodes. In the following section, we will outline the experimental setup, describe methods used for data acquisition and processing, and summarize the resulting data set. The section is concluded by a description of the similarity measures we used in order to compare spectrum information and device sets.

3.1   Experimental Setup

We carried out the experiment in an indoor office scenario. The experiment took place on the topmost floor of a modern, four-floor office building. The building has both drywalls and walls of reinforced concrete, solid wooden doors, and insulated glazing windows.

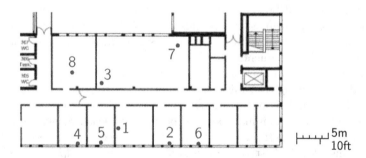

Fig. 1. Section of a floor plan showing the positions of all eight measurement devices

For measuring both spectrum occupancy and observation set, we used purpose-built *measurement devices* based on consumer WiFi hardware. A total of eight identical measurement devices was installed across seven rooms on both sides of a corridor as shown in Fig. 1. One room contains a public computer pool (#3, #7), one is a lab room (#8), and the remaining five rooms are offices.

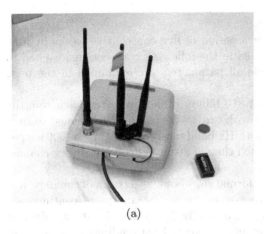

(a)   (b)

Fig. 2. Photo of one of the measurement devices (a) with 9-volt battery and 2 Euro coin for size comparison and photo of an AirView spectrum analyzer device (b) prior to its installation in the measurement device

We built the measurement devices from Ubiquiti RouterStation Pro boards and used 802.11abgn-capable, 2×2-MIMO WiFi network cards using Qualcomm Atheros AR 9220 chipsets. Each device had two 2-dBi omni-directional antennas. For measuring spectrum occupancy, we used an Ubiquiti AirView USB spectrum analyzer connected to an external omni-directional antenna. The spectrum analyzer is a swept-tuned type built using a proprietary 2.4 GHz RF transceiver[2]. The device's accuracy has been evaluated earlier in [8]. Figure 2 shows the hardware used in the experiment.

On the measurement devices, we ran a stock version of OpenWRT[3] 12.09 with Linux kernel 3.3.8. The system clocks of all devices were synchronized using NTP. The WiFi network cards were configured to operate in monitor mode, i.e. they passed all received frames along with their 802.11 header and Radiotap header[4] to the userspace. The headers (but not data parts) of the received frames were recorded using `tcpdump`. The WiFi network cards were not used for transmitting any frames. All collected data was transmitted over a wired network connection.

In the office building, a campus wireless network is operated in both 2.4 GHz and 5 GHz bands. The access points of the campus network offer access to four different networks by using multiple SSID and four different MAC addresses, respectively. The network is used by students, staff members, and visitors with laptops, smartphones, tablets, and desktop computers. Non-WiFi devices used in the building include cordless mice and keyboards, wireless presenters, Bluetooth-enabled phones and headsets, proprietary indoor positioning systems, and microwave ovens.

---

[2] Texas Instruments CC2532F, based on CC2500 with added USB device capability.
[3] More information available at `https://openwrt.org/`
[4] More information including a description of all defined headers can be found at `http://www.radiotap.org/`

3.2 Data Set

We carried out the experiment over a period of five consecutive weeks in June and July 2013. For the steps described in the following two sections, we had to decide on several parameters. While all parameters are explained in the text, Tab. 1 summarizes them.

During the experiment, a total of 810 billion frames were received from the measurement devices. The WiFi network cards were continuously tuned to each of the 13 available channels in the 2.4 GHz band with a dwell time of 500 ms per channel and an average channel switch time of 20 ms. Effectively, every channel was observed for 500 ms every 6.76 s.

In parallel to the WiFi data, information about spectrum occupancy was recorded using the AirView spectrum analyzers. The analyzers continuously sweep through the frequency range 2,399 MHz–2,485 MHz in steps (bins) of 500 kHz. After each sweep, an array of 173 power level readings in dBm is reported, one level per frequency bin. The devices send ≈ 3.67 reports/s. During the experiment, a total of 88.9 million reports was received from all eight measurement devices.

Since the AirView spectrum analyzers do not provide any facility to synchronize the sweeps, both the spectrum measurements and the channel switching of the WiFi network cards were not synchronized. Also, there was no synchronization across the different measurement devices. However, the precise time for each channel switch and the completion of each spectrum report was recorded.

3.3 Data Processing

Separately for each measuring device, each frame was processed and information about active devices ("sightings") were extracted. Here, we distinguish *direct sightings* and *indirect sightings*. A direct sighting results from a frame that physically originates from a particular WiFi device, while an indirect sighting results from processing a frame which contains a device's address but does not originate from that device. For computing the set of observed devices, we solely used direct sightings. In the extraction process, any data frame, a relevant subset of control frames (Block-ACK, RTS, PS-poll types), and a relevant subset of management frames (Beacon, Action, and all types related to probing, authentication and association) were processed. All other frame types were discarded.

To create the sets of *observed devices*, we defined two threshold values. First, a device will be added to the set of observed devices only if at least two frames with this device's address had been received. This measure avoids the addition of "phantom addresses"[5]. The second threshold value is the amount of time until a device is removed from the observation set after the last received frame. This is necessary since devices can disappear without any explicit notification (i. e. leave reception range). The selection of an appropriate threshold depends

---

[5] Although the WiFi network card was configured to discard frames with incorrect frame checksum (FCS), infrequently frames with incorrect address fields were recorded.

Table 1. Summary of all parameters and design considerations regarding data acquisition, data processing, and similarity computation

WiFi scanning parameters	
Channel scan scheme	round-robin
Channel dwell time	500 ms
Channel switch delay	≈ 20 ms
Channels scanned	1–13

Spectrum analyzer parameters	
Frequency range covered	2,399 MHz–2,485 MHz
Frequency resolution	500 kHz
Time resolution	$\mu = 3.674$ sweeps/s ($\sigma = 0.023$)

WiFi processing parameters	
Processed frame types	(see text)
Include hidden stations	no (direct sightings only)
Minimum received frames	2
Signal level threshold	none, -82 dBm, -62 dBm
Window size	60 s
Idle timeout	300 s

Spectrum processing parameters	
Measure	average duty-cycle
Window size	60 s
Power level threshold	-96, -82, -62 dBm

Observation set similarity parameters	
BSS weighting factor	1, 2, 5, 9

Spectrum occupancy similarity parameters	
Measure	Sum of differences, Number of differing bins
Difference threshold	0.05

on assumptions about device's activity and the likelihood of transmissions to be captured. Based on the recommendations for the "BSS Max idle period" [4, § 4.3.13.2] we chose a period of 300 s.

We also evaluated including a device only if the received frames exceed a certain signal level threshold and used two different threshold values (-82 dBm and -62 dBm).

For the spectrum measurements, we start with applying a power level threshold to each per-frequency-bin power reading in each spectrum measurement array in order to classify it as either "idle" or "busy". If the measured value in a bin exceeds the threshold, a value of is 1.0 assigned, otherwise 0.0 is assigned. We evaluated three different thresholds (-96 dBm, -82 dBm, and -62 dBm) for that, targeting signals close to noise floor, signals from devices which are most likely not in the same room, and signals from devices likely in the same room, respectively. The threshold values -82 dBm and -62 dBm were selected considering the Channel Clear Assessment levels as defined in 802.11 [4]; the value of -96 dBm is the minimal receiver sensitivity of the WiFi cards used in our experiment. These values have also been used in [3]. Finally, we computed the fraction of "busy" samples in each frequency bin within a time window of 60 s duration, eventually obtaining the mean duty cycle of each bin within the window.

Calibration experiments revealed that 8 out of the 173 frequency bins showed significantly higher power readings than all other bins throughout the entire experiment regardless of the measurement device and location. We assumed a systematic error and excluded these bins, leaving 165 bins in each array for further analysis steps.

3.4   Similarity

To evaluate the similarity of the spectrum occupancy measurements of two devices, we have to compare two arrays (165-tuples) of average duty cycle readings. Out of the numerous existing distance functions, we selected two measures. For the first measure, we simply count all array elements (e. g. frequency bins) where the element-wise absolute difference of both arrays exceeds a certain threshold. For our purposes, we used a threshold of 0.05 corresponding to a maximum allowed error of 5 % of channel duty time. A result of 0 would mean that both arrays are identical within the allowed tolerance range. A result of 165 would mean that all frequency bins differ above the allowed tolerance range. For the second measure, we compute the sum of all element-wise absolute differences between two arrays. This second measure will reflect small and large differences more accurately.

To quantify the similarity of the sets of observed WiFi devices, we employ the Jaccard index which is defined as follows:

$$J(A, B) = \frac{|A \cap B|}{|A \cup B|}. \tag{1}$$

Here, A and B are the sets of observed WiFi devices on two measurement devices. The Jaccard index will be 1 if both observation sets are identical and 0 for sets without common elements.

Based on the assumption that access points have a far lower mobility than client devices, we also evaluate emphasis of those WiFi devices which act as BSS in the set comparison. To do so, we define our observation set as multiset, e. g. a set that can contain unique elements more than one time. We then introduce a weighting factor for BSS that describes how often a BSS device is included in the multiset of observed devices. Client devices are included one time in the multiset. For computing the Jaccard index on multisets, we use the operations cardinality, union, and intersection as defined in [9].

4   Results

The following section describes the experiment's results. We start with giving an outline on the number of active WiFi devices. Following, we evaluate the relationship between Euclidean distance and both similarity of spectrum occupancy and similarity of observation sets. Finally, we target our main research question and investigate the relationship between observed devices and spectrum occupancy.

4.1   Number of Active WiFi Devices

First, we take a look at the absolute number of active WiFi devices observed during our experiment. Figure 3 shows a typical course (measurement device #4, 2nd week of experiment). We can see a distinct day/night pattern occurring from Monday to Friday with a day-peak of 58 active devices. At night, almost all detected devices are access points. The number of access points shows low variations which can be explained by varying propagation conditions and automatic reconfigurations of the campus network. Since the experiment was carried out in a university office building, only few devices are found on the weekends.

While all measurement devices show trends similar to the one described above, the absolute number of detected devices differs depending on the location. In Tab. 2, we can find a summary of the number of detected devices for all eight measurement devices. It can be seen that the numbers are consistently higher for those locations closer to the inner yard of the building (#3, #7, #8) than those near the outer edge of the building.

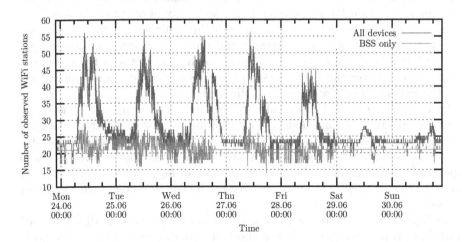

Fig. 3. Typical time series of number of observed WiFi devices. Graph shows data from measurement device #4 during 2nd week of experiment.

Table 2. Number of observed WiFi devices (BSS) on each measurement device during the experiment (columns list minimum, mean, maximum, and quartiles)

	#1	#2	#3	#4
Min	0.00 (0.00)	22.00 (13.00)	18.0 (11.00)	15.00 (9.00)
1st Q.	20.00 (17.00)	24.00 (21.00)	31.0 (29.00)	23.00 (21.00)
Median	25.00 (19.00)	27.00 (22.00)	34.0 (29.00)	26.00 (21.00)
Mean	26.73 (19.94)	29.73 (23.18)	37.8 (30.09)	28.87 (21.74)
3rd Q.	30.00 (22.00)	33.00 (25.00)	43.0 (32.00)	31.00 (23.00)
Max	58.00 (31.00)	63.00 (38.00)	87.0 (50.00)	68.00 (33.00)

	#5	#6	#7	#8
Min	12.00 (6.00)	22.00 (17.00)	0.0 (0.00)	21.00 (14.00)
1st Q.	20.00 (17.00)	24.00 (21.00)	31.0 (29.00)	31.00 (28.00)
Median	23.00 (18.00)	27.00 (21.00)	33.0 (29.00)	34.00 (29.00)
Mean	25.11 (18.57)	29.13 (22.55)	36.3 (29.46)	38.65 (30.42)
3rd Q.	29.00 (21.00)	32.00 (25.00)	40.0 (29.00)	44.00 (31.00)
Max	52.00 (29.00)	57.00 (33.00)	78.0 (41.00)	104.00 (60.00)

4.2   Euclidean Distance

Next, we assess the relationship between Euclidean distance and similarity of spectrum occupancy in order to verify our assumption that the Euclidean distance is not a sufficient measure to predict said similarity. For completeness, we also compare the Euclidean distance to the similarity of observed devices.

Our eight measurement devices form 28 distinct pairs. For each pair, we compute both the mean *sum of differences* and the mean *number of differing frequency bins* and compare this to the Euclidean distance between both measurement devices. We compute the Pearson's correlation coefficient across all 28 pairs and throughout the entire experiment duration.

In Tab. 3 we can find the results for the spectrum occupancy. One would expect a positive correlation since with growing distance a lower similarity is expected and both our distance functions result in higher values for higher dissimilarity. We can see such correlation only for the lowest power level threshold (-96 dBm) and much more distinct for the *sum of difference* measure than for the *number of differing bins* measure. For the higher thresholds, the results are inconsistent.

We found the reason for the decreasing correlation coefficients with increased thresholds in the fact that only few spectrum samples exceed these thresholds and consequently, an increasing number of computed duty cycle readings are zero. As a result, the similarity measures indicate a growing similarity independent of the Euclidean distance. In case of the -62 dBm threshold, this effect is dominant, resulting in a negative correlation coefficient.

Table 3. Correlation between Euclidean distance and spectrum occupancy similarity

Threshold	Correlation between Euclidean distance and mean...	
	...sum of differences	...number of differing bins
-96 dBm	0.655	0.248
-82 dBm	0.153	0.075
-62 dBm	-0.349	-0.360

For comparing the Euclidean distance to the similarity of observed active WiFi devices, we compute the Jaccard index for each pair of measurement devices and compare the result again to the Euclidean distance by calculating the correlation coefficient across all 28 device pairs. We repeat this step for all combinations of *device detection threshold* and *BSS weighting factor*.

Table 4 shows the resulting correlation coefficients. Since the Jaccard index decreases with lower set similarity and we assume a lower similarity with increasing Euclidean distance, a negative correlation is to be expected. We can see negative correlations throughout all parameter combinations although a marked correlation is only visible for high detection thresholds. Also, the correlations get weaker with increasing BSS weighting factor.

Table 4. Correlation between Euclidean distance and device observation set similarity

BSS weighting factor	Threshold	Correlation between Euclidean distance and Jaccard index
1	-62 dBm	-0.5466
1	-82 dBm	-0.4274
1	none	-0.1131
2	-62 dBm	-0.4673
2	-82 dBm	-0.3863
2	none	-0.0655
5	-62 dBm	-0.3774
5	-82 dBm	-0.3523
5	none	-0.0305
9	-62 dBm	-0.3404
9	-82 dBm	-0.3401
9	none	-0.0188

4.3 Observed Devices and Spectrum Occupancy

For our main question, the relationship between set of observed devices and spectrum occupancy similarity, we again compute the Pearson's correlation coefficient across all 28 pairs of measurement devices throughout the entire experiment duration. Nevertheless, this time we compare the *Jaccard index* to both the *sum of differences* measure and the *number of differing bins* measure. Then we compute the correlation separately for each combination of *BSS weighting factor*, *device detection signal level threshold*, and *spectrum occupancy power level threshold*.

The results are summarized in Tab. 5. Since a high similarity of observed WiFi devices will result in a high Jaccard index (close to 1) while a high similarity will result in low error measures for spectrum occupancy, one would expect a negative correlation. We can see significant correlations only for the highest device detection threshold of -62 dBm while the results are inconsistent for the lower detection threshold and for the cases without threshold applied.

The results across the *BSS weighting factor* are inconsistent. When focusing on the cases with a device detection threshold of -62 dBm, we can see increasing correlation with lower spectrum occupancy signal threshold only for the cases with a BSS weighting factor of 1, while the correlation decreases with all other BSS weighting factors.

This behavior can be found for both the *sum of differences* measure and the *number of differing frequency bins* measure, while we can state that the first measure performs generally better than the latter measure.

5 Discussion

In this section, we discuss the experimental setup and possible artifacts from the data acquisition followed by a brief discussion of our obtained results with emphasis on similarity measures.

5.1 Data Acquisition

The data acquisition, both RF spectrum and WiFi, deals with some challenges due to the utilized hardware. WiFi monitoring suffers from channel hopping, which makes it likely to miss transmissions and therefore makes device detection inherently inaccurate. As stated in section 3.2, every channel is observed for a duration of 500 ms every 6.76 s. A device will only be "seen" if it is active within this time window. Given current WiFi devices, use cases and energy saving strategies, there may be several cases, in which a device is present but unlikely to be noticed, especially if it is only present for a short time. Such a hard-to-detect device could be a smartphone in standby which is carried around by a person walking down the corridor and passing the measurement setup in less than 30 seconds (which is a typical value for this specific corridor). Besides channel hopping, devices may be overlooked because their frames cannot be decoded due to low signal levels or collisions (hidden node problem).

The RF spectrum measurement suffers less from this effect as the spectrum analyzer performs sweeps over the entire frequency range in a much shorter time (≈ 272 ms). Albeit, the time resolution of the hardware used is still rather coarse compared to typical durations of WiFi frames which are in the range of and below 1 ms. As a consequence, short transmissions might be missed. However, since the measurement is not synchronized with any transmissions, periodic transmissions

Table 5. Correlation between device observation set similarity and spectrum occupancy similarity

(a) Sum of differences

BSS weighting factor	Observation set threshold	Spectrum occupancy signal threshold		
		-62 dBm	-82 dBm	-96 dBm
1	-62 dBm	-0.2724	-0.4041	-0.4130
1	-82 dBm	0.1468	-0.0639	-0.2417
1	none	-0.0947	-0.1714	0.1117
2	-62 dBm	-0.3898	-0.3536	-0.3593
2	-82 dBm	0.1196	-0.0723	-0.2470
2	none	-0.1027	-0.1408	0.1473
5	-62 dBm	-0.4755	-0.2971	-0.2928
5	-82 dBm	0.0977	-0.0764	-0.2469
5	none	-0.1087	-0.1181	0.1721
9	-62 dBm	-0.5020	-0.2738	-0.2641
9	-82 dBm	0.0898	-0.0772	-0.2460
9	none	-0.1108	-0.1104	0.1801

(b) Number of differing frequency bins

BSS weighting factor	Observation set threshold	Spectrum occupancy signal threshold		
		-62 dBm	-82 dBm	-96 dBm
1	-62 dBm	-0.2352	-0.2234	-0.2098
1	-82 dBm	0.1493	-0.2340	-0.2145
1	none	-0.0908	-0.1170	0.0222
2	-62 dBm	-0.3528	-0.1503	-0.1575
2	-82 dBm	0.1226	-0.2293	-0.1947
2	none	-0.0996	-0.1041	0.0423
5	-62 dBm	-0.4407	-0.0859	-0.1109
5	-82 dBm	0.1010	-0.2231	-0.1780
5	none	-0.1062	-0.0943	0.0568
9	-62 dBm	-0.4686	-0.0629	-0.0943
9	-82 dBm	0.0932	-0.2204	-0.1719
9	none	-0.1085	-0.0909	0.0616

will likely be detected. To increase the probability of such a detection, we chose a rather long time window of 60 s for the spectrum occupancy measurement which might underestimate short, bursty channel occupancies.

Additional problems arise from the combination (comparison) of two unsynchronized sweeps. It may happen that short WiFi transmissions are missed by one spectrum analyzer but are detected by a neighboring analyzer resulting in a decreased similarity measure when comparing both spectrum occupancy arrays.

5.2 Obtained Results

Regarding the Euclidean distance, we can state that this measure is a questionable predictor for similarity of spectrum occupancy. On the other hand, when looking at the relationship between observed WiFi devices and similarity in spectrum occupancy, we can state that the chosen combination of parameters and distance functions shows encouraging results especially for high power levels and high device detection thresholds.

The first point is important since high interference levels result in a higher probability of a channel being detected as busy and in a higher probability of collisions. The second point indicates that more emphasis could be put on WiFi devices in immediate proximity. The fact that the correlations get higher with increasing *BSS weighting factor* support the hypothesis that known stationary WiFi devices should get emphasis for locality detection.

Nevertheless, the obtained results show still room for improvement and leave some questions regarding the counter-intuitive trends for some of the parameter combinations.

6 Conclusion

In this paper, we presented an experimental study carried out to assess the possibility for using information about present WiFi devices as basis for deciding about re-use of spectrum occupancy information in an indoor scenario. Summarizing the results, we find similar spectrum occupancy for devices that also detect a similar set of present WiFi devices, while we cannot state a clear relationship between Euclidean distance and observed spectrum occupancy. The latter finding complies with our initial assumptions. While the results support the general hypothesis, the accuracy of prediction has room for improvement. Future research should evaluate other approaches to express set similarity. Next to various similarity measures and indexes, fuzzy sets could be used to incorporate certainty of device sightings, signal levels, and device roles into this process.

Acknowledgements. Till Wollenberg is supported by a grant of the German National Research Foundation (DFG), research training group "MuSAMA" (GRK 1424). Andreas Dähn is supported by Landesgraduiertenförderung Mecklenburg-Vorpommern. We thank our colleagues at the Institute of Computer Science who supported our experiment.

References

1. Dely, P., Kassler, A.J., Sivchenko, D.: Theoretical and Experimental Analysis of the Channel Busy Fraction in IEEE 802.11. In: Future Network and Mobile Summit. IEEE (2010)

2. Halperin, D., Hu, W., Sheth, A., Wetherall, D.: Predictable 802.11 Packet Delivery from Wireless Channel Measurements. ACM SIGCOMM Computer Communication Review 40, 159–170 (2010)
3. Hanna, S.A., Sydor, J.: Distributed Sensing of Spectrum Occupancy and Interference in Outdoor 2.4 GHz Wi-Fi Networks. In: 2012 IEEE Global Communications Conference, GLOBECOM, pp. 1453–1459 (2012)
4. IEEE Computer Society. IEEE Standard for Information Technology–Telecommunications and Information Exchange Between Systems–Local and Metropolitan Area Networks–Specific Requirements Part 11: Wireless LAN Medium Access Control (MAC) and Physical Layer (PHY) Specifications (2012)
5. Rayanchu, S., Mishra, A., Agrawal, D., Saha, S., Banerjee, S.: Diagnosing Wireless Packet Losses in 802.11: Separating Collision from Weak Signal. In: The 27th Conference on Computer Communications, INFOCOM 2008, pp. 735–743. IEEE (2008)
6. Rayanchu, S., Patro, A., Banerjee, S.: Airshark: Detecting Non-WiFi RF Devices using Commodity WiFi Hardware. In: Proceedings of the 2011 ACM SIGCOMM Conference on Internet Measurement Conference, pp. 137–154. ACM (2011)
7. Wollenberg, T.: Estimation of Expectable Network Quality in Wireless Mesh Networks. In: Becvar, Z., Bestak, R., Kencl, L. (eds.) NETWORKING 2012 Workshops. LNCS, vol. 7291, pp. 126–132. Springer, Heidelberg (2012)
8. Wollenberg, T., Bader, S., Ahrens, A.: Measuring Channel Occupancy for 802.11 Wireless LAN in the 2.4 GHz ISM Band. In: Proceedings of the 15th ACM International Conference on Modeling, Analysis and Simulation of Wireless and Mobile Systems, pp. 305–308. ACM (2012)
9. Yager, R.R.: On the Theory of Bags. International Journal of General Systems 13(1), 23–37 (1986)
10. Zubow, A., Sombrutzki, R.: Adjacent Channel Interference in IEEE 802.11n. In: 2012 IEEE Wireless Communications and Networking Conference (WCNC), pp. 1163–1168. IEEE (2012)

Analyzing Coexistence Issues in Wireless Radio Networks: Simulation of Bluetooth Interfered by Multiple WLANs

Roland Neumeier and Gerald Ostermayer

FH OÖ Forschungs & Entwicklungs GmbH/ Research Center Hagenberg,
Softwarepark 11, 4232 Hagenberg, Austria
{roland.neumeier,gerald.ostermayer}@fh-hagenberg.at

Abstract. In many fields of technology more mobile transmission paths will be used in the future. In order to ensure a secure transmission of data, studies for coexistence of the used radio technologies with other currently wide used radio systems (WLAN, Bluetooth, ZigBee, etc.), are needed. Since an analytical treatment is too complex and a real test set is usually too expensive, the objective is the construction of a suitable simulation environment to investigate the performance of co-existing wireless systems in an economical way. Investigations of a variety of representative application scenarios indicated, that a universal applicability and adaptability of such a simulation framework can be achieved by a high-grade modular design. To keep the simulation results as realistic as possible, the use of statistical radio channel data was largely omitted. Instead, an accurate recording of the simulated scenario is done to compute the required channel characteristics by ray-tracing/-launching algorithms. The signal processing chains of the transmitters and receivers (user- and jammer-radio) were reproduced precisely to their specifications and for easy interchangeability they are connected to the channel via a universal defined interface. Finally an application scenario (Bluetooth connection interfered by multiple WLAN transmitters) is presented and the results of the simulations are shown and discussed.

Keywords: Attenuation, Bit error rate, Bluetooth, Ray tracing, Receivers, Wireless LAN, Wireless communication.

1   Introduction

Nowadays, wireless data transmission paths are used for a large number of applications. For example, such applications could be in logistics management, control and monitoring of industrial plants as well as management and billing of electric charging stations etc., however, there are virtually no limits in application areas.

Since many other systems, that operate in the same frequency band (WLAN, Bluetooth, ZigBee, etc.), often are in spatial proximity, there may be mutual interference. Therefore one objective of this project was to explore strategies to ensure reliable and high quality transmission of the data in coexistence scenarios. Therefore an investigation of the effects of coexistence of different wireless and / or mobile radio systems in

M. Jonsson et al. (Eds.): MACOM 2013, LNCS 8310, pp. 128–138, 2013.

close spatial proximity is needed. Since an analytical treatment is too complex and a real test set is usually too expensive, the objective is the construction of a suitable simulation environment to investigate the performance of co-existing wireless systems in an economical way.

Investigations of a variety of representative application scenarios indicated, that the requirements for such a simulator are very different and partly opposite. For example, errors, which occur on the transmission of control data for an industrial robot, require different handling than errors on video or audio streaming transmissions. Send/receive chains that act as probed connection in one scenario can act as jammer in the next scenario. In order to manage these requirements within one universal applicable and customizable simulation environment, a high-grade modular design is needed.

To keep the simulation results as realistic as possible, the use of statistical radio channel data was largely omitted. Instead, an accurate recording of the simulated scenario (space, position transmitter/receiver/jammer, etc.) is done to compute the required channel characteristics by ray-tracing/-launching algorithms. This ray-tracing/-launching simulator was built as separate, independent module to allow multiple simulations with different radio parameters in the same environment. The signal processing chains of the transmitters and receivers (user- and jammer-radio) were reproduced precisely to their specifications. For easy interchangeability of the individual radio technologies these signal processing chains are connected to the channel via a universal defined interface.

1.1   Related Work

Because it is not possible to discuss all the related work we will show based on a few examples the differences to our work. In [7] interference mitigation techniques for Bluetooth when operating in close proximity to WLAN systems based on interference avoidance techniques (adaptive frequency hopping, scheduling) are given. [8] deals with hardware interference avoidance technologies from Texas Instruments for the case where both radios are collocated in the same device. In [10] the author also investigates possibilities to avoid interference between Bluetooth and WLAN radios collocated in the same device. In [9] the performance of WLAN, Bluetooth and Zig-Bee is examined by real test environments.

Our work on the other hand investigates the performance of coexisting wireless technologies by simulation using ray tracing technologies for the channel modulation. This solution has the advantage to get quick performance results for a given scenario at low cost.

In the first section this paper describes the motivation and the objectives to build such a simulation environment. In the next part the structure of the simulator and its components, which was fully implemented in MATLAB Simulink, is explained. Main focus is on the modular design of the simulator and the aspects of the selected division of the single modules. In this context an application scenario (Bluetooth connection is disrupted by two WLAN transmitters) is presented and the results of the simulations are shown and discussed.

2   Simulation Framework

This section describes the structure of the simulation framework. One objective of this project was not to build the wireless transmission channel out of statistical data. Instead the geometrical dimensions and surfaces in the investigated scenario should be used. To build a channel model out of the geometrical room data and the position of sender and receiver a ray-tracing simulator is needed. In order to get a simulation environment that is independent from commercial, expensive ray-tracing suites, a simple and for now rudimentary ray-tracing simulator was built.

2.1   Ray-Tracer

For most simulation scenarios it is necessary to run a simulator many times with different parameters on send/receive-chains using the same channel model. Generating a channel model from a ray-tracer is a computationally intensive process, so running this process each time a new parameter set is simulated would lead to exorbitant execution time extension. Also saving a generated channel model for later use or reproduction of a previous simulation campaign would be beneficial. For that reason the ray-tracing simulator was built as separate, independent module. One more benefit of this breakup is the possibility to exchange this still simple module with a commercial software suite for channel generation or to use data from channel measurements in real environments.

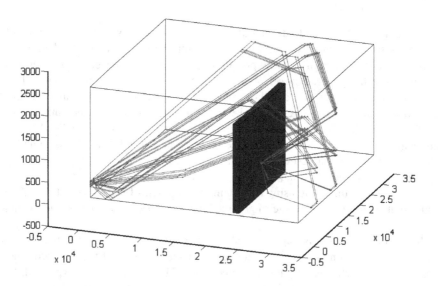

Fig. 1. Result of ray-tracing simulation: room model with signal paths

According to [1] and [2] the ray-tracing simulator was built in *Mathworks MATLAB*. The current implementation allows defining a rectangular or trapezoid room with one or more objects inside the room. These objects also have to be in rectangular or trapezoid shape. Sender and receiver can be positioned anywhere in the room. Each surface or only parts of surfaces can be assigned with different reflection and transmission coefficients. With this features a simple room model is created which can be saved for later use. After starting the channel model generation the ray-tracer computes all possible ray-paths from the sender to the receiver. These paths can contain line of sight, reflection on objects or walls and transmission through objects. The current implementation does not support effects like refraction, diffraction and scattering. At each reflection or transmission point all relevant data (distance from recent to current point, attenuation, angle of incidence etc.) are stored for later analysis purposes. The calculated full paths can contain multiple reflections and transmissions from sender to receiver. This can lead up to an infinite number of possible paths, although not all of them are relevant for channel model generation, because signals over those paths would get too weak to be recognized by the receiver. To limit these paths all paths reaching a total attenuation level higher than a given threshold are omitted.

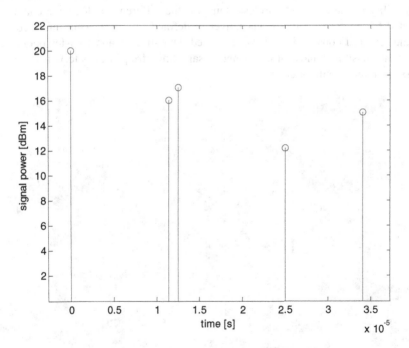

Fig. 2. Raytracer result: Tapped delay line model

Fig. 1 shows the ray-tracer result of a very simple room with one object in it and transmission through objects disabled (enabling transmission would lead to a result not suitable for graphical representation in this paper). Out of the stored data while calculating the possible signal paths from the sender to the receiver a tapped delay line model as shown in Fig. 2 is calculated.

2.2   Simulator Structure

This section explains the design of the whole simulation framework and its components as well as the aspects of the selected division of the single modules. Fig. 3 shows the block diagram of the framework. Main components of the simulator are the send/receive chains, the core simulator with signal channel management and the analysis component (throughput and bit error rate (BER) calculation).

In order to have the main engineering focus on the core simulator, the send/receive chains used in this simulator are extracted of the Simulink examples. Depending on the selected model, these examples are very accurate and with little or no modification they exactly follow the corresponding standards. In the current version Wireless LAN 802.11g [3] and Bluetooth in Version 1.1 [4] are implemented, for future research 802.15.4 [5] adoption is in progress. One requirement for all of these send/receive chains are that they have to be dividable between sender and receiver. The included channel model must be removable to be exchanged by the core simulator. Several control information between sender and receiver may remain. For interchangeability of the different wireless standards the different send/receive chains are connected to the core simulator via universal defined interface. This Interface contains the required constitution of the delivered data streams and transfer parameters (used transmission bandwidth, channel, sampling frequency etc.) needed for processing in the simulator core.

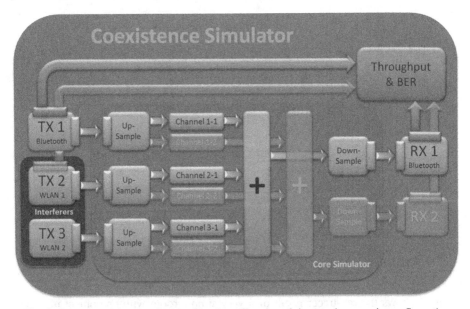

Fig. 3. Structure of the Coexistence Simulator Framework in sample scenario configuration

The core simulator is responsible for processing and combining the input data streams of the connected senders and forwarding them to the appropriate receivers. Minimum requirement for investigations in coexistence scenarios is one complete send/receive chain, this is the one which will be tested, and an interfering sender. This sender does not necessarily need a receiver if it works standalone. As shown in Fig. 3, multiple interferers of different technology or multiple receivers (more than one connection that will be investigated) are also possible. Fig. 3 shows the configuration of the sample scenario with an investigated Bluetooth connection and two different interfering WLAN transmitters.

First, the delivered baseband signals of the connected senders are up sampled with different factors to get a common sampling rate for all given data streams. The destination sampling frequency depends on the connected wireless technologies and will be calculated from the parameters given through the sender interfaces. The channel models are represented by Rayleigh fading in combination with Additive White Gaussian Noise (AWGN) and attenuation signal processing blocks. The block parameters are given by the tapped delay line (TDL) models extracted from the ray tracing simulations. The delays of these TDL models are matched to the used common sampling frequency. The attenuation blocks are needed because the gain vector of the Rayleigh fading blocks is normalized to 0dBm overall gain. So the attenuation blocks are used to model the distance dependent path loss. The AWGN blocks are used to form the thermal noise at the investigated receiver. As shown in Fig. 3, each sender-receiver pair needs its own channel block. This is necessary because each sender and receiver is located on a different position in the simulated room, so there is also a different channel between each unit. For example, an investigated connection has one channel between sender and receiver, but the interfering sender, located elsewhere in the room, experiences different channel effects to the disturbed receiver. The number of channel blocks needed is given by the product of the number of senders and receivers used in a simulation scenario. After passing the channel blocks the signals are combined. This combination has to be performed separately for each connected receiver. After combination the signals are down sampled to the corresponding receiver sampling rate. This sampling rate is given by the interface parameters of the connected receivers.

Finally, the connected receivers try to decode the given signals correctly. To perform this operation the use of channel filtering in the receivers as described in the corresponding standards is required. To be able to manage different signal levels at the various sender outputs, separate attenuation blocks have been implemented. This block is freely adjustable and may also be used to simulate different transmitter power levels if not possible by the used send/receive chains. For example, in the following scenario this attenuation block is used to model the different signal powers of the WLAN interferers to investigate the influence of these interferences to the Bluetooth transmission (data rate and BER).

The analysis component matches the data streams from the senders and the corresponding receivers. For that operation the delays of all components involved in signal transmission are needed. For that reason each sender and receiver has a small analysis interface. That interface contains the transmitted or received data and the entire delay of the component. The delay produced by the core simulator is known by the analysis component and does not have to be forwarded separately. In the current version, calculation of throughput in [bits/s] and bit error rate (BER) in [%] is implemented. For each investigated wireless connection (all connections where a receiver is present) a separate analysis component is required.

3   Example Scenario / Results

This section presents a sample scenario that was used for creating the first simulation results with multiple interferers. After that the obtained results are presented and discussed.

3.1   Configuration

The sample scenario consists of a room with one wall in the middle of the room, but this wall does not reach the top and one side wall of the room. The investigated

Table 1. Simulator configuration parameters

	Parameter	Value
Bluetooth	Role	Investigated Connection
	Connection type	Data
	Packet type	DM1
	Data transmission	continuous
	Number of hop frequencies	79
WLAN 1	Role	Interferer
	WLAN standard	802.11g
	Channel	1
	Data transmission	30 % of time
	Signal power	-44 – 16dBm in 10 dB steps
WLAN 2	Role	Interferer
	WLAN standard	802.11g
	Channel	11
	Data transmission	60 % of time
	Signal power	-54 – 6dBm in 10 dB steps
Sim. Core	Number of taps Bluetooth	3
	Number of taps WLAN 1	3
	Number of taps WLAN 2	3
	AWGN Noise Bluetooth	-60.89 dBm

wireless connection is a Bluetooth connection with the receiver on one side of the middle wall and the receiver on the other side. The interfering technology is Wireless LAN with two independent transmitters on different positions on the same side of the wall as the Bluetooth receiver. The signal powers of the interfering WLAN transmitters are controlled with attenuation blocks on the output of the transmitters. Table I shows the main parameters used for the simulations. The signal power of the Bluetooth connection was constant over all simulation runs, the WLAN interferer signal power for each transmitter increased each simulation run by 10dB using the attenuation blocks (independent for each transmitter).

3.2   Simulation Results

Simulations on the sample scenario using the above parameters have been run. On each simulation cycle the signal power of one of the interferers has been increased by 10 dB. The signal power of the Bluetooth connection remained the same over all simulation cycles. Fig. 4 shows the BER of transmitted data over the Bluetooth connection in a 3D view. On the two bottom axes (X and Y) we have the signal power of the two WLAN interferers, on the Z axis the BER of the Bluetooth connection is shown. Fig. 5 also shows the BER of the Bluetooth connection as a 2D cut through the 3D figure in Fig. 4. Both lines in Fig 4 show the BER for one interferer signal power range with the other interferer fixed to the lowest output power.

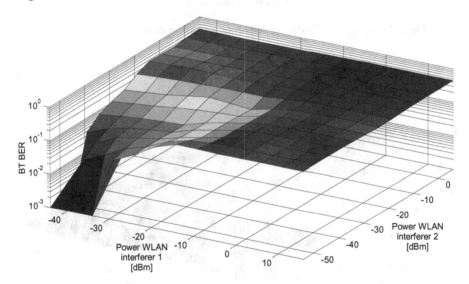

Fig. 4. Simulation result: Bluetooth BER on increasing interferer signal powers

From -60 to -40 dBm WLAN interferer power the BER remains very low, because the interfering power is too low to be recognized by the Bluetooth connection. From --40 to -20 dB the BER rises dramatically. After that, most of the jammed Bluetooth packets could not be decoded by the receiver. At -15 dBm the curve flattens and will not rise very much. This occurs, because the WLAN interferers only send 30 and 60% of the time and the used WLAN channel bandwidth is narrower than the whole frequency hopping bandwidth of the Bluetooth connection, so not all Bluetooth packets are interfered.

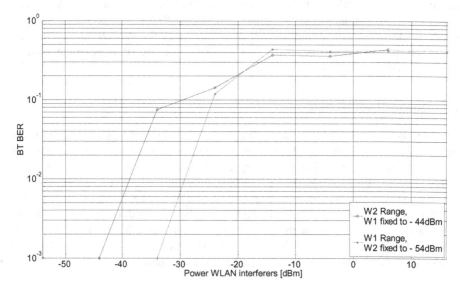

Fig. 5. Simulation result: Bluetooth BER on increasing interferer signal powers

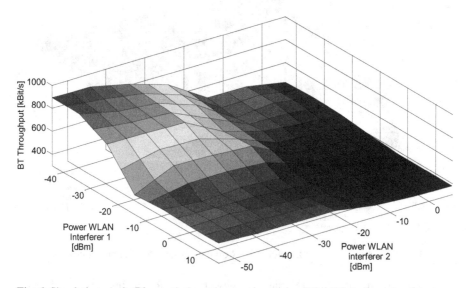

Fig. 6. Simulation result: Bluetooth throughput on increasing WLAN interferer signal powers

Fig. 6 and 7 show the throughput of the Bluetooth connection in the same manner as Fig. 4 and 5. In general the development of the throughput is analog to the BER curve. Starting at -60 dB to -40 dB the throughput decreases only moderate. After that a big drop in data rate occurs, but then the throughput gets constant at rate of 500 kbit/s.

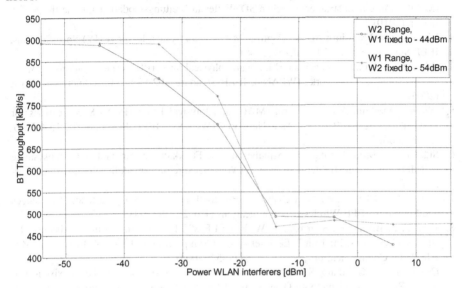

Fig. 7. Simulation result: Bluetooth throughput on increasing WLAN interferer signal powers

4   Conclusion

We proposed a first version of a simulation framework for investigating coexistence issues on wireless connections in close spatial proximity. We explained why such a framework is needed and presented the structure of this framework and the motivations why this structure was selected. Finally we presented the first simulation results of a defined sample scenario. Future work is the implementation of additional radio technologies and the refinement of the ray tracing and analysis components.

Acknowledgments. This project was supported by the program *Regionale Wettbe-werbsfähigkeit OÖ 2010-2013*, which is financed by the European Regional Development Fund and the Government of Upper Austria.

References

1. Hoppe, R.: Effiziente Modellierung der Wellenausbreitung für die Funknetzplanung in urbanen Szenarien und innerhalb von Gebäuden. Shaker (2002) ISBN 3-832-20749-X
2. Stäbler, O.: Modellierung und Simulation von Funkkanälen für Mehrantennensysteme (MIMO) mit einem strahlenoptischen 3D Wellenausbreitungsmodell. Diploma thesis, Erlangen (2010)
3. Wireless LAN Medium Access Control (MAC) and Physical Layer (PHY) Specifications, IEEE Standard 802.11-2007. IEEE (2006)
4. Wireless medium access control (MAC) and physical layer (PHY) specifications for wireless personal area networks (WPANs), IEEE Standard 802.15.1-2005 (Bluetooth). IEEE (2005)
5. Wireless Medium Access Control (MAC) and Physical Layer (PHY) Specifications for Low-Rate Wireless Personal Area Networks (WPANs), IEEE Standard 802.15.4-2006. IEEE (2006)
6. Stäbler, O.: Modellierung und Simulation von Funkkanälen für Mehrantennensysteme (MIMO) mit einem strahlenoptischen 3D Wellenausbreitungsmodell. Diploma thesis, Erlangen (2010)
7. Golmie, N., Chevrollier, N., Rebala, O.: Bluetooth and WLAN Coexistence: Challenges and Solutions. IEEE Wireless Communications (10), 22–29 (2003)
8. Herzlia, I., Bitran, Y., Sherman, I.: Wi-Fi (IEEE 802.11) and Bluetooth Coexistence: Issues and Solutions. In: 15th IEEE International Symposium on Personal, Indoor and Mobile Radio Communications, vol. 2, pp. 847–852 (2004)
9. Gazzarrini, L., Giordano, S., Tavanti, L.: Experimental Assessment of the Coexistence of Wi-Fi, ZigBee, and Bluetooth Devices. In: IEEE International Symposium on a World of Wireless, Mobile and Multimedia Networks, pp. 1–9 (2011)
10. Wojtiuk, J.: Bluetooth and WiFi Integration: Solving Co-existence Challenges. Defense Electronics Magazine, 20–26 (October 2004)

Capacity Analysis of IEEE 802.11ah WLANs for M2M Communications

T. Adame, A. Bel, B. Bellalta, J. Barcelo, J. Gonzalez, and M. Oliver

NeTS Research Group
Universitat Pompeu Fabra, Barcelona
{toni.adame,albert.bel,boris.bellalta,jaume.barcelo,
javier.gonzalez,miquel.oliver}@upf.edu

Abstract. Focusing on the increasing market of the sensors and actuators networks, the IEEE 802.11ah Task Group is currently working on the standardization of a new amendment. This new amendment will operate at the sub-1GHz band, ensure transmission ranges up to 1 Km, data rates above 100 kbps and very low power operation. With IEEE 802.11ah, the WLANs will offer a solution for applications such as smart metering, plan automation, eHealth or surveillance. Moreover, thanks to a hierarchical signalling, the IEEE 802.11ah will be able to manage a higher number of stations (STAs) and improve the 802.11 Power Saving Mechanisms. In order to support a high number of STAs, two different signalling modes are proposed, TIM and Non-TIM Offset. In this paper we present a theoretical model to predict the maximum number of STAs supported by both modes depending on the traffic load and the data rate used. Moreover, the IEEE 802.11ah performance and energy consumption for both signalling modes and for different traffic patterns and data rates is evaluated. Results show that both modes achieve similar Packet Delivery Ratio values but the energy consumed with the TIM Offset is, in average, 11.7% lower.

Keywords: IEEE 802.11ah, WLANs, M2M, WSNs, Power Saving Mechanisms.

1 Introduction

In the last years, several draft amendments to IEEE 802.11 are being developed to support its growth into the future of wireless networking. These amendments seek to respond to the new needs of wireless communications, such as very-high throughput WLANs (IEEE 802.11ac [1], IEEE 802.11ad [2]), occupancy of TV Whitespaces (IEEE 802.11af [3]) or sensor networks (IEEE 802.11ah [4]), among others.

With respect to the Wireless Sensor Networks (WSNs), IEEE 802.11 is not suitable for applications based on this kind of devices as it was originally designed to offer high throughput to wireless communications without having into account energy consumption concerns. Many MAC protocols in general wireless ad-hoc networks assume more powerful radio hardware than the common one

M. Jonsson et al. (Eds.): MACOM 2013, LNCS 8310, pp. 139–155, 2013.

in sensor nodes, which is needed to run for months or years with just a pair of AA+ batteries [5]. Therefore, these particular constraints of sensors in terms of energy consumption require the design of new energy saving mechanisms which force them to remain asleep the maximum time possible during their operation periods.

In fact, the cost benefit offered by wireless sensors when compared with traditional wired sensors is inducing to predict that the Compound Annual Growth Rate (CAGR) of these systems could range 55% to 130% over the 2012-2016 time frame [6]. Excluding consumer short-range standards, this could amount to a market differential of as few as 300 million WSN connections in 2016 or as many as over 2 billion connections.

The IEEE 802.11ah Task Group is nowadays working for enlarging the Wi-Fi applicability area, by designing a sub-1GHz protocol which will allow up to 8191 devices attached to a single Access Point (AP) to get access for short-data transmissions [7]. The standardization work was started in November 2010 and the final standard is expected not before January 2016, when it will be suitable for supporting Sensor Networks, Backhaul Networks for Sensors and Machine-to-Machine (M2M) Communication.

As for energy consumption, IEEE 802.11ah introduces new power saving features based on the segmentation of channel access into different contention periods, that are allocated to groups of stations according to a hierarchical distribution. Besides, ultra-low power consumption strategies are being developed from the former Power Saving Mode (PSM) of IEEE 802.11, so that they could extend up to 5 years the time that a STA can remain asleep without being disassociated from the network. Moreover, two signalling modes are defined in the draft amendment: the TIM Offset and Non-TIM Offset. While the first one uses two levels from the hierarchical distribution, has a high beacon transmission rate and sends little signalling information, the second one uses only one hierarchical level, has a low beacon rate and sends more signalling information.

In this paper, the feasibility of IEEE 802.11ah WLANs to support a large number of stations with a low energy consumption is analyzed. A theoretical model of the network capacity, in terms of the maximum number of supported STAs, for the TIM Offset and Non-TIM Offset signalling modes defined in the draft amendment is presented. The presented results show that, for low traffic loads, the maximum number of stations defined in the draft amendment (8191) could be supported in non-saturated conditions if the data rate is higher than 2.4 Mbps. Besides, the low energy consumption of STAs is demonstrated from the comparison of the time spent in sleeping and non-sleeping states. As for the signalling modes, although Non-TIM Offset supports a slightly higher amount of stations without being saturated, TIM Offset offers a better global performance by saving up to 15% of energy in high traffic scenarios.

The remainder of this paper is organized as follows: In Section 2, the main features of the amendment in terms of PHY and MAC layer are described. A description of IEEE 802.11ah appears in Section 3, while the theoretical model about its capacity is proposed in Section 4. The results obtained in simulations, related to capacity and energy consumption, are shown in Section 5. Finally, in Section 6, we present our conclusions and propose future work.

2   IEEE 802.11ah

IEEE 802.11ah is being designed for supporting applications with the following requirements [8]: up to 8191 devices associated to an AP, adoption of Power Saving strategies, minimum network data rate of 100 kbps, operating carrier frequencies around 900 MHz, coverage up to 1 km in outdoor areas, one-hop network topology and short and infrequent data transmissions (data packets $\sim$ 100 bytes).

One of the goals of the IEEE 802.11ah Task Group (TGah) is to offer a standard that, apart from satisfying these previously mentioned requirements, minimizes the changes with respect to the widely adopted IEEE 802.11. In that sense, the proposed PHY and MAC layers are based on the IEEE 802.11ac standard and moreover, try to achieve an efficiency gain by reducing some control/management frames and the MAC header length.

Technologies like Orthogonal Frequency Division Multiplexing (OFDM), Multi Input Multi Output (MIMO) and Downlink Multi-User MIMO (DL MU-MIMO) - which was firstly introduced in the IEEE 802.11ac - are also employed by the 802.11ah system.

2.1   PHY Layer

Channelization As commented above, the IEEE 802.11ah operates at the sub-1 GHz band, by being a 10 times down-clocked version of IEEE 802.11ac. This new standard defines different channel widths: 1 MHz, 2 MHz, 4 MHz, 8 MHz and 16 MHz.

The available sub 1 GHz ISM bands differ depending on the country regulations, so that the IEEE 802.11ah has defined the channelization based on the wireless spectrum in different countries [9].

Transmission Modes. The common channels adopted by the IEEE 802.11ah are 2 MHz and 1 MHz. Hence, the PHY layer design can be classified into 2 categories: transmission modes greater or equal than 2 MHz channel bandwidth and a transmission mode of 1 MHz channel bandwidth.

For the first case, the PHY layer is designed based on 10 times down-clocking of IEEE 802.11ac's PHY layer; i.e. the PHY layer uses an OFDM waveform with a total of 64 tones/sub-carriers (including tones allocated as pilot, guard and DC), which are spaced by 31.25 kHz. The modulations supported include BPSK, QPSK and 16 to 256 QAM (Table 1). It will also support multi user MIMO and single user beam forming. For the second case, the tone spacing is maintained, but the waveform is formed with 32 tones, instead of 64 [10].

Table 1. IEEE 802.11ah Modulation and Codification Schemes and their corresponding Coding and Data Rates for Bandwidth (BW) = 1MHz, and Number of Spatial Streams (NSS) = 1 [7]

MCS Idx	Mod	R	Data Rate (kbps)
0	BPSK	1/2	300
1	QPSK	1/2	600
2	QPSK	3/4	900
3	16-QAM	1/2	1200
4	16-QAM	3/4	1800
5	64-QAM	2/3	2400
6	64-QAM	3/4	2700
7	64-QAM	5/6	3000
8	256-QAM	3/4	3600
9	256-QAM	5/6	4000
10	BPSK	1/4	150

2.2 MAC Layer

Hierarchical Grouping. IEEE 802.11 MAC layer defines that the AP assigns an Association IDentifier (AID) to each STA. The maximum number of stations mapped is only 2007, due to the length of the partial virtual bitmap of Traffic Indication Map (TIM) Information Element (IE).

In order to support a larger number of STAs, TGah has defined a novel and hierarchical distribution of them [11]. With this novel structure, the IEEE 802.11ah achieves the objective of supporting up to 8191 STAs. In this manner, the AIDs are classified into pages, blocks (from now on called *TIM Groups* in this paper), sub-blocks and STAs' indexes in sub-blocks.

The number of pages (N_P) and TIM Groups per page (N_{TIM}) is configurable according to the size and requirements of the network. An example of hierarchical distribution with $N_P = 4$ and $N_{TIM} = 8$ is shown in Figure 1.

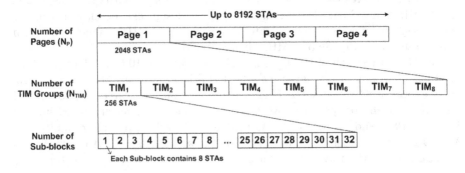

Fig. 1. Hierarchical distribution of stations in an IEEE 802.11 network

The IEEE 802.11ah AID assigned is unique and consists of 13 bits (see Figure 2) that include the different hierarchical levels. It could be an effective way to categorize STAs with respect to their type of application, battery level or required QoS (Figure 3). Thus, QoS differentiation could be achieved by restricting the number of stations in high-priority groups, in order to limit the contention in them.

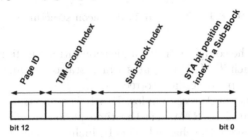

Fig. 2. AID Structure

AID Map					
#TIM	**STAs**				
TIM$_1$	1	2	3	...	256
TIM$_2$	257	258	259	...	512
TIM$_3$	513	514	515	...	768
TIM$_4$	769	770	771	...	1024
TIM$_5$	1025	1026	1027	...	1280
TIM$_6$	1281	1282	1283	...	1536
TIM$_7$	1537	1538	1539	...	1792
TIM$_8$	1793	1794	1795	...	2048

☐ Associated STA   ☐ Non-Associated STA   ☐ Non-allowed

Fig. 3. Example of AID Map

Beacon Structure. There are two classes of signalling beacons. The first one, which is called Delivery Traffic Indication Map (DTIM), informs about which groups of STAs have pending data at the AP and also about multicast and broadcast messages. The second class of beacons is called simply TIM. Each TIM informs a group of STAs about which of them have pending data in the AP.

Both DTIM and TIM beacon structures (Figure 4) are based in one Short Beacon Frame plus optional Information Elements (IE) for different purposes:

– SBF (Short Beacon Frame): Its primary functions are: advertizing the AP presence and synchronizing the STAs.
– DTIM IE: It is only transmitted in DTIM beacon frames and not in TIM segments. From this element, STAs can deduce their assignment in TIM Groups and their wake-up intervals. Besides, STAs with their TIM Group bit set to 0 may not wake up at assigned TIM Group interval.

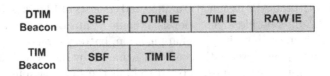

Fig. 4. DTIM and TIM Beacon structure

- TIM IE: When the complete traffic indication bitmap is divided into multiple TIM Groups, each TIM IE indicates which stations from its corresponding TIM Group have pending data to receive.
- RAW IE (Restricted Access Window IE): It is responsible for signalling all information related to RAW; i.e. the time period in which selected STAs contend for accessing the channel. This IE includes: time from the beacon to the RAW, duration of the RAW as well as mechanisms to generate sub-slots within the RAW contention period.

Types of Stations. As defined in IEEE 802.11ah draft, there are 3 different kinds of STAs, each with its procedures and time periods to access the channel:

1. *TIM Stations:* They have to listen to both DTIM and TIM beacons to send or receive data.
2. *Non-TIM Stations:* They only have to listen to DTIM beacons to send or receive data.
3. *Unscheduled Stations:* These STAs do not need to listen to beacons and can transmit data anytime.

3   Power Saving Mechanisms in IEEE 802.11ah

3.1   TIM and Page Segmentation

Compared to IEEE 802.11 power management mode, IEEE 802.11ah amendment tries to improve that power saving mode by means of using a scheme called *TIM and page segmentation*. This new scheme aims to save STA's energy consumption not only when they do not have to send or receive any data, but also during their operation time, by allocating them in shorter contention periods with other few STAs. To achieve this goal, IEEE 802.11ah extends some of the mechanisms already introduced in the former IEEE 802.11 PSM version [12].

IEEE 802.11 PSM is based on the inclusion of an IE field in each TIM beacon, responsible for signalling the existence of packets in the downlink buffer for each STA associated to the AP. Thus, any node can enter into a power saving state if it observes in the TIM beacon that there is no downlink traffic aimed at it.

However, this mechanism has two major drawbacks:

- Firstly, all STAs in power saving mode are forced to listen to all TIMs and, therefore, to shorten their sleeping periods.

– Secondly, each TIM must be able to map all STAs in the network (they could be up to 2048), so in a densely populated network such mapping would be very long in size and expensive in terms of energy.

TGah, trying to overcome the drawbacks mentioned above, proposes a scheme based on hierarchical signalling. This hierarchy is reflected both in the organization of the STAs in groups and in the signalling beacons. Therefore, the STAs only remain active during the time assigned to their group, the signalling data is shorter than the former PSM and the network can manage a higher number of STAs.

Between two consecutive DTIMs, an AP broadcasts as many TIMs per page as groups of STAs. Each one of these TIMs informs STAs about buffered downlink packets. These packets will be dropped after a certain time determined by the size of the AP buffer and the association parameters chosen by the STA.

TIM Offset. The draft specification also includes the *TIM Offset*, a 5-bit field that is contained in the DTIM IE and allows the AP to indicate the TIM beacon offset with respect to the DTIM beacon. The corresponding TIM beacon for the first TIM Group of a specific page can be allocated at the indicated TIM offset. Thus, TIM Groups of different pages can be flexibly scheduled over beacon intervals.

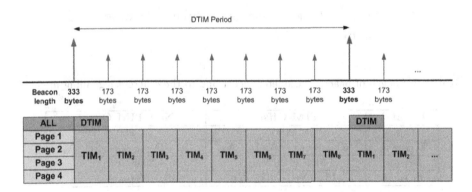

Fig. 5. Beacon distribution using Non-TIM Offset signalling mode in a four-page IEEE 802.11ah network

If TIM Offset is not used (Figure 5), signalling information of a determined TIM Group is transmitted in the same beacon as many times as existing pages in the network. This fact implies that the STAs are forced to listen the information related to pages that they do not belong to.

Otherwise, with the use of TIM Offset (Figure 6), all beacons except DTIM contain signalling information addressed to STAs from a single page, reducing in this manner the time spent in the receiving state and, consequently, the energy consumed by STAs. In this mode, TIM beacons are sequentially sent from the

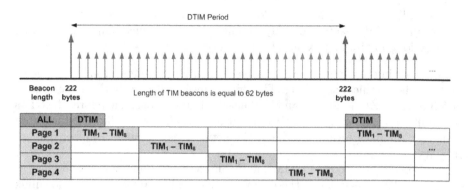

Fig. 6. Beacon distribution using TIM Offset signalling mode in a four-page IEEE 802.11ah network

first to the last page with a rate N_P times higher than in the Non-TIM Offset case.

Length of DTIM and TIM beacons becomes an important parameter in the network, as the more pages it has, the more bits it will need to map all contained stations. The equations of the length of both beacons are shown in Table 2, with different $L_{\text{TIM } IE}$ values depending on the activation of the TIM Offset field.

$$L_{\text{DTIM}} = L_{\text{SBF}} + L_{\text{DTIM IE}} + L_{\text{TIM IE}} + L_{\text{RAW IE}}$$
$$L_{\text{TIM}} = L_{\text{SBF}} + L_{\text{TIM IE}}$$

Table 2. Length of beacon parameters according to the different signalling modes

L (bits)	TIM Offset	Non-TIM Offset
L_{SBF}	200	200
$L_{\text{DTIM IE}}$	$(32 + N_{\text{TIM}} + N_{\text{TIM}}) \cdot N_P$	$(32 + N_{\text{TIM}} + N_{\text{TIM}}) \cdot N_P$
$L_{\text{TIM IE}}$	$(40 + 2048/N_{\text{TIM}})$	$(40 + 2048/N_{\text{TIM}}) \cdot N_P$
$L_{\text{RAW IE}}$	$(16 + N_{\text{TIM}} \cdot 32) \cdot N_P$	$(16 + N_{\text{TIM}} \cdot 32) \cdot N_P$

Channel Access. Once a node associates to an AP, it is included in a TIM Group and in its corresponding Multicast distribution group along with the other TIM Group stations. Figure 7 shows how time between 2 consecutive TIMs is split into one Downlink (DL) segment, one Uplink (UL) segment as well as one Multicast (MC) segment placed immediately after each DTIM beacon. In our proposal, the proportion between $\psi \in \{\text{DL}, \text{UL}\}$ segments size is equal to the DL/UL traffic proportion (β_ψ), and we assume that the multicast segment is able to accommodate only one data packet.

The operation modes for the downlink and uplink cases are detailed below:

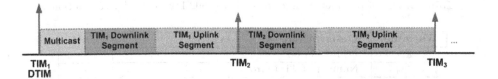

Fig. 7. Distribution of channel access into downlink and uplink segments

- Downlink: When an AP needs to send a packet to a STA, the DTIM beacon has to include the TIM Group to which belongs that STA in its bitmap. Similarly, the corresponding TIM beacon has to include that STA, also, in its bitmap. Each signalled STA has to listen its TIM to know when to contend. This contention will be done using the Distributed Coordination Function (DCF), by sending first a PS-Poll frame, in order to get its corresponding data.
- Uplink: When a STA has to send an uplink message to the AP, it must listen its corresponding TIM Group for knowing when to contend the channel. In this case, the contention is also done through an DCF scheme. Both Basic Access (BA) and RTS/CTS mechanisms can be used.

3.2 Long Sleeping Periods

Apart from the *TIM and Page Segmentation* scheme, an important feature in terms of energy savings of IEEE 802.11ah is the ability to set longer doze times (up to years) to STAs than IEEE 802.11. This is achieved by extending several system parameters during the initial handshake between an AP and its associated STAs.

However, an important drawback that has to be considered is the corresponding clock drift produced by such long doze times. Thus, the more time a STA has been asleep, the further in advance it should wake up to avoid possible synchronization problems with the network [13].

4 Maximum Number of Supported STAs

From the study of the channel access features in an IEEE 802.11ah WLAN, a theoretical model of the channel capacity for both the TIM Offset and Non-TIM Offset signalling modes is developed. The variables used to build the model are shown in Table 3.

The maximum number of packets in a DTIM period (N_ψ) is obtained from an equation formed by two summands: one corresponding to the DL/UL packets contained in the first TIM period ($N_{\psi,\text{DTIM}}$) and the other corresponding to those contained in the rest of TIM periods ($N_{\psi,\text{TIM}}$).

The value of N_ψ also depends on the $\omega \in \{\text{TIMO}, \text{non-TIMO}\}$ signalling mode chosen (TIM Offset or Non-TIM Offset, respectively) through a scale factor M_ω,

Table 3. List of parameters used in the IEEE 802.11ah capacity calculation

Variable	Description	Unit
T	DTIM Period	s
N_{TIM}	Number of TIM Groups	-
N_P	Number of Pages	-
$M\omega$	Signalling mode Scale factor	-
r	Network Data Rate	bps
$CW_{\min}$	Size of minimum contention window	slots
t_{slot}	Duration of an IEEE 802.11ah time slot	s
α_ψ	Traffic Pattern for DL/UL	-
β_ψ	Proportion of DL/UL traffic	-
T_{DTIM}	DTIM Beacon time $T_{DTIM} = \frac{L_{\text{DTIM}}}{r}$	s
T_{TIM}	TIM Beacon time $T_{DTIM} = \frac{L_{\text{TIM}}}{r}$	s
T_ψ	Duration of a packet transmission	s
T_{MC}	Duration of a multicast packet transmission $T_{MC} = \frac{L_{\text{DATA}}}{r} + T_{\text{DIFS}}$	s
T_{DL}	Duration of a DL packet transmission $T_{DL} = \frac{L_{\text{PS_POLL}}}{r} + T_{\text{SIFS}} + \frac{L_{\text{DATA}}}{r} + T_{\text{SIFS}} + $ $+ \frac{L_{\text{ACK}}}{r} + T_{\text{DIFS}}$	s
T_{UL}	Duration of an UL packet transmission $T_{UL} = \frac{L_{\text{RTS}}}{r} + T_{\text{SIFS}} + \frac{L_{\text{CTS}}}{r} + T_{\text{SIFS}} + $ $+ \frac{L_{\text{DATA}}}{r} + T_{\text{SIFS}} + \frac{L_{\text{ACK}}}{r} + T_{\text{DIFS}}$	s

that has been defined as $M_{\text{TIMO}} = N_{\text{TIM}} \cdot N_P$ for the TIM Offset case and as $M_{\text{non-TIMO}} = N_{\text{TIM}}$ for the Non-TIM Offset case.

$$N_\psi = N_{\psi,\text{DTIM}} + (M_\omega - 1) \cdot N_{\psi,\text{TIM}}$$

In the theoretical model, $N_{\psi,\text{DTIM}}$ and $N_{\psi,\text{TIM}}$ are calculated dividing the corresponding DL/UL segment time by the duration of a DL/UL packet transmission, and finally taking the integer part. Due to the allocation of a multicast transmission in the first TIM period, $N_{\psi,\text{DTIM}}$ is always lower than $N_{\psi,\text{TIM}}$. In order to obtain a conservative result, the time corresponding to a whole backoff $CW_{min} \cdot t_{\text{slot}}$ has also been included in the DL/UL segments.

$$N_{\psi,\text{DTIM}} = \left\lfloor \frac{\left(\frac{T}{M_\omega} - T_{\text{MC}} - T_{\text{DTIM}}\right) \cdot \beta_\psi - CW_{\min} \cdot t_{\text{slot}}}{T_\psi} \right\rfloor$$

$$N_{\psi,\text{TIM}} = \left\lfloor \frac{\left(\frac{T}{M_\omega} - T_{\text{TIM}}\right) \cdot \beta_\psi - CW_{\min} \cdot t_{\text{slot}}}{T_\psi} \right\rfloor$$

To obtain the maximum number of stations in an IEEE 802.11ah WLAN, we assume that a STA is only capable of receiving and transmitting one data packet per DTIM interval (two packets in total). Besides, the network traffic pattern

(α_ψ) has to be taken into account. This value, between 0 and 1, represents the proportion of stations that have data to receive from or to transmit to the AP. Once applied this proportion to N_ψ, the resulting minimum between both operators corresponds to the maximum number of supported stations by the network.

$$N_{\text{STA}} = min\left(\frac{N_{\text{DL}}}{\alpha_{\text{DL}}}, \frac{N_{\text{UL}}}{\alpha_{\text{UL}}}\right)$$

5 Performance Evaluation

We simulate a fully connected IEEE 802.11ah WLAN in MATLAB with different number of scheduled TIM STAs, where packets are delivered from the source to the destination in just one hop and there are no hidden terminals. We also assume ideal channel conditions, without communication errors, delays or capture effects. It is considered that the AP and all STAs have infinite buffers, although a packet could be dropped if it is retransmitted, inside the same segment, more than R_{max} times.

The IEEE 802.11ah defines four different power states for the STAs: receiving, idle, transmitting and sleeping. We consider that STAs are only capable of receiving and transmitting one data packet per DTIM interval. These intervals have been split into 8 TIMs (N_{TIM}) and also into 4 pages (N_P). We have not considered the presence of Non-TIM or Unscheduled STAs.

The parameters considered in the different simulations are presented in Table 4, where N_{DTIM} corresponds to the simulation duration, in number of DTIMs. The list of Modulation and Codification Schemes used, as well as their corresponding data rates, appears in Table 1.

Table 4. List of Simulation Parameters

T_{DTIM}	1.6 s	T_{SIFS}	16μs	L_{DATA}	100 bytes
N_{TIM}	8	T_{DIFS}	34μs	$L_{\text{PS-POLL}}$	14 bytes
N_{DTIM}	100	CW_{min}	16	L_{ACK}	14 bytes
N_P	4	CW_{max}	1024	L_{RTS}	20 bytes
T_{slot}	9 μs	R_{max}	7	L_{CTS}	14 bytes

We have considered three different scenarios (Table 5). At every DTIM, depending on the traffic pattern, only a percentage of the STAs will have a message from/to the AP; i.e., the AP generates a data message addressed to a percentage of randomly selected STAs (α_{DL}). Similarly, a fraction of randomly selected STAs generate a data message addressed to the AP (α_{UL}). From that information, the proportion of downlink/uplink traffic in our network, $\beta_{\text{DL}} = \frac{\alpha_{\text{DL}}}{\alpha_{\text{DL}}+\alpha_{\text{UL}}}$ and $\beta_{\text{UL}} = 1 - \beta_{\text{DL}}$ respectively, and the data generation rate per station (λ_ψ) can be determined.

Table 5. Traffic Patterns Definition

	% STAs		% Traffic		Data gen. rate / STA	
	α_{DL}	α_{UL}	β_{DL}	β_{UL}	λ_{DL}	λ_{UL}
Scenario A	15%	15%	50%	50%	75 bps	75 bps
Scenario B	15%	30%	33.3%	66.6%	75 bps	150 bps
Scenario C	15%	45%	25%	75%	75 bps	225 bps

In order to evaluate the capacity of IEEE 802.11ah WLANs using both the TIM Offset and Non TIM Offset signalling modes (see Subsection 3.1), we present several theoretical and simulated results for different traffic patterns by means of analyzing different figures of merit.

- Firstly, using the theoretical model presented in Section 4, we evaluate the maximum number of STAs that the network is capable of supporting (i.e., point at which the network is not able to deliver all generated packets) for the two signalling modes.
- Secondly, in order to provide more insights on the IEEE 802.11ah WLAN operation with a large number of STAs, the performance of the network in terms of PDR (Packet Delivery Ratio) and η (Network Efficiency) has been evaluated by simulation. In this manner, the influence of important effects like the different density of STAs within TIM Groups or packet collisions can be studied.
- Finally, the feasibility of both signalling modes in terms of energy consumption has also been studied.

5.1   Maximum Number of STAs

First of all, using the model presented in Section 4, we find the maximum number of STAs supported by an IEEE 802.11ah WLAN. The parameters considered are shown in Table 4.

Figure 8 shows the maximum number of supported STAs in an IEEE 802.11ah WLAN depending on the data rate. Results reflect some cases in which the maximum number of STAs supported by the network surpasses the 8191 STAs. Two traffic patterns (DL=15% UL=15% and DL=15% UL=30%) are able to support the 8191 stations. While the first one achieves this goal with r=2.4 Mbps, the second one does it with r=3.6 Mbps. Traffic pattern with DL=15% and UL=45% is only capable of supporting 6967 stations with r=4 Mbps. Besides, the differences between the Non-TIM and TIM Offset signalling modes are also shown. Results reflect a higher value in the maximum number of supported STAs for the Non-TIM Offset mode in all scenarios considered.

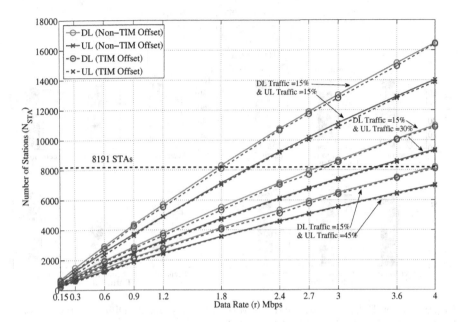

Fig. 8. Maximum number of supported STAs by an IEEE 802.11ah WLAN in function of different PHY Layer data rates, traffic patterns and signalling modes

5.2   Packet Delivery Ratio and Network Efficiency

In this section we evaluate the PDR and the Network Efficiency (η_ψ) in a specific scenario where the number of STAs is large. These two figures of merit are calculated as:

$$\text{PDR}_\psi = \left(\frac{\text{Packets Delivered}_\psi}{\text{Packets Generated}_\psi} \right)$$

$$\eta_\psi = \left(\frac{\text{Packets Delivered}_\psi}{\text{Channel Capacity}_\psi} \right)$$

with Channel Capacity$_\psi$, i.e. the maximum number of DL/UL data packets that the network could be able to deliver in a simulation, and is computed as:

$$\text{Channel Capacity}_\psi = N_\psi \cdot N_{\text{DTIM}}$$

We assume a data rate of $r = 1.8$ Mbps, and set the number of STAs to 7140 for Scenario A, 4770 for Scenario B and 3571 for Scenario C. It is worth noting that these values are the maximum number of STAs supported when the Non-TIM Offset signalling mode is used.

The results shown in Figure 9 reflect a high value of PDR for both modes: more than 90% in any studied case and always better when using the Non-TIM Offset. Nevertheless, the difference in terms of PDR, has a minimum value of

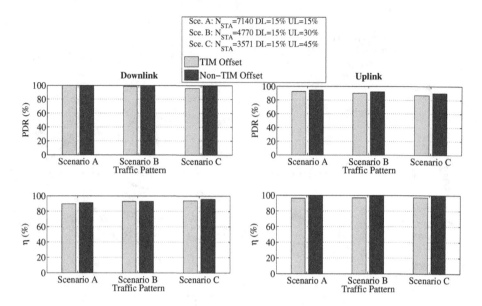

Fig. 9. Packet Delivery Ratio and Network Efficiency versus Different Transmission Rates and for TIM and Non-TIM Offset Schemes

1.9% and a maximum value of 3%. Therefore, these results reflect the efficient operation of an IEEE 802.11ah WLANs when the number of STAs is very high. As one can observe, the results of the Network Efficiency achieved are always above 89%.

5.3   Energy Consumption

Finally, the last figure of merit evaluated is the energy consumed by the STAs. The same scenarios and number of STAs as in previous case are considered.

The results are shown in Figure 10 and reflect one of the major issues that IEEE 802.11ah amendment aims for: the reduction of the energy consumption through the use of low power mechanisms, as described in Section 3. The energy consumed is divided in four states:

- **Receiving:** STAs in PSM which have not entered into a Long Sleeping Period must listen to all the DTIM beacons. If a STA is signalled in a DTIM beacon with downlink data or it has data to transmit, it will also listen to its corresponding TIM beacon. A STA receiving a data packet, a CTS or an ACK is also in receiving state. Overhearing of packets addressed to other STAs is also affecting the time a STA is in receiving mode.
- **Idle:** It is referred to Backoff periods and interframe spaces such as SIFS and DIFS.
- **Transmitting:** When STAs have to transmit certain frames both in the downlink (PS-Poll, ACK) and the uplink (RTS, DATA) communications.
- **Sleeping:** When STAs switch off their radio module.

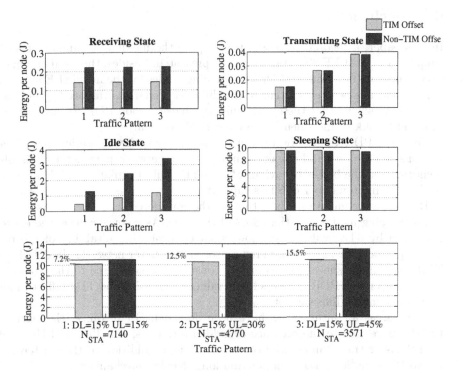

Fig. 10. Energy Consumed per Node (*Tx mode = 1400 mW; Rx mode = 900 mW; Id mode = 700 mW; Sl = 60 mW [14]*)

Although in both signalling modes, Non-TIM and TIM Offset, nodes remain the majority of the time in sleeping state, the major differences of consumption are reflected in the receiving and in the idle state. The Non-TIM Offset mechanism consumes more energy in these two states.

As presented in Section 3, the beacons used in Non-TIM mechanism are larger due to the increase of signalling data. Hence, STAs receive longer beacons, which results in that they have to remain more time in the receiving state. On the other hand, the TIM Offset mode divides each DL\UL time period in different page segments. This time division allows to distribute the STAs among more segments, compared to the Non-TIM signalling mode. Hence, STAs, that are only allowed to transmit inside their assigned segment, remain asleep during the rest of them. For that reason, their consumption in the idle state is reduced.

These two facts are reflected in the total energy consumed per STA shown in Figure 10. The TIM Offset mode achieves lower values of total energy consumed than the Non-TIM Offset mode. For the first traffic pattern simulated the reduction corresponds to 7.2%. For the second pattern, the gain achieved is 12.5%, while for the third one, the energy consumed is reduced in 15.5%.

6   Conclusions

In this paper, a theoretical model to compute the maximum number of STAs supported in an IEEE 802.11ah WLAN is presented. Besides, the comparison between the Non-TIM and TIM Offset signalling modes for the new IEEE 802.11ah amendment has been evaluated. In the different scenarios evaluated, simulation results have shown that these mechanisms achieve a good PDR for both Downlink and Uplink traffic when the number of STAs is large.

From the PDR values obtained in the simulations, the theoretical model can be considered as a valid upper bound for that network parameter. It is also demonstrated the better behaviour of Non-TIM Offset signalling mode in terms of the maximum number of STAs supported.

Besides, our simulations show that, in the considered scenarios, STAs remain in the sleeping mode more than 98% of the time. As a consequence, the energy consumed by STAs will be very low, what confirms the suitability of the presented protocol for battery-powered sensor and actuator networks. In detail, the TIM Offset mode shows a lower energy consumption compared to the Non-TIM one. However, the PDR achieves lower values when using the TIM Offset mode, with a maximum difference of 3%.

Some areas for future work have been detected. For instance, the study of the effects related to the presence of hidden terminals, non-TIM and Unscheduled STAs or traffic differentiation mechanisms, in addition to the existence of network association/disassociation and long sleeping mechanisms.

Acknowledgements. This work has been partially supported by the Spanish Government under projects TEC2012-32354 and IPT-2012-1028-120000 and by the Catalan Government (SGR2009#00617).

References

1. Ong, E.H., Kneckt, J., Alanen, O., Chang, Z., Huovinen, T., Nihtila, T.: IEEE 802.11ac: Enhancements for very high throughput WLANs. In: 2011 IEEE 22nd International Symposium on Personal Indoor and Mobile Radio Communications, PIMRC (2011)
2. Cordeiro, C., Akhmetov, D., Park, M.: IEEE 802.11ad: introduction and performance evaluation of the first multi-gbps wifi technology. In: Proceedings of the 2010 ACM International Workshop on mmWave Communications: From Circuits to Networks (2010)
3. Flores, A., Guerra, R., Knightly, E., Ecclesine, P., Pandey, S.: IEEE 802.11af: A Standard for TV White Space Spectrum Sharing. IEEE Communications Magazine (2013)
4. Aust, S., Prasad, R.V., Niemegeers, I.G.: IEEE 802.11ah: Advantages in Standards and Further Challenges for sub 1GHz Wi-Fi. In: IEEE International Conference on Communications, ICC (2012)
5. Zhou, G., Stankovic, J.A., Son, S.H.: Crowded spectrum in wireless sensor networks. In: Proceedings of Third Workshop on Embedded Networked Sensors, (EmNets) (2006)

6. HarborResearch, "Wireless Sensor Networks Report, 2013" (September 2013), http://harborresearch.com/product/wireless-personal-area-network-wpan-report/
7. IEEE, Proposed TGah Draft Amendment, https://mentor.ieee.org/802.11/dcn/13/11-13-0500-01-00ah-proposed-tgah-draft-amendment.docx
8. Aust, S., Ito, T.: Sub 1GHz Wireless LAN Propagation Path Loss Models for Urban Smart Grid Applications. In: International Conference on Computing, Networking and Communications (ICNC) (2012)
9. Hazmi, A., Rinne, J., Valkama, M.: Feasibility Study of IEEE 802.11ah Radio Technology for IoT and M2M Use Cases. In: IEEE Globecom Workshops (GC Wkshps) (2012)
10. Pratas, N.: First Impressions on the IEEE 802.11ah Standard Amendment, http://massm2m.wordpress.com/2013/01/25/first-impressions-on-the-ieee-802-11ah-standard-amendment/
11. Park, M.: IEEE P802.11 Wireless LANs: Specification Framework for TGah, http://www.ieee802.org/11/Reports/tgah_update.htm
12. IEEE Standard for Information technology–Telecommunications and information exchange between systems Local and metropolitan area networks–Specific requirements Part 11: Wireless LAN Medium Access Control (MAC) and Physical Layer (PHY) Specifications, IEEE Std 802.11-2012 (Revision of IEEE Std 802.11-2007), pp. 1–2793 (2012)
13. Yong, L., et al.: Active Polling, https://mentor.ieee.org/802.11/dcn/12/11-12-1101-01-00ah-active-polling.pptx
14. Orinoco wifi card datasheet, http://www.lema.lt/img/File/pdfs/Orinoco.pdf

Braess-Type Paradox
in Self-optimizing Wireless Networks

Ninoslav Marina*

University of Information Science and Technology "St. Paul the Apostle"
Ohrid, Macedonia
ninoslav.marina@gmail.com
http://www.uist.edu.mk

Abstract. The Braess's paradox, also called Braess paradox, in transportation networks states that adding extra capacity to a network, when moving entities with incomplete information selfishly choose their routes, can in some cases *reduce* the overall network performance. In this paper, we observe a similar phenomenon in wireless networks. More specifically, we consider a single-cell system with two different types of access points, one of them with a fixed rate and one of them with a variable rate, i.e., a rate that depends on the number of users connected to that access point. We observe that, under certain conditions, the intersystem connection between these two types of access points does not necessarily improve the overall system performance. In other words, after the interconnection, the individual rates of users as well as their sum rate might get worse. This is similar to the original Braess paradox where adding a new route does not necessarily improve the overall traffic throughput. We develop a general model that describes under which conditions and for which families of variable rate functions this paradox happens. *abstract environment.*

Keywords: Braess paradox, game theory, wireless networks, information theory, intersystem interconnection.

1 Introduction

In traffic networks, Braess paradox [1] states the following: Suppose a road network where cars go from a starting point to a destination through various routes. The delay incurred on each route depends on the number of users on that specific route. Hence, whether one street is preferable to another depends not only on the quality of the road, but also on the density of the flow. Under these conditions, one wishes to estimate the total time of travel at the equilibrium state. If each driver takes the path that looks most favorable for him, the resulting running times need not be minimal. It turns out that [1] an extension of the road network with a new road may cause a redistribution of the traffic that results in *longer* individual running times (which will not happen if a centralized approach

---

* The author is also with Princeton University, Princeton, NJ, USA.

M. Jonsson et al. (Eds.): MACOM 2013, LNCS 8310, pp. 156–167, 2013.

is used). This is known as the Braess paradox. Key reasons for Braess paradox are the greedy behavior of individual users and the lack of global information and coordination.

In the case of wireless networks, similar phenomena may occur if users are allowed to behave selfishly. The decentralized and selfish behavior of users have recently appeared in wireless networks as a solution to cope with the excess protocol signaling in highly mobile scenarios. Indeed, centralized approaches require feedback protocols and complex optimization, which turns out to be incompatible with the coherence time of mobile flexible networks, where terminals must decide on their own, on different resource allocation criteria [2, 3]. Decentralization appears also as a first step towards self-optimization networks, which are at the heart of future networks enabling to reduce monitoring and managing costs. Consequently, game theory turned out to be a natural mathematical framework to analyze the outcome of intelligent devices which make decisions based on their local information. As a result, many game theoretical approaches [4–6] have been proposed recently to let the users autonomously optimize their resources.

The general idea is to understand to what extent local optimization provides a global optimization of the network, which is difficult to achieve for scaling networks. Unfortunately, the distributed approaches often suffer from similar paradoxes as the original Baress's paradox, due to greedy and selfish behavior and lack of global information. In particular, in many cases and for a fixed number of devices, one can show that the equilibria states with respect to a given utility are Nash equilibria that are very often far from the Pareto optimal performance. Most solutions proposed in the literature are either to introduce some pricing mechanisms or to change the network architecture.

The goal of this paper is to show that the change in the network architecture, by interconnecting two different technologies (e.g., a technology with a fixed rate and a technology with a variable rate) in order to improve the network traffic has to be done carefully as it may worsen the utilities of different users and lead to a paradoxical situation in which network performs worse than the original one. Here we analyze to what extent the intersystem connection does not improve the network performance.

The rest of this paper is organized as follows: In Section 2, we describe three possible models of wireless networks, in which intersystem connection does not improve the downlink rate of the users. The general functions for the access points and conditions under which the Braess paradox happens is considered in Section 3. Finally, Section 4 concludes the paper.

2   System Models

We consider a single-cell network with two access points (APs). A number of mobile users (terminals) are connected (Fig. 1) to these two access points.

Assume that the first access point, denoted in Fig. 1 by AP_1, offers a fixed rate r_F and the rate offered by the second access point, denoted by AP_2, offers a per user rate that depends on the number of users connected to it $r_V(n)$. An

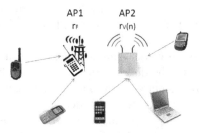

Fig. 1. A single cell with two different access points - one offering a fixed rate r_F and the other offering a rate that depends on the number n of users connected to it $r_V(n)$

example of such a system in practice could be a network that has two types of access points. The first type is an access point that uses an orthogonal multiple access scheme where each user gets a *fixed rate*. The second type is an access point that offers a *variable rate* depending on the number of users connected to it. An example of such an access point could be based on a system which offers a rate that depends on the number of users connected to it. In this system the more users are connected to it, the bigger the interference is. This leads to a lower signal-to-interference-and-noise ratio (SINR) and, therefore, to a lower rate. In the following text, we demonstrate that if one tries to improve the system by allowing an *intersystem connection*, i.e., connection between the two types of APs, this may lead to a performance that is worse than in the original system. In this section we present three different models of the variable rate access point that may lead to a Braess type of paradox in wireless networks.

2.1   Model 1

Assume that AP_2 in Fig. 1 offers the following per user rate as a function of the number of users connected to it

$$r_V(n) = \frac{r_0}{n+k}, \tag{1}$$

where n is the number of users connected to AP_2, $r_0 > 0$ is the total available rate and $k \geq 0$ is some fixed penalty that has to be paid when connected to AP_2. In other words, the total rate of the users connected to AP_2 is never equal to r_0. For instance, if we have ℓ users connected to AP_2, their sum rate will be $\ell r_0/(\ell + k)$ and is always smaller or equal to r_0.

At equilibrium, the total rate through both base stations will be the same and no user at that point will have an incentive to deviate to another access point. In that case if there are N users in the cell, we have

$$m \cdot \frac{r_0}{m+k} = (N-m)r_F, \tag{2}$$

where m is the number of users that are connected to AP_2 and the rest $(N-m)$ users are connected to AP_1. Solving (2) we get that in equilibrium:

$$m = \frac{N - k - \frac{r_0}{r_F}}{2} + \frac{\sqrt{(N - k - \frac{r_0}{r_F})^2 + 4kN}}{2}. \tag{3}$$

Note that each user connected to AP_1 has a rate of $r_1 = r_F$ and each user connected to AP_2 has a rate of $r_2 = r_0/(m + k)$. The number of users m that in equilibrium are connected to AP_2 as a function of r_0/r_f for different k is shown in Fig. 2. Note that for a given r_0/r_F, m is larger for larger k.

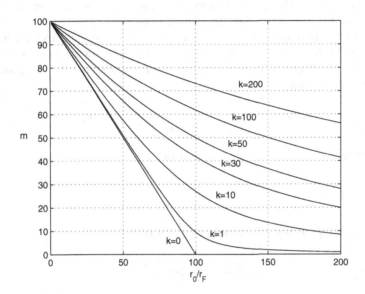

Fig. 2. The number of users m connected to AP_2 in equilibrium for the model (1), for $N = 100$ and various k

Assume now that the system provider decides to interconnect the two different technologies (and provide also terminals with the possibility to be connected on the two different technologies at the same time to split their packets), namely the access points with fixed and variable rates. With this new system, the network is no longer in equilibrium with the original rate flow since a new configuration has appeared. Users can, therefore, use a combination of the two links to send their packets. In particular, the individual rate of each user after interconnection is

$$\tilde{r}_2 = \frac{r_0}{N + k} > r_F.$$

Hence, all users would prefer to be connected to AP_2 since they get better rate than connecting to AP_1. In other words, no user has an incentive to change its access point, i.e., to connect back to AP_1.

Here, we consider two types of *paradox*. A paradox may happen with respect to the individual rate of users connected to AP_2, i.e., $\tilde{r}_2 \leq r_2$. For this model, this paradox happens since each user that was connected to AP_2 gets a smaller individual rate, since after interconnection

$$\tilde{r}_2 = \frac{r_0}{N+k} < \frac{r_0}{m+k} = r_2,$$

where m is given by (3). Note that the paradox happens if $1 \le m < N$. In the case $m = N$ noting changes after the interconnection, i.e., this case is trivial. In the case $m = 0$, the paradox does not happen, since all users previously connected to AP_1 get better rate by switching to AP_2.

More interesting paradox for the system designer is the paradox that happens with respect to the *total sum rate*. In other words, after interconnection is done, the total sum rate gets worse than before. The total sum rate in equilibrium, before interconnection is

$$r_T = (N-m)r_F + \frac{mr_0}{m+k} = 2(N-m)r_F.$$

Since after interconnection, the total sum rate is

$$\tilde{r}_T = \frac{Nr_0}{N+k},$$

the paradox happens with respect to the sum rate if

$$r_T = 2(N-m)r_F > \frac{Nr_0}{N+k} = \tilde{r}_T.$$

Example 1. Consider a system in which $N = 100$, $k = 10$, $r_0 = 120$ Mbps, and $r_F = 1$ Mbps. In this case, from (3), we get that $m = 20$. That means, in equilibrium, 20 users will be connected to AP_2 with a per user rate of $r_2 = r_0/(20+10) = 4$ Mbps, and the other 80 users will be connected to AP_1 with a fixed rate of $r_1 = r_F = 1$ Mbps. The sum rate is

$$r_T = (80 \cdot 1 + 20 \cdot 4) \text{ Mbps} = 160 \text{ Mbps}.$$

If an intersystem connection is applied, then all users will connect to AP_2 since in that case they get

$$\tilde{r}_2 = r_0/(N+k) = 120/110 \text{ Mbps} = 1.091 \text{ Mbps},$$

a rate larger than $r_F = 1$ Mbps. The paradox happens since the sum rate after interconnection is

$$\tilde{r}_T = N\tilde{r}_2 = \frac{Nr_0}{N+k} = 109.1 \text{ Mbps},$$

which is smaller than the sum rate $r_T = 160$ Mbps of the original system.

2.2   Model 2

Assume that AP_2 in Fig. 1 offers the following per user rate as a function of the number of connected users

$$r_V(n) = \frac{r_0}{n} + r_1. \tag{4}$$

Here n is the number of users connected to AP_2, $r_0 > 0$ is the total available rate and $r_1 \geq 0$ is some fixed rate that is guaranteed no matter how many users are connected to AP_2. In that case, since there are a total of N users in the cell, in equilibrium, if the access points are not interconnected we have the same amount of traffic through both access points, that is

$$m \cdot \left(\frac{r_0}{m} + r_1 \right) = (N - m)r_F. \tag{5}$$

Here, m is the number of users connected to AP_2, while the rest $(N - m)$ users are connected to AP_1. Solving (5) we get that at the equilibrium state:

$$m = \frac{Nr_F - r_0}{r_F + r_1} = \frac{N - r_0/r_F}{1 + r_1/r_F}. \tag{6}$$

Note that each user connected to AP_1 has a rate of $r_1 = r_F$ and each user connected to AP_2 has a rate of $r_2 = r_0/m + r_1$. The number of users m that in equilibrium are connected to AP_2 is shown in Fig. 3 for different r_1/r_F. Note that for a given r_0/r_F, m is larger for larger r_1/r_F.

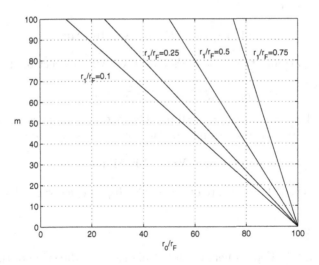

Fig. 3. The number of users m connected to AP_2 in equilibrium for the model (4), for $N = 100$ and various ratios r_1/r_0

Assume now that the system provider decides to interconnect the two access points with fixed and variable rates. In that case, if we assume that

$$\tilde{r}_2 = r_0/N + r_1 > r_F,$$

then all users prefer to be connected to AP_2 since they get a better rate if they are connected to AP_2 than to AP_1. Here again, no user has an incentive to connect to AP_1. In this case, the paradox happens since each user that was connected to AP_2 gets a smaller individual rate than in the previous case, since

$$\tilde{r}_2 = \frac{r_0}{N} + r_1 < \frac{r_0}{m} + r_1 = r_2,$$

where m is given by (6). The paradox happens if $1 \leq m < N$.

The sum rate before interconnection is

$$r_T = 2r_F(N - m) = 2m(r_0/m + r_1,)$$

while after interconnection it is

$$\tilde{r}_T = N(r_0/N + r_1).$$

Hence, the paradox happens with respect to the sum rate if

$$r_T = 2r_F(N - m) > r_0 + Nr_1 = \tilde{r}_T.$$

Example 2. Consider a system in which $N = 100$, $r_0 = 80$, $r_1 = 0.25$ Mbps, and $r_F = 1$ Mbps. In that case from (6), we get $m = 16$. This means that, in equilibrium, 16 users will be connected to AP_2 with a rate of $r_2 = 5.25$ Mbps and the other 84 users will be connected to AP_1 with a rate of $r_1 = r_F = 1$ Mbps. The sum rate is

$$r_T = (84 \cdot 1 + 16 \cdot 5.25) \text{ Mbps} = 168 \text{ Mbps}.$$

If an intersystem connection is done then all users will connect to AP_2, since in that case they get

$$\tilde{r}_2 = r_0/N + r_1 = 1.05 \text{ Mbps},$$

a rate that is larger than $r_F = 1$ Mbps. The paradox happens since $\tilde{r}_2 < r_2$ although the interconnection is applied. Moreover, the sum rate is

$$\tilde{r}_T = r_0 + Nr_1 = 105 \text{ Mbps}.$$

This is smaller than the sum rate of $r_T = 168$ Mbps in the original system.

2.3   Model 3

Assume that AP_2 in Fig. 1 offers the following rate as a function of the number of users connected to it

$$r_V(n) = \log_2\left(1 + \frac{P}{\sigma^2 + (n-1)P}\right), \tag{7}$$

where n is the number of users connected to AP_2, $P > 0$ is the received power of a given user, and σ^2 is the variance of the additive Gaussian noise. This model is used for CDMA based systems where if in the uplink, n users are connected to the access point. Here we assume an AWGN channel, however the extension to fading channels is straightforward. Since power equalization is applied, each user has the same received signal-to-interference-and-noise (SINR) ratio given by $P/(\sigma^2 + (n-1)P)$. In that case, since there are N users in the cell, we have that, in equilibrium,

$$m \cdot \log_2 \left(1 + \frac{P}{\sigma^2 + (m-1)P}\right) = (N-m)r_F. \tag{8}$$

Here again, m is the number of users connected to AP_2 and the rest $N - m$ is connected to AP_1. Equation (8) is a transcendental equation and can be solved only numerically. Fig. 4 depicts the number of users m that in equilibrium are connected to AP_2 as a function of r_F for different SNRs P/σ^2. Note that for low SNR= P/σ^2, using the approximation $\log_2(1 + x) \approx x/\ln 2$, (8) simplifies to

$$\frac{mP}{\sigma^2 + (m-1)P} \cdot \frac{1}{\ln 2} = (N-m)r_F.$$

For high SNR= P/σ^2, (8) simplifies to

$$m \cdot \log_2 \left(1 + \frac{1}{m-1}\right) = (N-m)r_F,$$

and does not depend on P/σ^2. Assuming that the solution m is large enough, using again $\log_2(1 + x) \approx x/\ln 2$ we get

$$\frac{m}{m-1} = (N-m)r_F \cdot \ln 2$$

Assume now that the system provider decides to interconnect the two access points with fixed and variable rates. In that case, if we assume that

$$\tilde{r}_2 = \log_2 \left(1 + \frac{P}{\sigma^2 + (N-1)P}\right) > r_F,$$

then all users prefer to connect to AP_2 since they get better rate if all are connected to AP_2 than to AP_1. The system is in equilibrium since no user wants to connect back to AP_1. The paradox happens since each user that was connected to AP_2 gets a smaller individual rate than in the previous case, since

$$\tilde{r}_2 = \log_2 \left(1 + \frac{P}{\sigma^2 + (N-1)P}\right)$$
$$< \log_2 \left(1 + \frac{P}{\sigma^2 + (m-1)P}\right) = r_2,$$

where m is given by the solution of (8). Note that the paradox happens only if $0 \le m < N$.

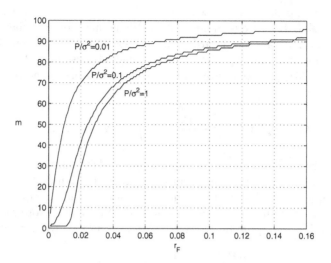

Fig. 4. The number of users m connected to AP_2 in equilibrium for the model (7), for $N = 100$ and various SNRs P/σ^2

The sum rate before interconnection is

$$r_T = 2r_F(N - m),$$

while after interconnection it is

$$\tilde{r}_T = N \log_2 \left(1 + \frac{P}{\sigma^2 + (N-1)P}\right) = N\tilde{r}_2.$$

The paradox happens for the sum rate if

$$r_T = 2r_F(N - m)$$
$$> N \log_2 \left(1 + \frac{P}{\sigma^2 + (N-1)P}\right) = \tilde{r}_T.$$

Example 3. Consider a system in which $N = 100$, $P/\sigma^2 = 0.1$, and $r_F = 12.5$ kbps. In that case solving numerically (8), we get that in equilibrium $m = 21$. This means that, in equilibrium, 21 users will be connected to AP_2 with a rate of $r_2 = 47.3$ kbps and the other 79 users will be connected to AP_1 with a fixed rate of $r_1 = r_F = 12.5$ kbps. The sum rate is $r_T \approx 1.981$ Mbps. By interconnecting the two access points, all users will connect to AP_2 since in that case they get

$$\tilde{r}_2 = \log_2 \left(1 + \frac{P}{\sigma^2 + (N-1)P}\right) \approx 13.18 \text{ kbps},$$

a rate larger than $r_F = 12.5$ kbps. The paradox happens since $\tilde{r}_2 < r_2$ although the interconnection is done. Moreover, the sum rate is $\tilde{r}_T = 1.318$ Mbps and it is smaller than the sum rate of $r_T = 1.981$ Mbps in the previous case.

3 General Model

In this section, we describe in general for what type of functions $r_V(n)$ for AP_2 in Fig. 1, the paradox happens, by interconnecting the fixed and variable rate access points. We describe the conditions under which paradox happens for both the individual and the sum rate of users.

From the previous analysis we see that $r_V(n)$ has to be a decreasing function of n, namely,

$$r_V : \mathbb{N} \mapsto \mathbb{R}_+$$
$$r_V(n+1) - r_V(n) \leq 0.$$

The paradox happens only if a certain number of users in the original system are connected to both access points. Mathematically, this means that the solution of

$$m \cdot r_V(m) = (N - m)r_F \tag{9}$$

gives a number between 1 and $N - 1$. In order to have an equilibrium in the new system and the paradox to happen for the individual rate, the following has to be satisfied

$$r_F < r_V(N) = \tilde{r}_2.$$

Then, the paradox with respect to the individual rate of users connected to the access point with variable rate happens since $r_V(N) < r_V(m)$. An example of such a variable rate function $r_V(n)$ and a fixed rate r_F is shown in Fig. 5.

It is of greater interest to consider under which conditions the paradox happens with respect to the sum rate. From the previous analysis we see that it happens if the following condition is satisfied

$$N \cdot r_V(N) < 2(N - m)r_F = 2m \cdot r_V(m)$$

where m is an integer solution to (9) and $1 \leq m < N$.

In summary, we give the conditions that the function $r_V(n)$ has to satisfy such that the performance gets worse after the interconnection of the two access points. Again we present the conditions for the two types of paradox.

In the first case the following conditions have to be satisfied such that the paradox happens with respect to the individual rate:

(1) $r_V(n+1) \leq r_V(n)$, for $1 \leq n < N$,
(2) $\tilde{r}_2 = r_V(N) > r_F$, and
(3) the solution m of $m \cdot r_V(m) = (N - m)r_F$ has to satisfy $1 \leq m < N$.

Note that the paradox follows directly from (1), since $r_2 = r_V(m) > \tilde{r}_2$.

In the second case the following conditions have to be satisfied such that the paradox happens with respect to the sum rate:

(1) $r_V(n+1) \leq r_V(n)$, for $1 \leq n < N$,
(2) $\tilde{r}_2 = r_V(N) > r_F$,
(3) the solution m of $m \cdot r_V(m) = (N - m)r_F$ has to satisfy $1 \leq m < N$, and
(4) $N \cdot r_V(N) < 2(N - m)r_F = 2m \cdot r_V(m)$.

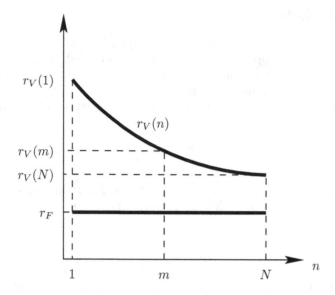

Fig. 5. An example of a network with $r_V(n)$ in which a Braess-type paradox happens

4   Conclusions

Based on the observation of Braess paradox in transportation, we investigate the impacts of greedy behaviors and lack of global information. From our analysis, we conclude that interconnecting two different access points (with the ability of the users to use these two access points at the same time, i.e., cross-system diversity) may not always improve the performance of the network. Under certain conditions, we showed that the rate of users connected to the access point with variable rate decreases after interconnection. We also identified the conditions under which the sum rate does not improve if a system interconnection is performed. Our analysis is based on game theory, and it suggests what are the conditions under which the Braess-type paradox happens. A future work will consist in designing a mechanism that encourages user cooperation in order to avoid the paradox under any scenario. In this case, users may also not cooperate, however, the design of a certain utility will have the same effect as in the case of cooperation.

References

1. Braess, D.: Uber ein paradoxen der werkehrsplannug. Unternehmenforschung 12, 256–268 (1968)
2. Mitola III, J.: Cognitive Radio: An Integrated Agent Architecture for Software Defined Radio, Ph.D. dissertation, Royal Institute of Technology (KTH) Stockholm, Sweden, May 8 (2000)

3. Haykin, S.: Cognitive radio: Brain empowered wireless communication. Journal on Selected Areas in Communications 23(2), 201–220 (2005)
4. Meshkati, F., Poor, H.V., Schwartz, S.C., Mandayam, N.: An energy-efficient approach to power control and receiver design in wireless data networks. IEEE Trans. on Communications 53(11), 1885–1894 (2005)
5. Meshkati, F., Poor, H.V., Schwartz, S.C.: Energy-efficient resource allocation in wireless networks: An overview of game theoretic approaches. IEEE Signal Process. Magazine 24(3), 58–68 (2007)
6. Bonneau, N., Debbah, M., Altman, E., Hjørungnes, A.: Non-atomic games for multi-user systems. IEEE Journal on Selected Areas in Communications 26(7), 1047–1058 (2008)
7. Altman, E., Kambley, V., Kamedaz, H.: A Braess type paradox in power control over interference channels. In: Proc. 6th Int. Symp. on Modeling and Optimization in Mobile, Ad Hoc, and Wireless Networks (WiOPT 2008), Berlin, pp. 555–559 (April 2008)
8. Saraydar, C., Mandayam, N.B., Goodman, D.J.: Efficient power control via pricing in wireless data networks. IEEE Trans. on Communications 50(2), 291–303 (2002)
9. Korilis, Y.A., Lazar, A.A., Orda, A.: Architecting noncooperative networks. IEEE J. on Selected Areas in Communications 13, 1241–1251 (1995)
10. Bean, N.: Secrets of network success. Physics World, 30–33 (February 1996)
11. Maugeri, A.: Variational and quasi-variational inequalities in network flow models: Recent developments in theory and algorithms. In: Giannessi, F., Maugeri, A. (eds.) Variational Inequalities and Network Equilibrium Problems, pp. 195–211. Plenum, New York (1995)
12. Bean, N.G., Taylor, P.G.: Can Braess's paradox occur in loss networks? University of Adelaide (November 1994), can be found online at http://citeseerx.ist.psu.edu/viewdoc/summary?doi=10.1.1.44.639
13. Calvert, B., Keady, G.: Braess's paradox and power-law nonlinearities in networks II. In: Lakshmanthan, V. (ed.), Proceedings of the First World Congress of Nonlinear Analysts, WC 528, Florida, August 1992, vol. III, pp. 2223–2230. W. de Gruyter (1996)
14. Han, Z., Liu, K.J.R.: Resource Allocation for Wireless Networks: Basics, Techniques, and Applications. Cambridge University Press, New York (2008)
15. Daganzo, C.: Two paradoxes of traffic flow on networks with physical queues. In: Symposium Ingeneria de los Transportes, Madrid, pp. 55–62 (May 1996)
16. Marinoff, L.: How Braess' paradox solves Newcomb's problem: Not! International Studies in the Philosophy of Science 10, 217–237 (1996)

Stationary Equilibrium Strategies
for Bandwidth Scanning

Andrey Garnaev[1] and Wade Trappe[2]

[1] Saint Petersburg State University, St. Petersburg, Russia
garnaev@yahoo.com
[2] WINLAB, Rutgers University, North Brunswick, USA
trappe@winlab.rutgers.edu

Abstract. In this paper we investigate the problem of designing a spectrum multi-step scanning strategy to detect an intelligent Invader who wants to utilize spectrum undetected for his/her unapproved purposes. To deal with this problem, we model it as a two stage game, along with specifying an algorithm of scanning the spectrum and evaluating the stationary bandwidth of spectrum to scan. The game is solved explicitly and reveal interesting properties. In particular, we have found a discontinuous dependence of the equilibrium strategies on the network parameters, fine and the Invader's intention for illegal activity, which can lead even to multi-equilibrium situation. To select a proper equilibrium strategy the best response strategy algorithm can be applied which in the multi-equilibria case always converges for a finite number of iteration, meanwhile for mono-equilibria situation it does not converge, circling around the equilibrium. Also, we have shown that the detection probability and payoffs in some situation can be very sensible to fine and the Invader's intention to intrude into the network longer, what yields that the network provider has to carefully make a value judgement of fine and estimation of the Intruder's intentions.

Keywords: Spectrum scanning, Intruder's detection, Repeating game, Stationary strategy, Nash equilibrium, Multi-equilibrium, Convergence of the best response strategy algorithm.

1 Introduction

Over the last few decades, the increasing demand for wireless communications has motivated the exploration for more efficient usage of spectral resources ([1, 2]). In particular, it has been noticed that there are large portions of spectrum that are severely under-utilized [3]. Recently, cognitive radio technologies (CR) have been proposed as a means to intelligently use such spectrum opportunities by sensing the radio environment and exploiting available spectrum holes for secondary usage[4]. In CR systems, secondary users are allowed to "borrow (or lease)" the usage of spectrum from primary users (licensed users), as long as they do not hinder the proper operation of the primary users' communications. Unfortunately, as we move to make CR technologies commercial, which

M. Jonsson et al. (Eds.): MACOM 2013, LNCS 8310, pp. 168–183, 2013.

will allow secondary users to access spectrum owned by primary users, we will face the inevitable risk that adversaries will be tempted to use CR technology for illicit and selfish purposes [5]. If we imagine an unauthorized user (Invader) attempting to sneak usage of spectrum without obeying proper regulations or leasing the usage of the spectrum, the result will be that both legitimate secondary users and primary users will face unexpected interference, resulting in significant performance degradation across the system.

The challenge of enforcing the proper usage of spectrum requires the notion of a "spectrum policing agent", whose primary job is to ensure the proper usage of spectrum and identify anomalous activities occurring within the spectrum[5]. As a starting point to being able to police the usage of spectrum, we must have the ability to scan spectrum and effectively identify anomalous activities. Towards this objective, there are several research efforts in signal processing techniques that can be applied to the spectrum scanning problem. For example, in [6, 7], the authors presented methods for detecting a desired signal contained within interference. Similarly, detection of unknown signals in noise without prior knowledge of authorized users was studied in [8, 9]. As another example, in [5], the authors proposed a method to detect anomalous transmission by making use of radio propagation characteristics. In [10] authors investigated what impact on spectrum scanning can have information about the over-arching application that a spectrum thief might try to run.

However, these works tend to not examine the important "interplay" between the two participants inherent in the problem– the Invader, who is smart and will attempt to use the spectrum in a manner to minimize the chance of being detected and fined, while also striving to maximize the benefit he/she receives from illicit usage of this spectrum; and the Scanner, who must be smart and employ a strategy that strategically maximizes the chance of detecting and fining the smart Invader, with minimal cost. To deal with this problem a one-step scanning model was suggested in [11]. This paper generalizes one short scanning model [11] to multi-step scanning and focus on finding explicitly the optimal stationary scanning strategy by selecting the scanning (and, similarly, the invading) bandwidth that should be employed in spectrum scanning. Note that game-theoretical approach has been widely employed in dealing with different problems in networks, for example, in intrusion detection [12–15]. Also, [16] supplies a structured and comprehensive survey of the research contributions that analyze and solve security and privacy problems in computer networks by game-theoretic approaches.

The organization of this paper is as follows: in Section 2, we first define the problem by formulating a two-stage game. In the first stage, each player determines the optimal algorithm of scanning and intrusion for fixed size of bandwidth which allows to obtain detection probability (Section 3). In the second stage of the game, based on this detection probability the rivals look for the optimal size of bandwidth for a multi-step scanning by taking into account their technical parameters, as well as those of the network and also their utilities (Section 4).

In Section 5 numerical illustrations and discussions are supplied. Finally, in Section 6 and 7 conclusions the proofs of the results are offered to close the paper.

2   Formulation of the Scanning Problem as a Two-Stage Game

In this section we set up our problem formulation. Our formulation of the spectrum scanning problem involves two players: the Scanner and the Invader. The Scanner, who is always present in the system, scans a part of the band of frequencies that are to be monitored, in order to prevent illegal usage by a potential Invader of the primary (Scanner) network's ownership of this band. We assume that the amount of bandwidth that needs to be scanned is much larger than is possible using a single scan by the Scanner. So, the Scanner faces a dilemma: the more bandwidth that is scanned, the higher the probability of detecting the Invader but it needs bigger scanning becomes more expensive to employ.

We assume that if the Scanner scans a particular frequency band B_S and the Invader uses the band B_I then the invasion will be detected with certainty if $B_S \cap B_I \neq \emptyset$, and it will not be detected otherwise. In our future work we will extend our model for other interesting scenarios of detection, such as: (a) detection takes place with certainty if measure of bands intersection $B_S \cap B_I$ is greater or equal some threshold value, and (b) detection probability is an increasing function of measure of this intersection. Without loss of generality we can assume that the size of the protected frequency band is normalized to 1. The Invader wants to use spectrum undetected for some illicit purpose. The reward for the Invader is related to the width of the frequency band he uses if he is undetected. If he is detected he will be fined.

2.1   Formulation of the Problem in the First Stage of the Game

In the first step of the game the Scanner selects the band $B_S = [t_S, t_S + x] \subseteq [0, 1]$ with a fixed upper bound of frequency width x to scan i.e. $t_S \leq 1 - x$. The Invader selects the band $B_I = [t_I, t_I + y] \subseteq [0, 1]$ with a fixed upper bound frequency width y to intrude, i.e. $t_I \leq 1 - y$. So, B_S and B_I are pure strategies for the Scanner and the Invader. The Scanner's payoff $v(B_S, B_I)$ is 1 if the Invader is detected (i.e. $B_S \cap B_I \neq \emptyset$) and his payoff is zero otherwise. The goal of the Scanner is to maximize his payoff meanwhile the Invader wants to minimize it. So, the Scanner and the Invader play a zero-sum game. The saddle point [17] of the game is a couple of strategies (B_{S*}, B_{I*}) such that

$$v(B_S, B_{I*}) \leq v := v(B_{S*}, B_{I*}) \leq v(B_{S*}, B_I) \text{ for any } (B_S, B_I),$$

where v is the value of the game. The game does not have a saddle point in the pure strategy if $x + y < 1$. To find the saddle point we have to extend the game by mixed strategies, where we assign a probability distribution over pure strategies. Then instead of the payoff v we have its expected value. The game has a saddle point when we consider mixed strategies. Let $P(x, y)$ be the value of the game. Then $P(x, y)$ is the maximal probability of detecting the Invader under worst conditions.

2.2   Payoffs and Strategies for One-Step Scanning on the Second Stage of the Game

A strategy for the Scanner is to scan a width of frequency of size $x \in [a, b]$, and a strategy for the Invader is to employ a width of frequency of size $y \in [a, c]$, where $c \leq b < 1/2$. So, we assume that the Invader's technical characteristics (e.g. its radio's capabilities) are not better than the Scanner's ones.

If the Scanner and the Invader use the strategies x and y, then the payoff to the Invader is the expected award (which is a function $U(y)$ of bandwidth y illegally used by the Invader) minus intrusion expenses (which is a function $C_I(y)$ of bandwidth y) and expected fine F to pay, i.e.

$$v_I(x, y) = (1 - P(x, y))U(y) - FP(x, y) - C_I(y).$$

The Scanner wants to detect intrusion taking into account scanning expenses and the damage caused by the illegal use of the bandwidth. For detection he is rewarded by a fine F imposed on the Invader. Thus, the payoff to the Scanner is difference between the expected reward for detection, and damage from intrusion into the bandwidth (which is a function $U(y)$ of bandwidth y illegally used by the Invader) with the scanning expenses (which is a function $C_S(x)$ of scanned bandwidth x),

$$v_S(x, y) = FP(x, y) - U(y)(1 - P(x, y)) - C_S(x).$$

Note that introducing transmission cost is common for CDMA [18, 19] and ALOHA networks ([20, 21]).

2.3   Payoffs and Stationary Strategies for Multi-step Scanning on the Second Stage of the Game

We assume that the rivals play the considered game repeatedly at time slot $t = 0, 1, \dots$ Let $\delta \in [0, 1]$ stand for a discount factor which is applied to losses at future stages of the game. The discount factor can be interpreted as capturing the Invader's desire to stay 'in the network longer'. Of course, while there is a threat of illegal intrusion in the network the Scanner has to be on, and so as to not make the result bulky, we use a common discount factor for the Invader and the Scanner. The discount factor equal to zero means that the network's intrusion as well as scanning efforts last just for one time slot (this case was detailed studied in [11]). In this paper we investigate how the Intruder's intent to be present longer impact the scanning strategy to detect him.

A stationary strategy for the Scanner is $x \in [a, b]$ which denotes a width, chosen once and used for all time. A stationary strategy for the Invader is $y \in [a, c]$ which denotes a width, chosen once and used for all time.

The game is played in stationary strategies as follows On the first step of the game the Scanner and the Invader spend scanning and intrusion expenses $C_S(x)$ and $C_I(y)$ independently on the result. With probability $P(x,y)$ the Invader is detected and fined by F and the Scanner is awarded by F. Then the game is over. With probability $1-P(x,y)$ the Invader is not detected. The Scanner faces damage $U(y)$ and the Invader gains reward $U(y)$, and the game moves to the next step with all the payments discounted by δ. Thus, the discounted expected payoff to the Scanner $v_S^\delta(x,y)$ is given as follows:

$$
\begin{aligned}
v_S^\delta(x,y) &= -C_S(x) + P(x,y)F \\
&\quad + (1-P(x,y))\Big(-U(y)+ \\
&\quad + \delta\Big(-C_S(x) + P(x,y)F + (1-P(x,y))\Big(-U(y)+\ldots \\
&= -C_S(x)\sum_{i=0}^\infty \delta^i(1-P(x,y))^i + P(x,y)F\sum_{i=0}^\infty \delta^i(1-P(x,y))^i \\
&\quad - (1-P(x,y))U(y)\sum_{i=0}^\infty \delta^i(1-P(x,y))^i \\
&= \sum_{i=0}^\infty \delta^i(1-P(x,y))^i v_S(x,y) = \frac{v_S(x,y)}{1-\delta(1-P(x,y))}.
\end{aligned}
\tag{1}
$$

Similarly, the discounted expected payoff to the Invader $v_I^\delta(x,y)$ are given by:

$$
v_I^\delta(x,y) = \sum_{i=0}^\infty \delta^i(1-P(x,y))^i v_I(x,y) = \frac{v_I(x,y)}{1-\delta(1-P(x,y))}.
\tag{2}
$$

We look for a stationary Nash equilibrium, i.e. a couple of the strategies (x_*,y_*) such that for any (x,y) the following inequalities hold:

$$
v_S^\delta(x,y_*) \le v_S^\delta(x_*,y_*) \text{ and } v_I^\delta(x_*,y) \le v_I^\delta(x_*,y_*).
$$

3   Equilibrium Strategies for the First Stage of the Game

In the following theorem we gives the equilibrium strategies for the first step, so for fixed bound width of the rivals, and show that they have tiling structure [22].

Theorem 1. *[11] In the first stage of the game with fixed width to scan x and to invade y, the rivals employ uniform tiling behavior. Namely,*
(a) Let $1-(x+y)M \le y$ with $M = \lfloor 1/(x+y)\rfloor$, where $\lfloor \xi \rfloor$ is the greatest integer less or equal to ξ. Then the Scanner and the Invader will, with equal probability $1/M$, employ a band of the set A_{-S} and A_{-I} correspondingly.

(b) Let $1 - (x + y)M > y$. Then the Scanner and the Invader will, with equal probability $1/(M + 1)$, employ a band of the set A_{+S} and A_{+I} correspondingly, where

$$A_{-S} = \{[k(x + y) - x, k(x + y)], k = 1, ..., M\},$$

$$A_{-I} = \{[k(x + y) - y - \epsilon(M + 1 - k), k(x + y) - \epsilon(M - k)], k = 1, ..., M\}, \quad 0 < \epsilon < \frac{x}{M},$$

$$A_{+S} = A_{-S} \cup [1 - x, 1],$$

$$A_{+I} = \{[(k - 1)(x + y + \epsilon), (k - 1)(x + y + \epsilon) + y],$$

$$k = 1, ..., M\} \cup [1 - y, 1], \quad 0 < \epsilon < \frac{1 - y - M(x + y)}{M - 1}.$$

The value of the game (detection probability) $P(x, y)$ is given as follows:

$$P(x, y) = \begin{cases} 1/M, & 1 - (x + y)M \le y, \\ 1/(M + 1), & 1 - (x + y)M > y. \end{cases}$$

4   Stationary Equilibrium Strategy for the Multi-step Scanning on the Second Stage of the Game

In this section, which is split into three subsections, we find explicitly the stationary equilibrium strategies for multi-step scanning in the second stage of the game. First in Subsection 4.1 we linearize our model to get an explicit solution, then in Subsection 4.2 the best response stationary strategies are given, and they are employed in Subsection 4.3 to construct stationary equilibrium strategies.

4.1   Linearized Model

In order to get an insight into the problem, we consider a situation where the detection probability $P(x, y)$ for $x \in [a, b], y \in [a, c]$ is approximated by a linear function as follows: $P(x, y) = x + y$.

We assume that the scanning and intrusion cost as well as the rival's utilities are linear in the bandwidth involved, i.e. $C_S(x) = C_S x$, $C_I(y) = C_I y$, $U(y) = Uy$, with $C_S, C_I, U > 0$. Then the payoffs to the Invader and the Scanner, if they use strategies $x \in [a, b]$ and $y \in [a, c]$ respectively, become:

(i) For one-step scanning:

$$v_I(x, y) = U(1 - x - y)y - F(x + y) - C_I y,$$

$$v_S(x, y) = F(x + y) - Uy(1 - x - y) - C_S x.$$

(ii) For multi-step scanning in stationary strategies:

$$v_I^\delta(x, y) = \frac{U(1 - x - y)y - F(x + y) - C_I y}{1 - \delta(1 - x - y)},$$

$$v_S^\delta(x, y) = \frac{F(x + y) - Uy(1 - x - y) - C_S x}{1 - \delta(1 - x - y)}.$$

Note that linearized payoffs have found extensive usage for a wide array of problems in wireless networks [20, 23–26]. Of course, such approach simplifies the original problem and only gives an approximated solution. Meanwhile it can also be very useful: sometimes it allows one to obtain a solution explicitly, and allows one to look inside of the structure of the solution as well as the correlation between parameters of the system.

4.2 Best Response Stationary Strategies

In this section we give best response strategies for the Scanner and the Invader, i.e. such strategies that $BR_S^\delta(y) = \arg\max_x v_S^\delta(x, y)$ and $BR_I^\delta(x) = \arg\max_y v_I^\delta(x, y)$.

Theorem 2. *In the second multi-step stage of the considered game the Scanner the best response strategies $BR_S^\delta(y)$ are given as follows:*

$$BR_S^\delta(y) = \begin{cases} a, & (U - \delta C_S)y/(1 - \delta) < C_S - F, \\ \text{any from } [a, b], & (U - \delta C_S)y/(1 - \delta) = C_S - F, \\ b, & (U - \delta C_S)y/(1 - \delta) > C_S - F, \end{cases} \tag{3}$$

Thus, the Scanner's best response strategy is piecewise constant function with at most one jump depending on whether D_δ does not or does belong to $[a, c]$ with

$$D_\delta = (1 - \delta)\frac{C_S - F}{U - \delta C_S}.$$

The Invader best response strategies $BR_I^\delta(x)$ are given as follows:

$$BR_I^\delta(x) = \begin{cases} c, & \delta c^2 + 2H_1(x)c < H_2(x)/U, \\ L(x), & \delta a^2 + 2H_1(x)a < H_2(x)/U < \delta c^2 + 2H_1(x)c, \\ a, & H_2(x)/U < \delta a^2 + 2H_1(x)a \end{cases} \tag{4}$$

with

$$\begin{aligned} H_1(x) &= 1 - \delta + \delta x, \\ H_2(x) &= -U\delta x^2 + ((2\delta - 1)U - C_I \delta)x + (1 - \delta)(U - F - C_I), \end{aligned} \tag{5}$$

$$L(x) = \frac{\delta - \delta x - 1}{\delta} + \frac{\sqrt{\delta(U - \delta C_I)x + (1 - \delta)(U - \delta(F + C_I))}}{\delta\sqrt{U}}. \tag{6}$$

Note that function $L(x)$ in the Scanner's best response strategy (4) has the following properties:

(a) $L(x)$ is well defined only if either

$$U \geq (F + C_I)\delta \text{ for any } x \in [a, b]$$

or

$$(F + C_I)\delta > U \geq C_I \delta \text{ for } x \geq \frac{1 - \delta}{\delta}\frac{(F + C_I)\delta - U}{U - C_I \delta}.$$

The function $L(x)$ is concave for such x, it gets unique maximum at

$$x_* = \frac{U - \delta C_I}{4U\delta} + \frac{1 - \delta}{\delta} \frac{(F + C_I)\delta - U}{U - C_I\delta}. \tag{7}$$

Thus, depending on location of x_*, the function $L(x)$ is either decreasing, or increasing in $[a, b]$ or it has unique interior maximum in (a, b).

4.3   Stationary Equilibrium Strategies

The stationary equilibrium can be found as a couple of strategies (x, y) which are the best response to each other, i.e. as a solution of the equations: $x = \mathrm{BR}_S^\delta(y)$ and $y = \mathrm{BR}_I^\delta(x)$. The following theorem shows that the best response strategy curves have at least one and at most three intersections and it supplies all the stationary Nash equilibrium strategies.

Theorem 3. *The considered game in the second multi-step scanning stage has at least one and at most three stationary Nash equilibrium. All possible equilibrium are listed below.*
  The first two cases deal with situation the Scanner's best response strategy has to be constant in $[a, c]$ (so $D_\delta \notin [a, b]$).
  (i_1) If

$$C_S > \max\left\{F, \frac{U}{\delta}\right\} \ or \ \left(\frac{U}{\delta} > C_S > F, D_\delta > c\right) \ or \ \left(F > C_S > \frac{U}{\delta}, D_\delta < a\right) \tag{8}$$

then $BR_S^\delta(y) \equiv a$ and the unique equilibrium is $(a, BR_I^\delta(a))$.
  (i_2) If

$$\min\left\{F, \frac{U}{\delta}\right\} > C_S \ or \ \left(\frac{U}{\delta} > C_S > F, D_\delta < a\right) \ or \ \left(F > C_S > \frac{U}{\delta}, D_\delta > c\right) \tag{9}$$

then $BR_S^\delta(y) \equiv b$ and the unique equilibrium is $(b, BR_I^\delta(b))$.
  The following two cases supply condition where the Invader's best response strategy is a constant in $[a, b]$.
  (i_3) If

$$\varphi_{x,c} \geq 0 \ for \ any \ x \in [a, b] \ with \ \varphi_{x,\xi} = H_2(x)/U - \delta\xi^2 - 2H_1(x)\xi \tag{10}$$

then the Invader's best response strategy $BR_I^\delta(x) \equiv c$ and the unique equilibrium is $(BR_S^\delta(c), c)$.
  (i_4) If

$$\varphi_{x,a} \leq 0 \ for \ any \ x \in [a, b] \tag{11}$$

then the Invader's best response strategy is $BR_I^\delta(x) \equiv a$, and the unique equilibrium is $(BR_S^\delta(a), a)$.
  If the conditions (8)-(11) do not hold then the best response strategies of both rivals are not constant, although there are still two subcases where the Invader

does not have interior equilibrium strategy (namely, his equilibrium strategy is either a or c). Below we assume that (8)-(11) do not hold.

(i_5) *If*

$$L(x) < D_\delta \text{ for any } x \in [a_*, b] \text{ with } a_* = \max\left\{a, \frac{1-\delta}{\delta} \frac{(F+C_I)\delta - U}{U - C_I\delta}\right\} \quad (12)$$

then there is the unique equilibrium

$$(x, y) = \begin{cases} (a, BR_I^\delta(a)), & U/\delta > C_S > F, \\ (b, BR_I^\delta(b)), & F > C_S > U/\delta. \end{cases}$$

(i_6) *If*

$$L(x) > D_\delta \text{ for any } x \in [a_*, b] \quad (13)$$

then there is the unique equilibrium

$$(x, y) = \begin{cases} (a, BR_I^\delta(a)), & F > C_S > U/\delta, \\ (b, BR_I^\delta(b)), & U/\delta > C_S > F. \end{cases}$$

(i_7) *Now we assume that neither conditions (8)-(13) hold. Then interior equilibrium strategy can arise as well as multi-equilibria situation can take place. All equilibria are given in Table 1 with*

$$R_\delta = (U - \delta C_I)^2 - 4\delta U((1-\delta)F + (U - \delta C_I)D_\delta),$$

$$x_\pm = \frac{2\delta U(1 - D_\delta) - U - \delta C_I \pm \sqrt{R_\delta}}{2\delta U}$$

and $x_\pm$ are the roots of the equations $L(x) = D_\delta$.

Table 1. The stationary equilibrium strategies (x, y)

Case	Condition	(x, y)
i_{71}	$x_\pm \in [a, b], U/\delta > C_S > F$	$(a, BR_I^\delta(a)), (x_-, D_\delta), (x_+, D_\delta)$
i_{72}	$x_\pm \in [a, b], F > C_S > U/\delta$	$(b, BR_I^\delta(b)), (x_-, D_\delta), (x_+, D_\delta)$
i_{73}	$x_+ \in [a, b], x_- \notin [a, b], U/\delta > C_S > F$	(x_+, D_δ)
i_{74}	$x_+ \in [a, b], x_- \notin [a, b], F > C_S > U/\delta$	$(a, BR_I^\delta(a)), (x_+, D_\delta), (b, BR_I^\delta(b))$
i_{75}	$x_+ \notin [a, b], x_- \in [a, b], U/\delta > C_S > F$	$(a, BR_I^\delta(a)), (x_-, D_\delta), (b, BR_I^\delta(b))$
i_{76}	$x_+ \notin [a, b], x_- \in [a, b], F > C_S > U/\delta$	(x_-, D_δ)

Finally note that two equilibria can arise only as extreme subcases when $x_- = a$ or $x_+ = a$. Thus, mainly the game has odd number of equilibrium: either one or three.

If multi-equilibrium situation arises then a problem associated with their choice arises, which in our case can be solved by applying the best response strategy algorithm. The best response strategy algorithm means that in the initial iteration, the width of bandwidth of one of the rivals is fixed. Each next iteration is given as the best response strategy based on the previous rival's response, i.e.

$$x_0 \text{ is fixed}, y_0 = \mathrm{BR}_I^\delta(x_0), x_1 = \mathrm{BR}_S^\delta(y_0), y_1 = \mathrm{BR}_I^\delta(x_1), \dots$$

or

$$y_0 \text{ is fixed}, x_0 = \mathrm{BR}_S^\delta(y_0), y_1 = \mathrm{BR}_I^\delta(x_0), x_1 = \mathrm{BR}_S^\delta(y_1), \dots$$

In the general case such an algorithm does not converge [17]. In our model such an algorithm in the multi-equilibria case always converges in a finite number of iterations, meanwhile for the mono-equilibria situation it does not converge, circling around the equilibrium, and does not approach it. Namely, the following result holds:

Theorem 4. *In the case of multiple stationary equilibrium the best response algorithm converges to the unique equilibrium for a finite number of iterations as it is given in Table 2.*

Table 2. Convergence of the best response strategy algorithm

Case	Condition	(x, y)
i_1	$x_\pm \in [a,b], U/\delta > C_S > F$	$(a, \mathrm{BR}_I^\delta(a))$
i_2	$x_\pm \in [a,b], F > C_S > U/\delta$	$(b, \mathrm{BR}_I^\delta(b))$
i_3	$x_+ \in [a,b], x_- \notin [a,b], F > C_S > U/\delta, ((x_0 < x_+) \text{ or } (y_0 > D_\delta))$	$(a, \mathrm{BR}_I^\delta(a))$
i_4	$x_+ \in [a,b], x_- \notin [a,b], F > C_S > U/\delta, ((x_0 > x_+) \text{ or } (y_0 < D_\delta))$	$(b, \mathrm{BR}_I^\delta(b))$
i_5	$x_+ \notin [a,b], x_- \in [a,b], U/\delta > C_S > F, ((x_0 < x_+) \text{ or } (y_0 > D_\delta))$	$(a, \mathrm{BR}_I^\delta(a))$
i_5	$x_+ \notin [a,b], x_- \in [a,b], U/\delta > C_S > F, ((x_0 > x_+) \text{ or } (y_0 < D_\delta))$	$(b, \mathrm{BR}_I^\delta(b))$

5   Numerical Illustrations and Discussions

As a numerical illustration we consider $U = 0.9, C_I = 0.6, C_S = 0.4; a = 0.01, c = 0.45, b = 0.45$. Figure 1(a) illustrates number of equilibrium as a function on discount factor δ and fine F. It is interesting that multiple equilibrium arise only for large enough discount factor. It is given by the fact that for a small enough discount factor (i.e., for the intent of longer illicit usage of bandwidth): (i) $L(x)$ is decreasing function, and (ii) the condition of Figure 3(b) does not hold, so the Invader's best response strategy has to have the form given by Figure 3(b). So, only one intersection of the best response strategy curves exists. Figures 1- 2 illustrates illustrate that the detection probability and payoffs in some situation can be very sensible to fine and the Invader's intention to intrude into the network longer, what yields that the network provider has to carefully make a value judgement of fine and estimation of the Intruder's intentions.

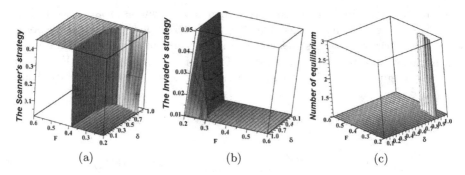

(a)   (b)   (c)

Fig. 1. (a) The Scanner's stationary equilibrium, (b) The Invader's stationary equilibrium, (c) Number of equilibrium

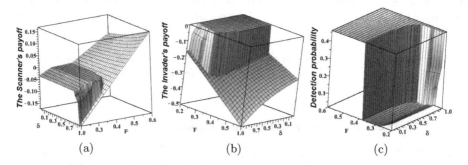

(a)   (b)   (c)

Fig. 2. (a) The Scanner's payoff, (b) The Invader's payoff, (c) Detection probability $P(x, y)$

6   Conclusions

In this paper we suggest a simple model for finding the optimal stationary bandwidth in multi-step scanning for the detection of an Invader. We have shown that the optimal stationary width essentially depends on the network's and agent's characteristics and the Invader's intention to use bandwidth illicitly for a longer time. Under some conditions a small change in network parameters, fine as well as the intent of the Intruder to act illegally in the network, could lead to jump changes in the optimal strategies and the payoffs of the rivals and could even cause multiple equilibria. This mixture between continuous and discontinuous behavior of the Invader under the influence of fine and intent of the Intruder to intrude implies that the Scanner has to carefully make a value judgement: some threshold values of fine as well as Intruder's intent could have a huge impact on the scanning outcome. If the Invader does not intend to intrude for a long time period, then there is a unique stationary equilibrium. If the Invader intends to intrude for a long time (it can be caused by the fact that the fine is improperly assigned compared to detection probability and the Intrude's utility) it could lead to a challenging situation for the Scanner with multiple equilibria where improperly choosing his equilibrium strategy can decrease his payoff. It is interesting that similar phenomena can be observed in OFDM networks when multiple equilibrium arise for enough large cross-talking coefficient [27] while uniqueness of the equilibrium holds for enough small cross-talking coefficient. In our model in the case multi-equilibria the best response strategy algorithm allows one to select proper equilibrium. Meanwhile in the case of mono-equilibrium the algorithm does not converge circling around it.

A goal for our future of course is to investigate the non-linearized detection probability model as well as to incorporate learning algorithm in multi-step scanning case. Also, we intend to extend our model to the case of multi-scanner [28] or multi-invader systems.

References

1. Haykin, S.: Cognitive radio: brain-empowered wireless communications. IEEE Journal on Selected Areas in Communications 23, 201–220 (2005)
2. Mitola, J.: Cognitive radio for flexible mobile multimedia communications. In: IEEE International Workshop on Mobile Multimedia Communications, pp. 3–10 (1999)
3. Akyildiz, I.F., Lee, W.Y., Vuran, M.C., Mohanty, S.: Next generation/dynamic spectrum access/cognitive radio wireless networks: a survey. Computer Networks 50, 2127–2159 (2006)
4. Fette, B.A.: Cognitive radio technology. Academic Press, NY (2009)
5. Liu, S., Chen, Y., Trappe, W., Greenstein, L.J.: ALDO: An anomaly detection framework for dynamic spectrum access networks. In: INFOCOM 2009, pp. 675–683 (2009)
6. Verdu, S.: Multiuser detection. Cambridge Univ. Press (1998)
7. Van Trees, H.L.: Detection, Estimation, and Modulation Theory, Radar-Sonar Signal Processing and Gaussian Signals in Noise. Wiley-Interscience (2004)
8. Digham, F.F., Alouini, M.S., Simon, M.K.: On the energy detection of unknown signals over fading channels. IEEE Transactions on Communications 55, 21–24 (2007)
9. Urkowitz, H.: Energy detection of unknown deterministic signals. Proceedings of the IEEE 55, 523–531 (1967)
10. Garnaev, A., Trappe, W., Kung, C.-T.: Dependence of Optimal Monitoring Strategy on the Application to be Protected. In: IEEE GlobeCom 2012, pp. 1072–1077 (2012)
11. Garnaev, A., Trappe, W., Kung, C.-T.: Optimizing Scanning Strategies: Selecting Scanning Bandwidth in Adversarial RF Environments. In: Crowncom 2013 (2013)
12. Liu, Y., Comaniciu, C., Man, H.: A Bayesian game approach for intrusion detection in wireless Ad Hoc networks. In: GameNets 2006 (2006)
13. Agah, A., Das, S.K., Basu, K., Asadi, M.: Intrusion detection in sensor networks: A non-cooperative game approach. In: NCA 2004, pp. 343–346 (2004)
14. Garnaev, A.: Remark on the Princess and Monster Search Game. International Journal of Game Theory 20, 269–276 (1992)
15. Garnaev, A., Garnaeva, G., Goutal, P.: On the Infiltration Game. International Journal of Game Theory 26, 215–221 (1997)
16. Manshaei, M.H., Zhu, Q., Alpcan, T., Basar, T., Hubaux, J.-P.: Game theory meets network security and privacy. J. ACM Computing Survey 453 (2013)

17. Owen, G.: Game Theory. W.B. Sanders, Philadelphia (1982)
18. Zhu, Q., Saad, W., Han, Z., Poor, H.V., Basar, T.: Eavesdropping and Jamming in Next-Generation Wireless Networks: A Game-Theoretic Approach. In: MILCOM 2011, pp. 119–124 (2011)
19. Altman, E., Avrachenkov, K., Garnaev, A.: Taxation for green communication. In: WiOpt 2010, pp. 108–112 (2010)
20. Sagduyu, Y.E., Ephremides, A.: A Game-Theoretic Analysis of Denial of Service Attacks in Wireless Random Access. Journal of Wireless Networks 15, 651–666 (2009)
21. Garnaev, A., Hayel, Y., Altman, E., Avrachenkov, K.: Jamming Game in a Dynamic Slotted ALOHA Network. In: Jain, R., Kannan, R. (eds.) GameNets 2011. LNICST, vol. 75, pp. 429–443. Springer, Heidelberg (2012)
22. Garnaev, A.: On a Ruckle problem in discrete games of ambush. Naval Research Logistics 44, 353–364 (1997)
23. Altman, E., Avrachenkov, K., Garnaev, A.: Jamming in Wireless Networks: the Case of Several Jammers. In: GameNets 2009, pp. 585–592 (2009)
24. Altman, E., Avrachenkov, K., Garnaev, A.: Transmission Power Control Game with SINR as Objective Function. In: Altman, E., Chaintreau, A. (eds.) NET-COOP 2008. LNCS, vol. 5425, pp. 112–120. Springer, Heidelberg (2009)
25. Kim, S.L., Rosberg, Z., Zander, J.: Combined power control and transmission rate selection in cellular networks. In: IEEE VTC 1999, pp. 1653–1657 (1999)
26. Koo, I., Ahn, J., Lee, H.A., Kim, K.: Analysis of Erlang capacity for the multimedia DS-CDMA systems. IEICE Trans. Fundamentals E82-A(5), 849–855 (1999)
27. Altman, E., Avrachenkov, K., Garnaev, A.: Closed Form Solutions for Water-Filling Problem in Optimization and Game Frameworks. Telecommunication Systems Journal 47, 153–164 (2011)
28. Comaniciu, C., Mandayam, N.B., Poor, H.V.: Wireless Networks Multiuser Detection in Cross-Layer Design. Springer, Heidelberg (2005)

7 Appendix

7.1 Proof of Theorem 2

First, note that

$$\frac{\partial v_S^\delta(x,y)}{\partial x} = \frac{(F - C_S)(1 - \delta) + (V - \delta C_S)y}{(1 - \delta - \delta(x + y))^2}.$$

So, for a fixed y the payoff $v_S^\delta(x, y)$ is increasing for $(V - \delta C_S)y > (C_S - F)(1 - \delta)$, it is decreasing for $(V - \delta C_S)y < (C_S - F)(1 - \delta)$ and it is constant for $(V - \delta C_S)y = (C_S - F)(1 - \delta)$ and (3) follows.

Note that, the Invader's payoff has the following form:

$$\frac{\partial v_I^\delta(x,y)}{\partial y} = \frac{-\delta U y^2 - 2U H_1(x)y + H_2(x)}{(1 - \delta - \delta(x + y))^2}$$

with H_1 and H_2 given by (5).

Since $H_1(x) > 0$ for $x \in [a, b]$ we have that for a fixed x: (a) payoff $v_I^\delta(x, y)$ gets maximum at $y = a$ for $-\delta U a^2 - 2U H_1(x)a + H_2(x) < 0$, (b) it gets maximum at $y = c$ for $-\delta U c^2 - 2U H_1(x)c + H_2(x) > 0$, and (c) it gets maximum at the unique positive root $y = \dfrac{-U H_1(x) + \sqrt{U^2 H_1^2(x) + \delta U H_2(x)}}{\delta U} = L(x)$ of the equation $-\delta U y^2 - 2U H_1(x)y + H_2(x) = 0$ for $-\delta U c^2 - 2U H_1(x)c + H_2(x) < 0 < -\delta U a^2 - 2U H_1(x)a + H_2(x)$ and (4) follows.

Finally we have to prove properties (a) and (b) of $L(x)$.
If $U \le \delta C_I$ then $U \le \delta(C_I + F)$. Thus, also, $\delta(U - \delta C_I)x + (1 - \delta)(U - \delta(C_I + F)) < 0$ for $x \in [a, b]$, and (a) follows.
Note that

$$\frac{d L(x)}{d x} = -1 + \frac{(U - \delta C_I)/(2\sqrt{U})}{\sqrt{\delta(U - \delta C_I)x + (1 - \delta)(U - \delta(C_I + F))}}$$

Thus, the equation $L(x) = 0$ has the unique root $x = x_*$ given by (7), and (b) follows. ∎

7.2   Proof of Theorem 3

The stationary equilibrium can be found as a couple of strategies (x, y) which are the best response to each other, i.e. as a solution of the equations: $x = BR_S^\delta(y)$ and $y = BR_I^\delta(x)$. By Theorem 2, function $L(x)$ from the Invader's best response strategy (4) is either decreasing, or increasing in $[a, b]$ or it has unique interior maximum in (a, b) depending on location of x_*. By Theorem 2 the Scanner's best response strategy (3) is piecewise constant function with at most one jump depending on whether D_δ does not or does belong to $[a, c]$. Thus, the best response strategy curves have at least one and at most three intersections in the roots $x_\pm$ of the equation $L(x) = D_\delta$ (Figure 3) and the result follows

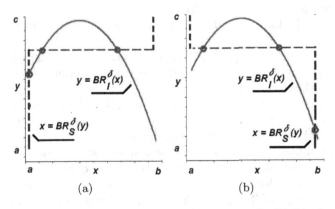

(a)   (b)

Fig. 3. (a) The best response strategies for $U/\delta > C_S > F$, (b) The best response strategies for $F > C_S > U/\delta$

If $D_\delta \notin [a, b]$ then the Scanner best response strategy by (3) is a constant and it equals to a if (8) holds and it equals to b if (9) holds, and (i_1) and (i_2) follow.

If $D_\delta \in [a, b]$ then by (4) the Intruder best response strategy can be constant only in two cases: it equals to c if (10) holds and it equals to a if (11) holds, and (i_3) and (i_4) follow.

If the conditions (8)-(11) do not hold then the best response strategies of both rivals are not constant, although there are still two subcases where $L(x)$ does not equal to D_δ in $[a, b]$ and, so, the Invader does not have interior equilibrium strategy. It takes if either (12) or (13) kolds. Then, by (3), (i_5) and (i_6) follow.

If neither conditions (8)-(13) hold, then the equation $L(x) = D_\delta$ has at least one and at most two roots $x_\pm$ in $[a, b]$. Then interior equilibrium strategy can arise as well as multi-equilibria situation can take place. Then, by Figure 3, the cases (i_{71})–(i_{76}) hold.   ∎

7.3   Proof of Theorem 4

The proof, that the best response strategy algorithm convergences in multi-equilibrium situation, consists of considering a lot of subcases depending on mutual location of the roots $x_\pm$ and the interval $[a, b]$. Here we consider only two basic ones. The rest cases can be considered similarly. Let condition of the case (i_1) from Table 2 hold. Then the best response strategies have the form given by Figure 4(a). In this case we have to consider two subcases: (a) $x_0 \in (x_-, x_+)$ and (b) $x_0 \notin (x_-, x_+)$.

(a) Let $x_0 \in (x_-, x_+)$. Then $y_1 = BR_I^\delta(x_0) = \min\{L(x_0), c\}$. Since $L(x_0) > D_\delta$, $x_1 = BR_S^\delta(y_1) = b$. So, $y_2 = BR_I^\delta(b) < D_\delta$. Thus, $x_2 = BR_S^\delta(y_1) = a$ and $y_3 = BR_I^\delta(a)$, that is an equilibrium point $(a, BR_I^\delta(a))$, and the algorithm terminates.

(b) Let $x_0 \notin (x_-, x_+)$. Then $y_1 = BR_I^\delta(x_0) = \max\{L(x_0), a\}$. Since $L(x_0) < D_\delta$, $x_1 = BR_S^\delta(y_1) = a$. So, $y_2 = BR_I^\delta(a)$, that is the same equilibrium point $(a, BR_I^\delta(a))$ as in case (a) and the algorithm terminates.

Let condition of the case (i_3) from Table 2 hold. Then the best response strategies have the form given by Figure 4(b). In this case we have to consider two subcases: (a) $x_0 < x_+$ and (b) $x_0 > x_+$.

(a) Let $x_0 < x_+$. Then $y_1 = BR_I^\delta(x_0) = \min\{L(x_0), c\}$. Since $L(x_0) > D_\delta$, $x_1 = BR_S^\delta(y_1) = a$. So, $y_2 = BR_I^\delta(a)$, that is the equilibrium point $(a, BR_I^\delta(a))$ and the algorithm terminates.

(b) Let $x_0 > x_+$. Then $y_1 = BR_I^\delta(x_0) = \max\{L(x_0), a\}$. Since $L(x_0) < D_\delta$, $x_1 = BR_S^\delta(y_1) = b$. So, $y_2 = BR_I^\delta(b)$, that is the other boundary equilibrium point $(b, BR_I^\delta(b))$, and the algorithm terminates.

In mono-equilibrium situation the best response strategy algorithm circling around the equilibrium. To prove it again we have to consider a lot of subcases depending on mutual location of the roots $x_\pm$ and interval $[a, b]$. Here we consider one basic case (i_{73}) of Table 2 with $x_0 < x_+$ (Figure 4(c)). Since $x_0 < x_+$, $y_1 = BR_I^\delta(x_0) = \min\{L(x_0), c\}$. Since $L(x_0) > D_\delta$, $x_1 = BR_S^\delta(y_1) = b$. So, $y_2 = BR_I^\delta(b) < D_\delta$. So, $x_2 = BR_S^\delta(y_2) = a$. Then $y_3 = BR_S^\delta(a) > D_\delta$ and on the next step we come to $x_3 = \mathrm{BR}_S^{\delta}(y_3) = b = x_1$, so the algorithm returned to the second step and never terminate.   ∎

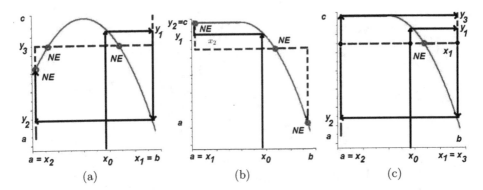

Fig. 4. (a) Convergence of the best response strategy algorithm in multi-equilibria situation with two interior equilibrium, (b) Convergence of the best response strategy algorithm in multi-equilibria situation with one interior equilibrium, (c) The best response strategy algorithm in mono-equilibrium situation circling around the equilibrium

Author Index